Machine Vision

Machine Vision

Automated Visual Inspection and Robot Vision

David Vernon

Department of Computer Science
Trinity College Dublin Ireland

Prentice Hall

New York   London   Toronto   Sydney   Tokyo   Singapore

First published 1991 by
Prentice Hall International (UK) Ltd
66 Wood Lane End, Hemel Hempstead
Hertfordshire HP2 4RG
A division of
Simon & Schuster International Group

Typeset in 10 on 12 point Times
by MCS Typesetters, Salisbury, Wiltshire, England

Printed and bound in Great Britain
by Cambridge University Press

Library of Congress Cataloging-in-Publication Data
is available from the publisher

British Library Cataloguing in Publication Data

Vernon, David
  Machine vision.
  I. Title
  006.3

    ISBN 0-13-543398-3

1 2 3 4 5   95 94 93 92 91

Everything that I can spy
Through the circle of my eye,
Everything that I can see
Has been woven out of me;
I have sown the stars, and threw
Clouds of morning and of eve
Up into the vacant blue;
Everything that I perceive,
Sun and sea and mountain high,
All are moulded by my eye:
Closing it, what shall I find?
– Darkness and a little wind.

James Stephens
The Hill of Vision

Contents

Contents

Preface

Machine vision is a multi-disciplinary subject, utilizing techniques drawn from optics, electronics, mechanical engineering, computer science, and artificial intelligence. This book is intended to be an in-depth introduction to Machine Vision which will allow the reader quickly to assimilate and comprehend the essentials of this evolving and fascinating topic. Significant emphasis will be placed on providing the reader with a solid grounding in the fundamental tools for image acquisition, processing, and analysis; a range of techniques, dealing with very simple two-dimensional systems, through more sophisticated robust two-dimensional approaches, to the current state of the art in three-dimensional robot vision, will be explained in some detail. Both application areas of automated visual inspection and robot vision are addressed. Recognizing that machine vision is just a component of a larger automation system, a brief introduction to robot programming will be provided, together with an explanation of the mechanisms by which robot vision modules interact with the programming language. It is important to recognize that the discipline of machine vision is presently undergoing a maturing process, with sophisticated techniques and tech drawn from current research being exploited more and more in industrial systems. Without doubt, there is a long way to go, but the die is well cast. Acknowledging this trend, the last chapter of the book is devoted to the more research-orientated topics of three-dimensional image understanding and early visual processing (e.g. stereopsis and visual motion). It would indeed be foolhardy to attempt an exhaustive treatment of these areas; each deserves a volume on its own. However, if the essence of the philosophy of robot vision in its broadest sense is cogently imparted to the reader, then the exercise will have been successful and worth while.

The book is directed at final-year undergraduate and first-year graduate students in computer science and engineering, and at practising industrial engineers; the fundamental philosophy being to impart sufficient knowledge so that the reader will be competent to begin the implementation of a simple vision system and to enable him/her to study each issue independently in more depth. To that end, care

xi

is taken to provide adequate references to supporting texts, reports, and research papers. In this way the book may be viewed both as a self-contained introductory text and as a spring-board to more detailed and specific study.

Acknowledgements

Special thanks are due to Kenneth Dawson of the Computer Vision Group, Department of Computer Sciences, Trinity College, Dublin, for his work on the raw primal sketch, the extended Gaussian image, and the polyhedral models; and to Massimo Tistarelli and Prof. Giulio Sandini at the University of Genoa for their help with the examples of camera motion and stereopsis. Many people in the Trinity Computer Vision Group read draft versions of this book and I am grateful for their contributions. I would also like to record a note of thanks to Dr R. Dixon, The University, Manchester, for his many valuable comments on an earlier draft of this book. Several of the examples in this book were facilitated by research funded by the Commission of the European Communities under the European Strategic Programme for Research and Development in Information Technology: Project 419 – Image and Movement Understanding.

1

An introduction to computer vision

1.1 Computer vision: image processing or artificial intelligence?

What is computer vision and why would one be interested in studying it? It is perhaps easier to answer these two questions in reverse order. There are several reasons why one would be interested in computer vision, but the following two will serve to illustrate the many directions from which one can view the subject area:

1. All naturally occurring intelligent life-forms exhibit an ability to interact with and manipulate their environment in a coherent and stable manner. This interaction is facilitated by on-going intelligent interplay between perception and motion-control (i.e. action); visual perception is fundamentally important to most intelligent life.

2. Most manufacturers are concerned with the cosmetic integrity of their products; customers quite often equate quality of appearance with functional quality. So, to ensure the successful long-term marketing of an item, it is highly desirable that its appearance is checked visually before packaging and shipping. Likewise, it is desirable that the inspection process be automated and effected without human intervention.

These two motivations for the study of perception characterize two possible extremes of interest in the processing, analysis, and interpretation of visual imagery: from the philosophical and perhaps esoteric to the immediate and pragmatic. And the subject matter of everything between these two extremes presents one with wide and varied spectrums of commercial interest, difficulty and, indeed, success.

The answer to the first question (what is computer vision?) now becomes a little easier to identify. The world we live in and experience is filled with an endless variety of objects, animate and inanimate, and, to borrow a phrase from David Marr (of whom we shall hear more later in the book), it is by looking and seeing

1

that we come to know what is where in this world. So, if vision is a means to an end – to know the world by looking – then computer vision is exactly the same except that the medium by which the knowledge is gained is now a computational instrument rather than the brain of some living creature. Without doubt, this is a very broad definition. But the subject matter of computer vision *is* this broad: topics such as image restoration, image enhancement, automated visual inspection, robot vision, computer-based image understanding of general three-dimensional scenes, and visual perception and cognition all fall under the umbrella of the term 'computer vision'.

Although for centuries man has been interested in solving the puzzle of how man comes to 'see', the first computational experiments in developing artificial machine vision systems were conducted in the late 1950s and, over the last twenty-five to thirty years computer-based vision systems of widely varying degrees of complexity have been used in many diverse areas such as office automation, medicine, remote sensing by satellite, and in both the industrial world and the military world. The applications have been many and varied, encompassing character recognition, blood cell analysis, automatic screening of chest X-rays, registration of nuclear medicine lung scans, computer-aided tomography (CAT), chromosome classification, land-use identification, traffic monitoring, automatic generation of cartographic projections, parts inspection for quality assurance industrial, part identification, automatic guidance of seam welders, and visual feedback for automatic assembly and repair. Military applications have included the tracking of moving objects, automatic navigation based on passive sensing, and target acquisition and range-finding.

As we have seen, computer vision is concerned with the physical structure of a three-dimensional world by the automatic analysis of images of that world. However, it is necessary to qualify the use of the word *image*. First, the image is a two-dimensional one and, hence, we inevitably lose information in the projection process, i.e. in passing from a three-dimensional world to a two-dimensional image. Quite often, it is the recovery of this lost information which forms the central problem in computer vision. Second, the images are digital images: they are discrete representations (i.e. they have distinct values at regularly sampled points) and they are quantized representations (i.e. each value is an integer value).

Computer vision includes many techniques which are useful in their own right, e.g. image processing (which is concerned with the transformation, encoding, and transmission of images) and pattern recognition (frequently the application of statistical decision theory to general patterns, of which visual patterns are but one instance). More significantly, however, computer vision includes techniques for the useful description of shape and of volume, for geometric modelling, and for so-called cognitive processing. Thus, though computer vision is certainly concerned with the processing of images, these images are only the raw material of a much broader science which, ultimately, endeavours to emulate the perceptual capabilities of man and, perhaps, to shed some light upon the manner by which he accomplishes his amazingly adaptive and robust interaction with his environment.

1.2 *Industrial machine vision vs. image understanding*

Computer vision, then, is an extremely broad discipline (or set of disciplines) and in order to get to grips with it, we need to identify some way of classifying different approaches. To begin with, we note that humans live and work within a general three-dimensional world, pursuing many goals and objectives in an unconstrained and constantly changing environment in which there are many varied and, often, ill-defined objects. Industrial automation, on the other hand, is given to performing single repeated tasks involving relatively few objectives, all of which are known and defined, in manufacturing environments which are normally constrained and engineered to simplify those tasks. Industrial systems do not yet work with *general* three-dimensional environments (although the environments they do work in are often much less structured than one would suppose) and vision systems for manufacturing still exploit many assumptions, which would not generally apply to unconstrained worlds with many objects and many goals, in order to facilitate processing and analysis. There is a considerable dichotomy between the two approaches – a situation which must change and is changing – it is for this reason that the final chapter is concerned with advanced techniques and their migration to the industrial environment. Let us look a little closer at each of these classes of computer vision.

Approaches associated with general environments are frequently referred to by the terms 'image understanding' or 'scene analysis'. The latter term is now quite dated as it typically refers to approaches and systems developed during the 1970s. Vision systems specifically intended for the industrial environment are often referred to generically as 'industrial machine vision systems'.

Image understanding vision systems are normally concerned with three-dimensional scenes, which are partially constrained, but viewed from one (and often several) unconstrained viewpoint. The illumination conditions may be known, e.g. the position of the room light might be assumed, but usually one will have to contend with shadows and occlusion, i.e. partially hidden objects. As such, the data or scene representation is truly a two-dimensional image representation of a three-dimensional scene, with high spatial resolutions (i.e. it is extremely detailed) and high grey-scale resolutions (i.e. it exhibits a large variation in grey-tone). Occasionally, colour information is incorporated but not nearly as often as it should be. Range data is sometimes explicitly available from active range-sensing devices, but a central theme of image understanding is the automatic extraction of both range data and local orientation information from several two-dimensional images using e.g., stereopsis, motion, shading, occlusion, texture gradients, or focusing. One of the significant aspects of image understanding is that it utilizes several redundant information representations (e.g. based on the object edges or boundaries, the disparity between objects in two stereo images, and the shading of the object's surface); and it also incorporates different levels of representation in

3

order to organize the information being made explicit in the representation in an increasingly powerful and meaningful manner. For example, an image understanding system would endeavour to model the scene with some form of parameterized three-dimensional object models built from several low-level processes based on distinct visual cues. [At present,] image-understanding systems utilize both explicit knowledge (or models) and software-embedded knowledge for reasoning, that is, for controlling image analysis.)

Most industrial machine vision systems contrast sharply with the above approach. The scenes in an industrial environment are usually assumed to be two-dimensional, comprising known isolated rigid parts, frequently with a contrasting visual backdrop. Lighting is almost always a critical factor and must be very carefully organized. Typically, the ambient room lighting will be totally inadequate, and even confusing, so that each inspection station will require its own set of dedicated lights, each designed for the task in hand. The images which industrial machine vision systems use are frequently two-dimensional binary images (pure black and white, with no intermediate grey-levels) of essentially two-dimensional scenes. There is normally just one simple internal object representation or model; the analysis strategy being to extract salient features (e.g. area, circularity, or some other measure of shape) and to make some decision, typically using feature-based discrimination. This process frequently uses software-embedded (hard-coded) knowledge of the scene.

There are two complementary areas of industrial machine vision: robot vision and automated visual inspection. Both of these use essentially the same techniques and approaches, although the visual inspection tasks are, in general, not as difficult as those involved in visual perception for robotic parts manipulation, identification, and assembly. This is because the inspection environment is usually easier to control and the accept/reject decisions required for inspection are often easier to determine than the location and identification information needed for assembly. The significant problems associated with robotic part handling, too, has meant that advanced three-dimensional robot vision has not received the attention it merits.

1.3 *Sensory feedback for manufacturing systems: why vision?*

The answer to this question must necessarily be double-barrelled:

1. We need feedback because the manufacturing system is not perfect and free of errors: we wish to ensure that we are informed when errors begin to creep into the process, so that we can take corrective action and ensure that quality and productivity are maintained.

2. We use vision because it is by far the most versatile sense available and conveys extremely rich information when compared with, e.g., sonar or infra-red sensing. Furthermore, unlike tactile sensing, it senses the environment in

a remote manner rather than having to be in contact with the objects being analysed.

Systems which are equipped with (useful) visual capabilities are inherently adaptive and can deal with uncertainty in the environment, or at least that is what one would hope for. The upshot of this is that, by incorporating vision in the manufacturing process, not only can we identify when things go wrong (e.g. in visual inspection) but the uncertain and variable nature of the manufacturing environment can be catered for.

Unfortunately, vision, while versatile, is also the most complex of the senses, due mainly to the fact that most information in visual images is implicitly coded and requires extensive processing and analysis to make it explicit. *Visual sensing is difficult*: in humans, ten of the estimated one hundred cortical areas in the brain are devoted to vision and much work remains to be done before we can claim to have even a modest grasp of visual sensing.

Given that one acknowledges that vision is (potentially) a very powerful sense, let us look at some of the motivations for using visual processes in the industrial workplace.

☐ *Safety and reliability*

Considerations of safety and reliability usually arise in environments which are hazardous for humans (e.g. in close proximity to a milling bit) or because manufactured parts are of critical importance and 100 per cent inspection is required (e.g. defects in a brake lining might conceivably cause loss of life).

Machine vision also facilitates consistency in inspection standards; such systems don't suffer from the 'Monday-morning' syndrome and their performance can be (and should be) quantitatively assessed.

☐ *Product quality*

High-volume production using humans seldom facilitates inspection of all parts but automated visual inspection techniques may make it feasible; this depends on the complexity of the task and the effective throughput that is required by the manufacturing system. The latter consideration is particularly important if the vision system is to be incorporated in an on-line manner, i.e. inspecting each part as it is manufactured.

☐ *Flexible automation*

In environments where quality assurance is performed by a machine, it is feasible to integrate the inspection task into the complete production or manufacturing cycle, and allow it to provide feedback to facilitate on-line control. This provides for the adaptive requirements of AMT (advanced manufacturing technology) systems and facilitates the overall control by computer, such as is found (or, more realistically, as will be found in the future) in advanced computer integrated manufacturing (CIM) environments.

5

Integration within a CIM system is, however, one of the problems that is forestalling the rapid deployment of vision technology in advanced manufacturing environments, not least because the vision system will not usually know how to communicate with, e.g., the CAD (computer aided design) database or another manufacturer's robotic palletizing system.

1.4 Examples of industrial machine vision problems and solutions

Of the two sub-sections of industrial machine vision, automated visual inspection is presently by far the most important area, accounting for at least 80 per cent of all current applications. Within inspection, there is a great diversity of uses in fields such as quality assurance, machine monitoring, and test and calibration. These applications may be classified on a functional basis as either gauging, inspection, or sorting:

- Gauging is concerned with the measurement of dimensional characteristics of parts and with checking tolerances.
- Inspection, *per se*, is concerned with performing part verification, i.e. establishing whether there are any parts or sections missing from the object being inspected or whether there are any extraneous parts which should not be present. Alternatively, one might be interested in performing flaw detection, i.e. effecting the *detection* and *classification* of flaws (usually surface flaws) on the part: for example, the detection of scratches on plastic housings.
- Sorting is concerned with the identification and recognition of parts. Parts will usually be on a conveyer system and it is pertinent to note that this does not necessarily involve robot manipulation as the part can quite simply be pushed into an appropriate bin using a simple pneumatically actuated flipper.

The applications of robot vision are less varied. At present, this is primarily due to the uncertain nature of the industrial environment within which a robot will be operating: there are typically three dimensions to deal with instead of two, partly manufactured objects tend to be poorly finished having spurious material attached (e.g. swarf) and they tend not to appear exactly where they are expected or are supposed to be. The two application areas which are well developed are materials handling and welding. The reasons for this are that these problems can often be reduced to two-dimensions; objects on a conveyer or pallet are visualized as two-dimensional silhouetted shapes and tracking a welding seam is conceived, locally, as a two-dimensional exercise in the estimation of the disparity between the position of the welding rod and the metal seam. The application which one would expect to be the main subject matter of robot vision – part assembly – is very poorly developed for the reasons given above and, additionally, because the assembly operation requires greater dexterity on the part of the robot than is currently offered by commercial manipulators. It is for this reason that the development of compliant manipulation and the incorporation of tactile sensors in the robot grippers are fundamentally important.

(Despite these negative comments, there is still a great deal of potential for existing vision technologies; there are many common industrial problems which can be successfully and cost-effectively solved with the judicious use of well-understood and simple vision tools. To illustrate this and some of the techniques that have been alluded to so far, a few very simple examples are in order; a more sophisticated application is described in detail in Chapter 8.) ↳ₒₙ

1.4.1 Measurement of steel bars

Raw material for steel ingots to be used in a casting process is delivered in four-foot long bars with a circular cross-section. Individual ingots are then cut from the bar and stacked in a wooden box before being moved to the next stage of the casting process. To ensure high-quality casting with minimal wastage of raw material, it is essential that the weight of the charges fall within acceptable tolerances. The nominal tolerances on weight are ±5 g.

If the cross-sectional area of the bar of raw material were constant, the required weight would be given by an ingot of fixed length. Unfortunately, the cross-sectional area is not constant and the outside diameter of the bar can vary considerably (a 1.25″ bar has a nominal variation of 0.01″ but often exceeds this limit). Thus, in order to ensure the correct weight of a cut charge, the cross-sectional area of the bar must be monitored and a length of bar chosen such that the volume (and hence weight) falls within the required tolerance.

To measure the cross-sectional area, an 'outside diameter' gauge comprising a diametrically opposed light source and an image sensor is mounted on a robot end effector and moved along the axis of the bar (see Figure 1.1). In this manner, the

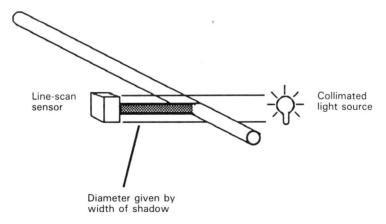

Line-scan sensor

Collimated light source

Diameter given by width of shadow

Figure 1.1 Measurement and inspection of steel bars.

bar will form a 'shadow' on the light sensor, the size of which corresponds to the diameter of the bar at that point. Thus, a profile of the bar can be built as the bar passes through the gauge. One pass of the sensor generates a single signature describing how the diameter varies over the scanned length. If it is assumed that the bar is truly circular in cross-section, this single measure is sufficient to compute the volume of the bar; several passes of the sensor at different orientations (i.e. rotating the sensor about the axis of the bar after each pass) allow this assumption to be dropped. The essential point to be noticed about this system is that the techniques used are inherently simple (measuring the length of a shadow cast directly on a sensor) and do not require any special sophisticated software. The gauging process is very fast and consequently can be integrated into the production system as a feedback device to control the ingot cutting operation directly.

1.4.2 Inspection of computer screens

Cathode ray tubes (CRTs) must be inspected and calibrated during the assembly of personal computers. The picture position, width, height, distortion, brightness, and focus need to be computed and, if any of these measurements lie outside specified tolerances, real-time feedback is required to facilitate on-line adjustment. Such a system has been configured using standard off-the-shelf equipment, comprising an

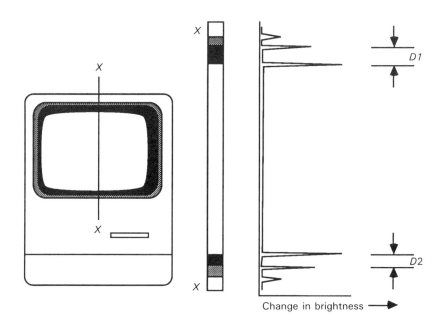

Vertical eccentricity $= D1 - D2$

Figure 1.2 Inspection of computer screens.

8

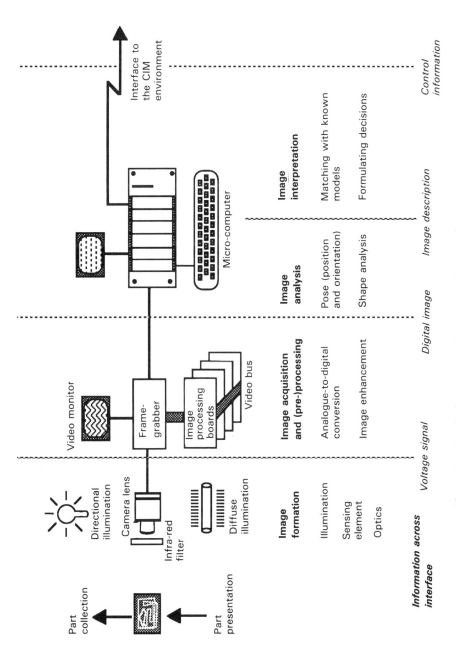

Figure 1.4 Typical system architecture (after Sanderson 1983).

11

interpretation is normally effected in software on a conventional computer, usually the same one which implements the image analysis.

Exercises

1. Comment on the validity of the statement that 'Industrial machine vision and image understanding have nothing in common'.
2. Given that an inspection task typically comprises three main stages of sensing, image processing, and image analysis, identify the component processes within each stage by describing the functional structure of a task involving the automated visual inspection of O-ring seals. The objective of the inspections task is to compute the outside and inside diameters and the diameter ratios and to check that each of the three values is within a certain tolerance. Pay particular attention to the components related to image analysis.
3. Describe briefly the essential difference between information contained in images and the information required to make a decision in a manufacturing environment.

References and further reading

Ballard, D.H. and Brown, C.M. 1982 *Computer Vision*, Prentice Hall, New Jersey.

Batchelor, B.G., Hill, D.A. and Hodgson, D.C. (eds) 1985 *Automated Visual Inspection*, IFS (Publications), Ltd, United Kingdom.

Besl, P.J., Delp, E.J. and Jain, R. 1985 'Automatic visual solder joint inspection', *IEEE Journal of Robotics and Automation*, Vol. RA-1, No. 1, pp. 42–56.

Binford, T.O. 1982 'Survey of model-based image analysis systems', *The International Journal of Robotics Research*, Vol. 1, No. 1, pp. 18–64.

Brady, J.M. (ed.) 1981 *Computer Vision*, Elsevier Science Publishers, The Netherlands.

Brady, M. 1982 'Computational approaches to image understanding', *ACM Computing Surveys*, Vol. 14, No. 1, pp. 3–71.

Bolles, R.C. 1981 *An Overview of Applications of Image Understanding to Industrial Automation*, SRI International, Technical Note No. 242.

Boyle, R.D. and Thomas, R.C. 1988 *Computer Vision – A First Course*, Blackwell Scientific Publications, Oxford.

Chin, R.T. and Harlow, C.A. 1982 'Automated Visual Inspection: A survey', *IEEE Transactions on Pattern Analysis and Machine Intelligence*, Vol. PAMI-4, No. 6, pp. 557–73.

Christiansen, D. 1984 'The automatic factory', *IEEE Spectrum*, Vol. 20, No. 5, p. 33.

Connors, R.W., McMillin, C.W., Lin, K. and Vasquez-Espinosa, R.E. 1983 'Identifying and locating surface defects in wood: part of an automated lumber processing system', *IEEE Transactions on Pattern Analysis and Machine Intelligence*, Vol. PAMI-5, No. 6, pp. 573–83.

Corby, N.R. 1983 'Machine vision for robotics', *IEEE Transactions on Industrial Electronics*, Vol. IE-30, No. 3, pp. 282–91.

Caudrado, J. L. and Caudrado, C. Y. 1986 'A.I. in computer vision', *Byte*, Vol. 11, No. 1, pp. 237–58.

Duda, R.O. and Hart, P.E. 1973 *Pattern Classification and Scene Analysis*, Wiley, New York.

Fairhurst, M.C. 1988 *Computer Vision for Robotic Systems*, Prentice Hall International (UK), Hertfordshire.

Fischler, M.A. 1981 *Computational Structures of Machine Perception*, SRI International, Technical Note No. 233.

Gonzalez, R.C. and Safabakhsh, R. 1982 'Computer vision techniques for industrial applications and robot control', *Computer* Vol. 15, No. 12, pp. 17–32.

Gonzalez, R.C. and Wintz, P. 1977 *Digital Image Processing*, Addison-Wesley, Reading, Mass.

Hall, E.L. 1979 *Computer Image Processing and Recognition*, Academic Press, New York.

Hanson, A.R. and Riseman, E.M. 1978 'Segmentation of natural scenes', in *Computer Vision Systems*, Hanson, A.R. and Riseman, E.M. (eds), Academic Press, New York.

Hara, Y., Akiyama, N. and Karasaki, K. 1983 'Automatic inspection system for printed circuit boards', *IEEE Transactions on Pattern Analysis and Machine Intelligence*, Vol. PAMI-5, No. 6, pp. 623–30.

Horn, B.K.P. 1986 *Robot Vision*, The MIT Press, Cambridge, Massachusetts.

Jarvis, J. 1982 *Computer Vision Experiments on Images of Wire-Wrap Circuit Boards*, Conference Record on 1982 Workshop on Industrial Applications of Machine Vision, pp. 144–50.

Kelley, R.B., Birk, J. R., Martins, H.A.S. and Tella, R. 1982 'A robot system which acquires cylindrical workpieces from bins', *IEEE Transactions on Systems, Man, and Cybernetics*, Vol. SMC-12, No. 2, pp. 204–13.

Kelley, R.B., Martins, H.A.S., Birk, J.R. and Dessimoz, J-D. 1983 'Three vision for acquiring workpieces from bins', *Proceedings of the IEEE*, Vol. 71, No. 7, pp. 803–21.

Mahon, J., Harris, N. and Vernon, D. 1989 'Automated visual inspection of solder paste deposition on surface mount technology printed circuit boards, accepted for publication in *Computers in Industry*.

Moore, F.W. 1987 'Remote visual inspection of nuclear fuel pellets with fibre optics and video image processing', *Optical Engineering*, Vol. 26, No. 2, pp. 152–5.

Nevatia, R. 1982 *Machine Perception*, Prentice Hall, New Jersey.

Pau, L.F. 1983 'Integrated testing and algorithms for visual inspection of integrated circuits', *IEEE Transactions on Pattern Analysis and Machine Intelligence*, Vol. PAMI-5, No. 6, pp. 602–8.

Pau, L.F. 1984 'Approaches to industrial image processing and their limitations', *Electronics and Power*, February, pp. 135–40.

Pinker, S. (ed.) 1984 'Cognition', *The International Journal of Cognitive Psychology*, Vol. 18, Nos. 1–3.

Pratt, W.K. 1978 *Digital Image Processing*, Wiley, New York.

Pugh, A. (ed.) 1983 *Robot Vision*, IFS (Publications) Ltd, United Kingdom.

Rosenfeld, A. 1984 *Why Computers Can't See (Yet)*, Abacus, Vol. 1, No. 1, pp. 17–26, Springer Verlag, New York.

Rosenfeld, A. and Kak, A. 1976 *Digital Picture Processing*, Academic Press, New York.

Rosenfeld, A. and Kak, A. 1982 *Digital Picture Processing*, Academic Press, New York.

Sanderson, R.J. 1983 *Machine Vision Systems: A Summary and Forecast*, Tech Tran Corp. Illinois.

Spoehr, K.T. and Lehmkuhle, S.W. 1982 *Visual Information Processing*, Freeman and Co., San Francisco.

Suresh, B., Fundakowski, R.A., Levitt T.S. and Overland, J.E. 1983 'A real-time automated visual inspection system for hot steel slabs', *IEEE Transactions on Pattern Analysis and Machine Intelligence*, Vol. PAMI-5, No. 6, pp. 563–72.

Vernon, D. (Rapporteur) 1987 *Sensoric Feedback for Control and Decision Support Systems*, Report of a Workshop in the Framework of ESPRIT Conference 1987, Directorate General XIII (eds.).

Vernon, D. 1989 'Computers See the Light', *Technology Ireland*, Vol. 21, No. 1, pp. 21–3.

2

Illumination and sensors

2.1 Illumination

Scene and object illumination play a key role in the machine vision process. The central purpose of imposing controlled constant illumination is to enhance visually the parts to be imaged so that their flaws, defects, and features are highlighted and so that their identification and classification by the vision system becomes somewhat easier. Although the choice of lighting will typically be application-dependent, some general points may be pertinent.

The common incandescent bulb is probably the simplest source of light. It is cost-effective and it is easily adjusted for light intensity; however, it generally provides directional illumination since it is, to an approximation, a point source of light. Hence, incandescent bulbs cast strong shadows which invariably cause problems for machine vision software. Special bulbs are normally required as degradation in emitted light intensity is common with age. Furthermore, incandescent bulbs emit considerable infra-red radiation; this does not cause problems for humans as we are not sensitive to such light but some camera sensors, particularly so-called CCD cameras, are sensitive and visual data can be washed out by the reflected infra-red rays.

For most machine vision applications, a diffuse source of light is the most suitable. Diffuse lighting is non-directional and produces a minimum amount of shadow. Fluorescent lighting is the simplest and most common method of obtaining diffuse illumination and is especially good for providing illumination of large areas.

In situations where the only features that need to be inspected are evident from the silhouette of the object, back-lighting is the most appropriate. Back-lighting, e.g. in the form of a light table, provides high contrast between the object and the background upon which the object rests. Its advantage is that it facilitates very simple object isolation or *segmentation*, a topic to which we will return in Chapter 5.

In some manufacturing environments, it is necessary to inspect moving objects. Depending on the characteristics of image sensor, it may be necessary to 'freeze' the motion of the object for an instant by the use of a strobe light or electronic flash. The lamp emits a short (1 ms) burst of light, thus the moving object is illuminated for a very short period and appears stationary. The activation of the strobe must be synchronized with the acquisition of the image. Alternatively, you can exploit cameras with a very fast 'shutter speed' or, rather, the electronic equivalent, a very short exposure time. The exposure is usually referred to as the integration time since it is the period over which the sensor integrates or averages the incident light. One would normally choose the latter option of a short integration time, since it is more ergonomic and less disruptive for humans.

☐   *Control of illumination and light levels*

As many inspection systems base much of their analysis on the absolute intensity of the incident light, the control of the object illumination can be important. In particular, if image processing and analysis decisions are being made on the basis of a fixed intensity datum (threshold), then some problems will occur if the illumination, and hence the reflected light, changes. If possible, the vision system should be able to adapt to such changes, although this does not necessarily mean that it should be capable of dealing with dynamic changes. Most illumination systems degrade quite slowly over time and it would be quite satisfactory if the system were capable of self-calibration at the beginning of each day.

Other alternatives exist, however, to this adaptive approach. One solution is to ensure that the illumination does, in fact, remain constant by monitoring it using light meters and adjusting the illumination system appropriately. Alternatively, the aperture of the camera lens might be altered. Note, however, that electronically controlled aperture lenses (so-called auto-iris lenses) should not be employed directly; their function is to alter aperture so that the average amount of light passing through the lens remains constant. This is not appropriate for machine vision systems as the grey-tone shade of a particular feature would vary, depending on the intensity of the ambient lighting.

It was mentioned above that incandescent lighting is not suitable for some cameras and, in general, one should ensure that the lighting system is compatible with the image sensor. For example, mains-powered lighting is inherently 'flickery' due to the a.c. characteristics of the mains electricity supply. Humans do not notice this, in general, because they effectively 'integrate' (or average) the incident illumination over a short period of time. This process also accounts for our ability to view moving objects in cinema films and perceive the motion to be continuous. Machine vision sensors, as we shall see in the next section, do not integrate in quite the same way and, when they acquire the image, the flicker can become apparent. The use of an appropriate (d.c., say) power supply can alleviate this problem, when it does occur.

2.2 Sensors

The task of a camera system is to convert an optical picture, typically representing a two-dimensional or three-dimensional scene, into some form suitable for use with electrical systems. Since the camera represents the direct link between the environment being examined and the information-processing system, it plays a particularly significant role and merits a good deal of attention.

2.2.1 Image formation: elementary optics

Before commencing a discussion of cameras, image sensors, and image acquisition components proper, we will first address a few fundamental issues on the optics of a vision system and of lenses in particular.

Lenses are required to focus part of the visual environment onto the image sensor. It is possible to construct an imaging system without lenses, using, for example, a collimated light source to project a shadow of a (small) object onto the sensor but such a configuration is not typical of the requirements of a vision system.

Lenses are defined by their *focal length* (quoted in millimetres: mm) and their *aperture* (the *f number*). These parameters determine the performance of the lens in terms of light-gathering power and magnification, and it often has a bearing on its physical size.

The focal length of a lens is a guide to the magnification it effects and its field of view. Selecting the focal length which is appropriate to a particular application is simply a matter of applying the basic lens equation:

$$\frac{1}{u} + \frac{1}{v} = \frac{1}{f}$$

where

v is the distance from the lens to the image,
u is the distance from the lens to the object,
f is the focal length.

Noting the magnification factor M is:

$$M = \frac{\text{image size}}{\text{object size}}$$

and, equivalently:

$$M = \frac{\text{image distance}}{\text{object distance}}$$

Thus:

$$f = \frac{uM}{M+1}$$

Hence, if we know the required magnification factor and the distance from the object to the lens, we can compute the required focal length.

For example, if a 10 cm wide object is to be imaged on a common 8.8 × 6.6 mm sensor from a distance of 0.5 m this implies a magnification factor of:

$$M = \frac{8.8}{100} = 0.088$$

So:

$$f = \frac{500 \times 0.088}{1.088} = 40.44$$

Thus, we require a 40.44 mm focal length lens. Typically, one would use a slightly shorter focal length (e.g. 35 mm) and accept the slight loss in resolution due to the larger field of view.

The *minimum focal distance* is the minimum distance between the front of the lens and the object at which the object can still be in focus. Generally speaking, lenses with short focal lengths have smaller minimum focal distances.

If the lens is required to focus on a relatively small object at short distances, the minimum focal distance (typically 300 mm) may be too large. In that case, an extension tube can be used to increase the distance, v, of the lens from the sensor and hence decrease the distance, u, from the lens to the object. For a given focal length, f, the lens equation stipulates that u decreases as v increases, if the image is to remain in focus.

The *f-number* is a measure of the amount of light allowed to pass through the lens and is a normalized measure of lens aperture. It is defined by the focal length divided by the diameter of the aperture. The standard scale is 1.4, 2, 2.8, 4, 5.6, 8, 11, 16; each increase *reduces* the amount of light passing through the lens by one-half.

The *depth of field* is the distance between the nearest and the furthest points of a scene which remains in acceptable focus at any one aperture setting. In general, the depth of field gets larger as the focused point moves away from the lens (given constant aperture and focal length). Also, the depth of field increases significantly as the aperture closes (i.e. as the f number increases) for any given focusing distance.

Lenses have many types of standard mounts, for example the Pentax, Olympus, Nikon bayonet mounts, but the standard on television, and CCTV (Closed Circuit TV), cameras is a screw mount called the C mount. Since there is a vast choice of 35 mm photographic lenses, it makes sense to be able to use these photographic lenses with C mount cameras and there are several types of bayonet adaptors available for C mount cameras. However, it should be remembered that these lenses are usually much more bulky than the miniature lenses which are specifically designed for CCD cameras. The reason for this is that a photographic lens is designed to image a 35 mm format and, for a given focal length, the optical surface must be much larger. CCD sensors (as we will see in the next section) are typically less than 10 mm in width and hence the optical surface can be much smaller.

Many of the visual problems which cause difficulty in interpreting a scene can often be solved by the use of simple filters on the camera lens. Filters are frequently used by the television and video industries to produce special effects, for example, the star-light filter used to make candlelight seem soft and star-like. Filters are just as often used to reduce, or remove, such effects; polaroid sunglasses are probably the most widely used 'filters' and are used to reduce glare. In machine vision, one of the most annoying and potentially disruptive problems is that due to specular reflection (mirror-like reflection on shiny objects). The use of a simple polarizing filter on the camera lens can often reduce the effect of these reflections.

Some sensors are sensitive to segments of the electromagnetic spectrum which do not convey visual data, e.g. infra-red radiation. The use of a simple infra-red blocking filter can solve this problem in a simple and effective manner.

2.2.2 Camera sensors

There are essentially two types of video camera available: one, the vidicon, is based on vacuum-tube technology and the other is based on semi-conductor technology.

Briefly, a vidicon tube is a photoconductive device which employs a photosensitive sensor layer consisting of several million mosaic cells insulated from one another on a transparent metal film (refer to the Figure 2.1). Each cell represents a small capacitor whose charge is a function of incident light. The sensor layer is scanned in a raster format with an electron beam over 625 lines in accordance with the television standard (discussed in the next section). This beam is deflected magnetically by a set of coils outside the tube bulb. The electron beam makes up charge lost through the incidence of light in individual mosaic cells and

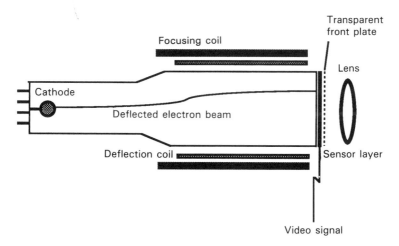

Figure 2.1 Schematic of the pickup tube of the Vidicon television camera.

so generates the video signal at the sensor element. This video signal is simply a continuous analogue signal proportional to the light intensity of the focused image. The camera electronics insert synchronization pulses (syncs.) to indicate scan lines, fields and frame ends (see Section 2.2.3).

A distinction is made between the following camera types depending on the sensor element: the standard vidicon has a sensor element comprised of antimony sulphide (Sb_2S_3), the silicon diode vidicon has a sensor element made from silicon (Si), while the plumbicon has a sensor element made of lead oxide (PbO).

Most solid-state cameras are based on charge-coupled device (CCD) technology, though there are several variations on the theme. In order for the reader to be at least acquainted with the names of these devices, they are listed here:

- charge transfer devices   CTD
- single transfer devices   STD
- bucket brigade devices   BBD
- charge coupled devices   CCD
- charge injection devices   CID
- surface charge coupled devices   SCCD
- bulk charge coupled devices   BCCD

CCD technology is the most widespread, the basic structure of which is that of an analogue shift register consisting of a series of closely spaced capacitors. Charge integration (accumulation) by the capacitors, photosites, caused by the photons comprising the incident light, provides the analogue representation of light intensity. At the end of the integration period (exposure time) these charges are read out of the sensor.

CCD sensors most commonly use one of three addressing strategies: interline transfer, frame transfer, and column–row transfer.

The interline transfer CCD is organized into column pairs of devices. An imaging column of photosensors is adjacent to an opaque vertical shift register (see Figure 2.2). Charge accumulates in the imaging column until the end of the integration period, when it is transferred to the opaque column. The signal then shifts vertically into a horizontal shift register that represents the picture sequentially, line by line. The advantage of the interline transfer is that the transfer time (to opaque storage) is short compared to the integration period. This is desirable because when transfer time approaches the integration time, solid-state sensors tend to exhibit a locally contained spreading of the image response, called smear. Thus, the interline transfer minimizes smear.

In the frame transfer organization (refer to Figure 2.3) the sensor consists of vertical columns of CCD shift registers divided into two zones. One zone, where charge accumulates during integration time, is photosensitive. When integration is complete, the whole array is transferred in parallel to the opaque storage area of the second zone.

A third type of solid-state sensor employs $x–y$ addressing to transfer charge from the photosite to the output signal amplifier. The sensor elements are addressed

time available for one line is:

$$T = 1/f = 1/15\,625 \text{ s} = 64 \times 10^{-6} \text{ s} = 64 \, \mu\text{s}$$

11.5 μs of this are used for the blanking and synchronizing signal. This consists of a 6.5 μs *porch* blanking signal and a 5 μs sync. The sync. pulse signals the beginning of one line and the end of another and the porch represents a quiescent voltage level which prevents the beam appearing as a bright line during the line flyback (when being displayed on a video monitor).

The end of the picture consisting of 625 lines, i.e. the frame, is characterized by several picture pulses which are significantly different from the line pulses. During these pulses, the picture is blanked and the beam returns to the top of the picture for the next frame. A (simplified) diagrammatic representation of a video signal is depicted in Figure 2.4.

Unfortunately for machine vision, the CCIR standard specifies a 4:3 horizontal-to-vertical aspect ratio for video signals. The television monitor has a similar aspect ratio and thus an image of a square will appear square. However, as we shall see shortly, image acquisition devices often have a 1:1 aspect ratio, meaning that the rectangular video picture is effectively squeezed into a square with a consequent geometric distortion. This has very severe repercussions for vision-based gauging applications which we will address in Chapter 3.

2.2.4 Characteristics of camera sensors

There are several measures of the usefulness and reliability of a camera sensor; these characteristics will be briefly considered in turn.

□ *Resolution*
Given that the purpose of the camera sensor is to convert an incident analogue optical image to some electrical signal, the resolution of a sensor can be defined as the number of optical image elements which can be discriminated by that sensor

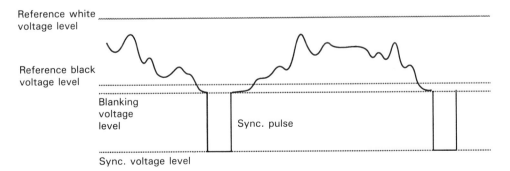

Figure 2.4 Composite video signal.

and represented by the resulting signal. The resolution is limited by the number of photosites in the sensor since this defines the frequency with which the optical image is sampled. The concept of image sampling is an important one and we will defer detailed discussion of this issue until Chapter 3. For the moment, note that in solid-state cameras the effective resolution of the sensor is approximately half that of the number of photosites in any given direction. Resolution is also limited by the array geometry and by how much opaque material separates the photosites: interline transfer sensors have less effective resolution than frame transfer sensors due to the presence of shielded buffers between each photosensitive line.

As we will see in Chapter 3, the resolution of the camera system is also constrained by the limitations imposed by the CCIR video standard and by the sampling frequency of the analogue-to-digital converter which converts the video signal to a digital image.

Tube camera resolution is a function of the electron-beam diameter relative to the area of the photoconductive layer. Tube camera resolution is generally higher than that of solid-state cameras and easily outstrips the limitations imposed by the CCIR standard.

☐　*Geometric faults*

For television cameras with electron-beam scanning, deviations in constancy of the vertical and horizontal deflection show up as faults in the geometrical placement of the picture content. Standard industrial cameras are not designed as measuring cameras but to generate a picture for subjective human examination, and they exhibit relatively large geometrical faults. For the standard industrial television camera it is usually ± 1 per cent or ± 2 per cent of the picture frame and it is usually much larger with cheaper cameras.

With CCD cameras there are no geometrical faults due to electron beam scanning; any geometric distortion is due to the lens.

☐　*Sensitivity and transfer linearity*

The input signal of an image sensor is a distribution of light or brightness. The output signal is a current or voltage which is related to the brightness. The sensitivity of the sensor is defined as the ratio of the output magnitude to the input magnitude.

In general, the output will be some power function of the input magnitude:

$$\text{output magnitude} = (\text{input magnitude})^{\gamma}$$

where γ (gamma) is the exponent of the transfer function which, rearranging the above equation, is given by:

$$\gamma = \frac{\log(\text{output magnitude})}{\log(\text{input magnitude})}$$

A linear sensor would have a γ of 1. The following are typical values of transfer linearity for common types of sensor:

Image sensor	Gamma
Sb_2S_3 vidicon	0.6
PbO plumbicon	0.95
CCD	1

☐ *Lag*

Lag is often defined as the percentage of the signal current at a certain point of the target some period after the illumination has been switched off. Typical values for an elapsed time of 60 ms are shown below:

Image sensor	Lag
Sb_2S_3	20%
PbO plumbicon	2%−5%
CCD	1%

The lag introduces a limitation in the practical industrial application of TV cameras in terms of the permissible speed of movement of an object under consideration.

☐ *Spectral sensitivity*

The spectral sensitivity of an image sensor system is defined as the variation of the output as a function of the wavelength of the incident light. Referring to Figure 2.5, we see that solid-state image sensors are sensitive to light in the near infra-red region of the spectrum, and since such radiation does not carry any useful visual information, an infra-red cut filter should be used with such cameras, particularly if they are to be used with incandescent lighting.

☐ *Blooming*

If the sensor of a television camera is subjected to intensive brightness, then the

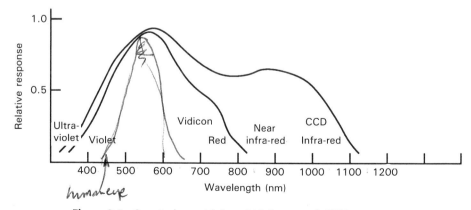

Figure 2.5 Spectral sensitivity of Vidicon and CCD cameras.

excess charge carriers spread into neighbouring zones and light is registered there also. Thus, a thin beam of very bright light will be sensed over an area considerably larger than the cross-sectional area of the beam. This effect is called 'blooming' and is especially noticeable with specular (mirror-like) reflections. While tube cameras are most susceptible to blooming, solid-state sensors, too, will exhibit this characteristic under extreme conditions.

☐ *Noise*

Noise, unwanted interference on the video signal, is defined quantitatively by the signal-to-noise ratio (S/N), i.e. the ratio of the amplitude of the wanted signal to the average amplitude of the interference. For television cameras, the signal-to-noise ratio is defined as the peak-to-peak video signal divided by the effective amplitude of the noise. If one follows general practice in telecommunications and

Table 2.1 CCD Camera systems

Vendor	Model	Camera type	Sensor resolution	Output signal	Interface required
Sony	XC-77CE	CCD Area	756×581	CCIR	Standard framestore
Sony	XC-57CE	CCD Area	500×582	CCIR	Standard framestore
Panasonic	WV50	CCD Area	500×582	CCIR	Standard framestore
Pulnix	TM-540	CCD Area	500×582	CCIR	Standard framestore
Fairchild	CCD3000	CCD Area	488×380	CCIR	Standard framestore
Hitachi	KP-120	CCD Area	320×240	CCIR	Standard framestore
Videk	Megaplus	CCD Area	1320×1035	Non-interlaced analogue; digital	Special framestore
Fairchild	CCD1600R	CCD Line-scan	3456×1	Analogue	Requires camera controller
Honeywell	HVS 256	CCD Line-scan	256×1	RS232; RS422	Conventional serial port
Fuji	PJ1	CCD Line-scan	2048×1	Analogue; Digital flags	Can be directly interfaced to PLC[a]
Analytic Vision Systems	IMS-90	CCD Line-scan	1024×1 2048×4 4096	Analogue; Digital	Slow-scan framestore; can be directly interfaced to PLC

[a]PLC: Programmable Logic Controller.

expresses the ratio of electrical variables of the same unit in logarithmic terms, one can compute the level, defined as twenty times the decimal log of the ratio of the linear variables and expressed in decibels (dB). Thus, a signal-to-noise ratio of 20 dB means that the picture quality is very bad (20 dB implies that $\log_{10}(S/N)$ equals 1 and, thus, the signal-to-noise ratio is 10:1). For satisfactory quality, a signal-to-noise ratio of 40 dB or more is required.

2.2.5 Commercially available cameras

Table 2.1 summarizes the characteristics of a number of popular CCD cameras which are available at time of writing. We have listed only CCD cameras since these are the most popular for industrial machine vision.

Exercises

1. Identify the basic operational differences between vidicon-tube cameras and solid-state cameras. Which type of camera is more appropriate for use in FMS (flexible manufacturing systems) requiring automated vision for either inspection or robot guidance? Why is this so?
2. What limitations does the European CCIR television standard impose on the effective resolving power of imaging equipment? Is it an appropriate standard for machine vision? Explain.
3. It is required to image a 5 cm wide object using a CCD camera, whose sensor measures 8.8 mm × 6.6 mm, at a distance of 0.5 m. What focal length lens should you choose? What options do you have if you wish to image an object which measures only 1 mm × 1 mm.

References and further reading

Batchelor, B.G., Hill, D.A. and Hodgson, D.C. (eds) 1985 *Automated Visual Inspection*, IFS (Publications) Ltd, U.K.

Blouke, M.M., Corrie, B., Heidtmann, D.L., Yang, F.H., Winzenread, M., Lust, M.L. and Marsh, H.H. 1987 'Large format, high resolution image sensors', *Optical Engineering*, Vol. 26, No. 9, pp. 837–43.

CCIR, International Radio Consultative Committee 1982 *Recommendations and Reports of the CCIR, 1982*, XVth Plenary Assembly, Geneva, Vol. XI, Part 1.

Dunbar, P. 1986 'Machine vision', *Byte*, Vol. 11, No. 1, pp. 161–73.

Herrick, C.N. 1972 *Television Theory and Servicing*, Reston Publishing Company, Virginia.

Market Intelligence Research Co. 1986 *Solid-state Cameras for Machine Vision*, Market Intelligence Research Company, 4000 Middle Field Road, Palo Alto, California, 94303, USA. (*Vision*, SME, Vol. 4, No. 1, p. 12.)

Tassone, J. 1987 'An illumination system for inspecting printed circuit boards with surface mounted components', *Vision*, SME, Vol. 4, No. 4, pp. 1–5.

3

Image acquisition and representation

3.1 Sampling and quantization

Any visual scene can be represented by a continuous function (in two dimensions) of some analogue quantity. This is typically the reflectance function of the scene: the light reflected at each visible point in the scene. Such a representation is referred to as an *image* and the value at any point in the image corresponds to the intensity of the reflectance function at that point.

A continuous analogue representation cannot be conveniently interpreted by a computer and an alternative representation, the *digital image*, must be used. Digital images also represent the reflectance function of a scene but they do so in a *sampled* and *quantized* form. They are typically generated with some form of optical imaging device (e.g. a camera) which produces the analogue image (e.g. the analogue video signal discussed in the preceding chapter), and an analogue-to-digital converter: this is often referred to as a 'digitizer', a 'frame-store', or 'frame-grabber'.

The frame-grabber samples the video signal in some predetermined fashion (usually in an equally spaced square grid pattern) and quantizes the reflectance function at those points into integer values called grey-levels (see Figure 3.1). Each integer grey-level value is known as a *pixel* and is the smallest discrete accessible sub-section of a digital image. The number of grey-levels in the (equally spaced) grey-scale is called the quantization or grey-scale resolution of the system. In all cases, the grey-scale is bounded by two grey-levels, black and white, corresponding to the minimum and maximum measurable intensity respectively. Most current acquisition equipment quantizes the video signal into 256 discrete grey-levels, each of which are conveniently represented by a single byte. In certain cases, a grey-scale of -128 to $+127$ is more convenient; processed images need not necessarily represent the reflectance function and pixels may assume negative values but the grey-level can still be represented by a signed-byte integer.

The sampling density, the number of sampling points per unit measure, is

Rectangular sampling pattern

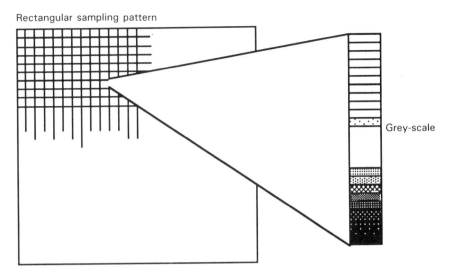

Grey-scale

Figure 3.1 Sampling and quantization.

usually referred to as the (spatial) resolution and, since the sampling device is usually arranged as a square grid, it is measured in terms of the number of sampling elements along each orthogonal axis. This normally corresponds to the extent of the number of pixels in both the horizontal and vertical directions. Most current commercial frame-grabbers have spatial resolutions of 512×512 pixels. In summary, digital image acquisition equipment is essentially concerned with the generation of a two-dimensional array of integer values representing the reflectance function of the actual scene at discrete spatial intervals, and this is accomplished by the processes of sampling and quantization. Since these are fundamentally important concepts, we will look at them in a little more depth in the remainder of this section.

3.1.1 Spatial frequency and the effects of sampling

Recall that the objective of the image acquisition system (which includes the sensor sub-system) is to convert an analogue optical image to a digital image in as faithful a manner as possible. As we have seen, this is achieved by first using the sensor to sample the analogue optical image, generating an analogue video signal, and then by subsequently re-sampling the video signal and generating the digital signal. Thus, there are three factors which can limit the effective resolution and fidelity of the final digital image:

    (a)   the sensor sampling frequency;
    (b)   the bandwidth of the video signal;
    (c)   the sampling frequency of the analogue-to-digital converter, i.e. the frame-grabber.

29

We shall consider each of these in turn. First, however, we need to look a little closer at the idea of sampling an analogue image and to develop the concept of spatial frequency. We will do this intuitively at first and then we will formalize the ideas somewhat. Readers who find this area interesting should consult Duda and Hart (1973) which contains a particularly lucid account of this topic.

High-frequency signals, such as high-pitch soundwaves, periodically change their value over a very short period of *time*. Similarly, a high-frequency spatial signal, such as an image, periodically changes its value (e.g. its intensity or grey-level) over a very short *distance*, i.e. it changes abruptly from one grey-level to another. Conversely, low spatial frequencies correspond to 'slower' changes in intensity where the change occurs gradually from one position in the image to another.

To make this idea more formal, consider a spatially unbounded analogue optical image $g(x, y)$. The *Fourier transform* $G(f_x, f_y)$ of the image $g(x, y)$ is defined by:

$$G(f_x, f_y) = \mathscr{F}(g(x, y))$$

$$= \int_{-\infty}^{\infty} \int_{-\infty}^{\infty} g(x, y) \exp[-2\pi i(f_x x + f_y y)] \, dx \, dy \qquad (3.1)$$

The *inverse Fourier transform* of $G(f_x, f_y)$ is defined by:

$$g(x, y) = \mathscr{F}^{-1}(G(f_x, f_y))$$

$$= \int_{-\infty}^{\infty} \int_{-\infty}^{\infty} G(f_x, f_y) \exp[2\pi i(f_x x + f_y y)] \, df_x \, df_y \qquad (3.2)$$

The variables f_x and f_y which identify the domain over which $G(f_x, f_y)$ is defined are known as the spatial frequencies in the x- and y-directions, respectively, and the domain is known as the *spatial frequency* domain. What do these variables and this domain represent? The integral in equation (3.2) can be viewed as a 'generalized sum' of complex exponentials, defined in terms of the spatial frequencies f_x and f_y, and in terms of the spatial coordinates x and y. Each exponential is weighted by a value given by $G(f_x, f_y)$ and, thus, equation (3.2) is an expansion (or expression) of the analogue optical function $g(x, y)$ in terms of this weighted generalized sum of exponentials. These weights are, in fact, given by equation (3.1), i.e. the Fourier transform of the image function, and will, of course, vary with image content. Since these complex exponentials can also be expressed in terms of sine functions,[*] a spatial frequency domain which has, for example, just two non-zero values at, say (f_{x_1}, f_{y_1}) and $(-f_{x_1}, -f_{y_1})$ corresponds to a sinusoidal variation in intensity in the spatial domain, i.e. to an image $g(x, y)$ which comprises sinusoidally undulating 'stripes' of alternating light and dark intensity. The period and orientation of these stripes depends on the exact values of f_{x_1} and

---

[*] $e^{i\theta} = \cos \theta + i \sin \theta$.

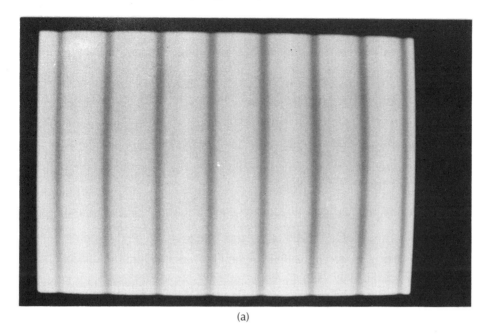

(a)

(b)

Figure 3.2 (a) An image comprising a sinusoidal variation in intensity along the x axis; and (b) its Fourier transform, comprising two spatial frequency components (f_{x_1}, f_{y_1}) and $(-f_{x_1}, -f_{y_1})$, both of which are spatial frequencies in the x direction.

f_{y_1}. Conversely, an image $g(x, y)$ which comprises a sinusoidal variation in intensity can be expressed in terms of the spatial frequencies (f_{x_1}, f_{y_1}) and $(-f_{x_1}, -f_{y_1})$; see Figure 3.2. The 'quicker' these sinusoidal variations, i.e. the greater the frequency of variation in the spatial domain, the further (f_{x_1}, f_{y_1}) and $(-f_{x_1}, -f_{y_1})$ are from the origin in the $G(f_x, f_y)$ domain. Of course, a sinusoidal variety in intensity is not a particularly common image. However, Fourier analysis tells us that more complex functions can be constructed by including more terms of varying weight in the 'generalized sum' of exponentials, i.e. *by including further spatial frequency components*. The exact weight is, again, determined by equation (3.1), i.e. the Fourier transform. An abrupt change in intensity will require the presence of a large number of terms which will correspond to high spatial frequencies, many of which are far removed from the origin of the $G(f_x, f_y)$ domain; see Figure 3.3. Thus, we now have arrived at the interpretation we required. That is: *high spatial frequencies correspond to the presence of abrupt, or sharp, changes in the intensity of the image.*

The next issue to which we turn is that of sampling. In particular, we would like to know what sampling frequency is required, i.e. how often one needs to sample in the spatial domain in order to represent an image faithfully. Shannon's sampling theorem tells us that a band-limited image (i.e. an image which does not comprise infinitely high spatial frequencies) can be faithfully represented (i.e. reconstructed) if the image is sampled at a frequency twice that of the highest spatial frequency present in the image. This sampling frequency is often referred to as the *Nyquist frequency*.

We are now in a position to return to address the three issues we raised at the beginning of this section: the effect of the sensor sampling frequency (resolution), the video signal bandwidth, and the analogue-to-digital (frame-grabber) sampling frequency on the effective resolving power of the image acquisition system.

First, we now see that a sensor which has, for example, 756 photosites in the horizontal direction, i.e. along a line, will only be capable of representing a sinusoidal variation in intensity which has a spatial frequency of 378 cycles per unit distance. A pattern of 378 alternately light and dark bars with abrupt edges, i.e. discontinuities in intensity, would obviously require a much higher sensor sampling frequency to represent the image faithfully.

Second, the resolution of a television picture is also limited by the number of lines and the frequency bandwidth of the video signal. We saw in Chapter 2 that the line frequency for the CCIR standard video signal is 15 625 Hz. In addition, the nominal bandwidth of the CCIR standard is 5.0 MHz, meaning that a signal can transmit a video image with five million periodic variations in the signal (brightness) levels. This results in an absolute maximum of $5 \times 10^6 \div 15\,625 = 320$ periodic (or sinusoidal) variations per line, that is, the maximum spatial frequency which can be faithfully represented by a video signal is 320 cycles per line.

Third, a frame-grabber which has, for example, a sampling frequency of 512 pixels in the horizontal direction, will only be capable of faithfully representing a sinusoidal variation in intensity which has a spatial frequency of 256 cycles per unit

(a)

(b)

Figure 3.3 (a) An image comprising a step discontinuity in intensity along the x axis; and (b) its Fourier transform, exclusively comprising spatial frequency components f_x, i.e. spatial frequencies in the x direction.

33

distance. Again, a pattern of 256 alternately light and dark bars with abrupt edges would require a much higher sampling frequency to represent the image faithfully.

3.2 Inter-pixel distances

As mentioned in the preceding chapter, video signals assume an aspect ratio of 4:3 (horizontal-to-vertical) and we noted in Section 3.1 that, although framestores with 4:3 aspect ratios are becoming available, they normally use a square aspect ratio of 1:1. The aspect ratio mis-match has serious repercussions for gauging or measuring functions of an inspection system: the rectangular picture is being squeezed into a

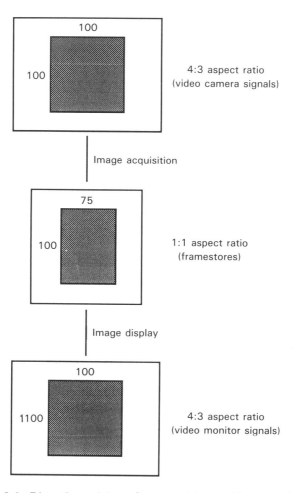

Figure 3.4 Distortion arising when acquiring a video signal with a conventional (square) framestore.

square image and, hence, the effective distance between horizontal pixels is $\frac{4}{3}$ times greater than that between vertical neighbours (see Figure 3.4).

The situation becomes even more unsatisfactory when one considers the distance between a pixel and its diagonal neighbour. While most discussions of inter-pixel distances usually assume the diagonal inter-pixel interval to be $\sqrt{2}$ (i.e. the length of the hypotenuse completing the right-angle triangle formed by the horizontal inter-pixel interval of length 1 and the vertical inter-pixel interval of length 1). However, if we are working with a framestore which has a square aspect ratio and has a video signal which as a 4:3 aspect ratio, then the diagonal inter-pixel interval is, in fact, $\sqrt{\frac{5}{3}}$, i.e. the length of the hypotenuse completing the right-angle triangle formed by the horizontal inter-pixel interval of length $\frac{4}{3}$ and the vertical inter-pixel interval of length 1 (see Figure 3.5).

Unfortunately, this is not the complete story. The CCIR standard stipulates that a picture comprises 625 lines. However, only 576 of these carry visual information while the remainder are used for other purposes. Framestores with a vertical resolution of 512 pixels (i.e. 512 lines) *do not* capture all 576 of these lines of video; they only capture the first 512 of them. This introduces a further distortion, resulting in an effective CCIR aspect ratio of $4:(3 \times \frac{512}{576}) = 4:2.66$ or $3:2$. The effective vertical, horizontal and diagonal inter-pixel distances are thus 1, $\frac{3}{2}$, $\sqrt{\frac{13}{4}}$.

3.3 Adjacency conventions

There is yet another problem which is associated with the representation of digital images: the exact spatial relationship of one pixel with its neighbours. In effect, this problem is one of defining exactly which are the neighbours of a given pixel. Consider the 3×3 neighbourhood in an image (shown in Figure 3.6) where the

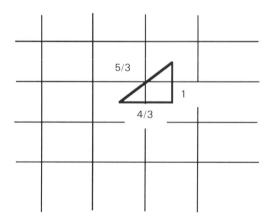

Figure 3.5 Inter-pixel distances.

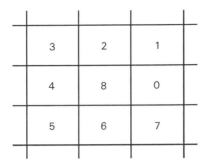

Figure 3.6 A 3 × 3 pixel neighbourhood.

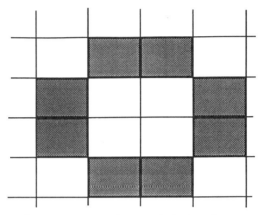

Figure 3.7 Adjacency conventions: a dark doughnut on a white table.

pixels are labelled 0 through 8; which pixels does pixel 8 touch? One convention, called 4-adjacency, stipulates that pixel 8 touches (i.e. is connected to) pixels 0, 2, 4, and 6, but does not touch (i.e. is not connected to pixels 1, 3, 5, and 7). An alternative convention, called 8-adjacency, stipulates that pixel 8 is connected to all eight neighbours.

Adopting either convention universally can, however, lead to difficulties. Figure 3.7 shows parts of a digital image depicting, in extremely simplified form, a dark doughnut on a white table. If we apply the 4-adjacency convention, then we have an obvious problem: there are four 'doughnut segments' (two vertical and two horizontal) but none of the segments is touching: the segments are not connected. Applying the 8-adjacency convention, the segments are now connected in a ring (as we would expect) but now so too is the inside of the doughnut connected to the outside: a topological anomaly.

In themselves, neither convention is sufficient and it is normal practice to use both conventions: one for an object and one for the background on which it rests. In fact, this can be extended quite generally so that the adjacency conventions are applied alternately to image regions which are recursively nested (or embedded)

within other regions as one goes from level to level in the nesting. Thus, one would apply 4-adjacency to the background region, 8-adjacency to the objects resting on the background, 4-adjacency to holes or regions contained within the objects, 8-adjacency to regions contained within these, and so on. This convention means that one never encounters topological anomalies such as the one described in the above example. Because the 8-adjacency convention allows diagonally connected neighbours, measurements of object features (e.g. its perimeter) will be more faithful with 8-adjacency. Consequently, if it is possible to stipulate which convention is to be applied to a particular object of interest, one should opt for the 8-adjacency convention.

The preceding discussion has been developed in the context of the acquisition of digital images from area cameras. As we have seen, however, line-scan cameras are extremely important imaging devices, particularly for high-resolution gauging applications. The same sampling and quantization processes must also be used with these linear array cameras, the only difference in this case is that only one line of video information needs to be digitized. Similarly, the discussion of adjacency conventions and inter-pixel distances applies equally. Image acquisition equipment for line-scan sensors will often be custom-designed for a particular application and configuration, although it is worth reiterating the point made earlier that matched line-scan cameras and digitizers and, indeed, line-scan digitizers are now appearing on the market. These line-scan digitizers are, in fact, general purpose devices which can deal with many different scan rates. They are often referred to as slow-scan digitizers. This is an unfortunate misnomer: they are really variable-scan digitizers and can deal with extremely high data rates.

3.4 Image acquisition hardware

A typical machine vision system can be configured in two ways: by building it yourself using off-the-shelf equipment or by buying a complete turnkey system. The former alternative is very cost-effective but a significant amount of work needs to be done to integrate the system, ensuring that the image acquisition and processing devices are correctly matched with the host computer and can be controlled by it. The latter alternative is more expensive but, depending on the application, turnaround time on development should be much reduced.

There are two mutually dependent components to be chosen when configuring a machine vision system with off-the-shelf equipment: the CPU and the framestore. Most of the commercial framestores are dedicated to just a few of the more popular computer buses, in particular, the VME bus, the Multibus, the Q-Bus, the IBM PC bus, the Nu-bus (Apple Macintosh II), and to some extent the IBM MicroChannel Architecture used in the newer PS-2 models. Each bus enforces certain restrictions on the way the framestore is used and most of the functional differences are related to the bus structure and the available support equipment (i.e. the framestore sister boards).

Table 3.1 Overview of commercial frame-grabber hardware

Feature	ITI[a] PCVision Plus	ITI Series 100	ITI 150/151 Family	ITI 200 Family	Matrox MVP-AT MVP-NB	Datacube Max Video Family	DT[b] 2851/ 2858	DT 2603	DT 2861	DT 225
Frame buffers	2	up to 4	2 per board[c]	up to 4 per board[c]	4	Many[c]	2	1	16	1
Spatial resolution	512 × 512	512 × 512	512 × 512	512 × 512	512 × 512	512 × 512	512 × 512	256 × 256	512 × 512	768 × 512
Bus compatibility	PC-AT	PC-AT VME Multibus Q-bus	VME 151: VME-AT adaptor	Q-bus	PC-AT	VME	PC-AT Q-bus VME	PC-AT	PC-AT	Nu-bus
RS-170	Yes	Yes	Yes	Yes	Yes	Yes	Yes	Yes	Yes	Yes
CCIR	Yes	Yes	Yes	Yes	Yes	Yes	Yes	Yes	Yes	Yes
Grey levels	256	256	256	256	256	256	256	64	256	256
Dedicated Graphics plane	0	4	—	—	4	Several	0	2	0	0
I/O mapped	No	Yes	—	Yes	—	—	Yes	—	—	—
Memory mapped	Yes	Yes	Yes	No	Yes	Yes	Yes	Yes	Yes	Yes
Input LUTS	Yes	Yes	Yes	Yes	Yes	Yes	Yes	Yes	Yes	Yes
Pseudo-colour	Yes	Yes	Yes	Yes	Yes	Yes	Yes	Yes	Yes	No
Pan/scroll/zoom	Yes	Yes	Yes[c]	Yes[c]	Yes	Yes[c]	—	No	—	No
Dedicated video bus	No	No	Yes	Yes	Yes	Yes	Yes	No	Yes	No
Video inputs	2	3	4	4	1	8	1	1	1	4
4:3 aspect ratio compensation	Yes	Yes	No	No	No	No	No	No	No	Yes

Feature	ITI[d] PCVision Plus	ITI Series 100	ITI 150/151 Family	ITI 200 Family	Matrox MVP-AT MVP-NB	Datacube Max Video Family	DT[e] 2851/2858	DT 2603	DT 2861	DT 225
Convolution	No	Binary images	Yes[c]	Yes[c]	Yes 3 × 3 400ms	Yes[c] up to 8 × 8 in realtime	Yes not in realtime	No	Yes not in realtime	No
Erosion	No	Binary images	Yes[c]	Yes[c]	Yes	Yes[c]	Yes	No	Yes	No
Dilation	No	Binary images	Yes	Yes[c]	Yes	Yes[c]	Yes	No	Yes	No
Sister boards	No	No	Yes	Yes	Yes	Yes	Yes	No	Yes	No
Real-time	No	No	Yes[c]	Yes	Yes	Yes[c]	Yes	No	Yes	No
ALU operations										
Histogram	No	No	Yes[c]	No	Yes	Yes[c]	Yes	No	—	No
Feature[f] extraction	No	No	Yes[c]	No	No	Yes[c]	No	No	No	No
Area of interest	No	No	Yes[c]	Yes[c]	Yes	Yes[c]	No	No	No	No
Prototyping board	No	No	Yes	No	No	Yes[c]	No	No	No	No
Variable	No	No	Yes	No	No	Yes[c]	No	No	Yes	No
Scan interface										

[a] Imaging Technology Corporation.
[b] Data Translation Corporation.
[c] Functionality provided by sister board.
[d] Imaging Technology Corporation.
[e] Data Translation Corporation.
[f] A feature in this context has an extremely restricted meaning: it is a region having a specified grey-level.

It would not be appropriate to enter into a discussion of different CPUs here; suffice it to say that most microprocessors are supported by VME bus and Multibus boards (e.g. 68030, 80386, 32032), while Q-bus computers are generally MicroVax based. The IBM PC AT bus is supported by IBM's PC-AT and the multitude of PC clones (most of which are now significantly faster than the AT).

Once an image has been digitized, it is stored on the frame-grabber in memory as a square two-dimensional array. It may now be accessed, processed, and analysed by the host computer. However, it is frequently desirable to process the digital image somewhat before the computer ever uses the information, mainly because the resultant image may be more amenable to subsequent analysis and it may take the computer an inordinately long time to perform such processing. This pre-processing can frequently be accomplished in one frame-time (40 ms) by hardware resident on the frame-grabber or by sister boards for the frame-grabber. This rate of processing is often called real-time image processing, as the image data can be processed at the same rate at which the camera system generates it. Recall, however, the comment in Chapter 1 that a more pragmatic definition of real-time in machine vision is simply that the vision process should keep up with production rates, i.e. if the vision system produces the information as quickly as it is required, it runs in real-time.

To provide the reader with some idea of the capabilities that are provided by some commercial frame-grabbers and sister boards, a brief summary of the main characteristics is given in Table 3.1. Unfortunately, many of the capabilities that are cited refer specifically to image processing techniques which are not covered until the next chapter. To describe them here, however briefly, would be pre-emptive and you should refer again to this section after having read Chapter 4.

Custom commercial systems, which can be bought complete with processing and analysis software, and subsequently programmed to accomplish a required function, tend to be significantly more expensive than a system configured from off-the-shelf equipment. Since such systems are by their very nature unique, a direct comparison is very difficult. However, a brief synopsis of some systems that are available is included so that the reader can form some idea of their capabilities.

Universal Instruments Corp. market several printed circuit board (PCB) inspection systems. Model 5511 exploits four high-resolution CCD cameras, each of which views a small portion of the board from a different angle in order to facilitate thorough inspection. The complete board is inspected by moving the PCB on an X–Y table. It uses high-speed strobed light emitting diode (LED) illumination to allow it to take images while the PCB is being moved on the X–Y table. This increases the overall speed of the system quite significantly since it removes the acceleration and deceleration time between snapshots. The quoted inspection performance is an impressive twelve square inches per second. The 5515 is based on the Motorola 68020 (nominally running at 20 MHz) and can use CAD data to drive the inspection strategy.

IRI (International Robomation Intelligence) Ltd offer a wide variety of systems, from development vision systems with imaging resolutions of 256×256

and 512 × 512, to fully fledged turnkey PCB inspection systems. The development systems are typically based on Motorola 680XX microprocessors and incorporate a real-time operating system and an extensive library of image processing functions. It should be emphasized that this library of functions is a collection of *image processing* routines, rather than *image analysis* routines. The distinction will be discussed in detail in the next chapter but suffice it for the present to note that a significant amount of software development will be required in most cases before a fully operational target system can be configured and incorporated in a manufacturing environment. A typical IRI development system, the SD512 Vision System, features 512 × 512 × 8 bit resolution, and can store eight images simultaneously. It can interface to normal video cameras, to line-scan cameras, and to special-purpose video cameras such as the Videk MEGAPLUS 1320 × 1035 sensor. Optional array processors are available to implement convolution and algebraic operations in near real time (250 million operations per second). A development system such as this would normally incorporate a MC68020 25 MHz host processor, a MC68851 memory management unit, 8 Mbytes of memory, a convolution processor, a correlation processor, CCD camera, colour monitor, terminal, 56 Mbyte hard disk, eight camera ports, and 2 Mbytes of image memory. Complete turnkey systems, e.g. the IRI PCB INSPECTOR would typically cost between two and three times the cost of a development system.

In a similar vein to IRI Ltd, Computer Recognition Systems Ltd, in the United Kingdom, offer a mix of configured development systems and application engineering expertise and have developed machine vision systems for several industries. A typical CRS development system comprises at least a VMEbus workstation (MC68020, 1 Mbyte program RAM, 40 Mbyte hard disk, 5.25″ floppy disk drive, Idris operating system, Pascal, and C), two 512 × 512 × 8 bit image memory, 8 bit resolution frame-grabber, extensive image processing algorithm library and development software, edge detector (simple 3 × 3 masks), and four video inputs.

Note that these summaries, and indeed Table 3.1, are provided for illustration only; while every effort has been made to ensure that this information is correct, manufacturers are continually upgrading their products and specific models often re-appear with much enhanced capabilities. As such, no responsibility can be accepted for errors in the functional specifications or prices. You should contact the vendor to ensure that the information is accurate and up-to-date.

3.5 Speed considerations

There are several issues which must be addressed when evaluating vision systems and their potential processing speed. The first of these is obviously the processing power of the host computer. An Intel 80286-based PC-AT will operate about three times faster than an 8086-based PC, while an 80386-based system can deliver nearly ten times the power of a PC. A DEC MicroVAX will outperform an LSI-11 or

PDP-11. Many of the newer, more powerful VME-bus systems are based on Motorola's 68030; but you should be sure to compare the processor clock frequencies and memory access times of otherwise similar CPU boards.

No matter how fast the CPU is, if it can't communicate effectively with the framestore then the effective image acquisition time will become significant, i.e. the image may be grabbed in $\frac{1}{25}$th second but it may take nearly one second to transfer it to the host. In general, memory-mapped framestores are the most efficient since transfer may not be necessary; this is the distinct advantage of VME systems, such as some of those marketed by Datacube and Imaging Technology. Many boards are input/output (I/O) mapped, however, and image transfer must take place pixel by pixel; some boards attempt to alleviate this bottleneck by offering DMA (direct memory access) transfer capabilities.

Most microprocessor systems do not support floating point arithmetic directly (the Inmos Transputer is one exception) and, if your application requires a significant number of floating point operations, this may be another computational bottleneck. Even if you can get a floating point co-processor, it is best to adhere to integer arithmetic wherever possible when writing image analysis software.

As is evident from the survey of imaging systems in the preceding section, most framestores facilitate simple image manipulation (such as contrast stretching, thresholding, trivial segmentation: see next chapter for detailed explanation) through the use of look-up tables (LUT). Each LUT will have an entry for every grey-level that the system can deal with, typically 256 of them. This entry corresponds to the value to which this grey-level is to be changed. When digitizing the video signal each incoming pixel is checked against the LUT, and the table value, not the digitized value, is stored in the frame buffer.

Most vendors now offer ALU (arithmetic logic unit) boards which contain high-speed pipe-line processors. Basic operation includes 8 bit 2's complement, logical AND, OR, XOR, multiplication, and 16 bit addition. A full frame can usually be processed in one frametime (40 ms). These boards are intended to provide real-time frame summation, thresholding, contrast enhancement, and relatively fast edge enhancement and filtering. If real-time filtering, such as edge detection, is required then sister boards can often be deployed. It is important to note that these systems generally utilize their own high-speed video bus to effect communication between the frame-grabber and the sister processing boards.

As a concluding note, remember that the application requirements will dictate the effective pixel throughout the inspection or robot vision system, which, in turn, will dictate the required architecture and whether or not the application is feasible. If real-time response is required, as it normally will be, this does not necessarily mean that it must process the part in, say, 10 ms; it means that the machine vision system must not delay the overall production system. If extremely fast on-the-fly processing is required then one may have to restrict the functionality of the system somewhat to ensure a feasible solution or, alternatively, one may have to deploy dedicated hardware to implement either the initial processing or subsequent analysis, or both.

Exercises

1. What compatibility problems would you encounter in measuring the perimeter of objects when the alternate 8-adjacency/4-adjacency convention is used?

2. What do you understand by the terms 'quantization resolution' and 'sampling density'? Identify two adjacency conventions and discuss the merits of each.

3. What adjacency convention would you choose in an application to measure visually the perimeter of coastlines in ordnance survey maps using a conventional 4:3 aspect ratio CCIR camera and a 1:1 aspect ratio framestore? How would you ensure that your measurement is as accurate as possible, given a fixed field of view?

4. What problems do you encounter when attempting to use line-scan cameras?

5. Dedicated video buses are used to alleviate the communication bottleneck between frame-grabbers and their sister boards. Why?

References and further reading

Agin, G. 1975 *An Experimental Vision System for Industrial Application*, SRI International, Technical Report No. 103.

Agin, G. 1977 *Servoing with Visual Feedback*, SRI International, Technical Report No. 149.

Agin, G. 1980 'Computer vision systems for industrial inspection and assembly', *Computer*, Vol. 13, No. 5.

Beedie, M. 1986 'Image IC detects edges in real time', *Electronic Design*, May, pp. 50–8.

Duda, R.O. and Hart, P.E. 1973 *Pattern Classification and Scene Analysis*, Wiley, New York.

Dunbar, P. 1986 'Machine vision', *Byte*, Vol. 11, No. 1, pp. 161–73.

Giordano, A., Maresca, M., Sandini, G., Vernazza, T. and Ferrari, D. 1985 *A Systolic Convolver for Parallel Multiresolution Edge Detection*, Internal Report, DIST, University of Genoa.

Giordano, A., Maresca, M., Sandini, G., Vernazza, T. and Ferrari, D. 1987 'VLSI-based systolic architecture for fast Gaussian convolution', *Optical Engineering*, Vol. 26, No. 1, pp. 63–8.

Healy, P. and Vernon D. 1988 *Very Coarse Granularity Parallelism: Implementing 3-D Vision with Transputers*, Proc. Image Processing '88, Blenheim Online Ltd., London, pp. 229–45.

Li, H.F., Tsang, C.M. and Cheung, Y.S. 1983 'A low-cost real-time imaging and processing system, *Software and Microsystems*, Vol. 2, No. 5, pp. 121–9.

Plessey Semiconductors Ltd 1986 *PDSP16401 2-Dimensional Edge Detector*, Preliminary product information.

Selfridge, P.G. and Mahakian, S. 1985 'Distributed computing for vision: architecture and a benchmark test, *IEEE Transactions on Pattern Analysis and Machine Intelligence*, Vol. PAMI/7, No. 5, pp. 623–6.

4

Fundamentals of digital image processing

Although the distinction between digital image processing and digital image analysis is not immediately obvious, it is an extremely important one. Image processing can be thought of as a transformation which takes an image into an image, i.e. it starts with an image and produces a modified (enhanced) image. On the other hand, digital image analysis is a transformation of an image into something other than an image, i.e. it produces some information representing a description or a decision. However, digital image analysis techniques are usually applied to previously processed (enhanced) images. Since the analysis of enhanced images is accomplished quickly and easily by human observers, it is often erroneously assumed that the analysis phase is easy, if not trivial. Although image processing techniques often provide more pleasing or more visually accessible images when viewed by a human observer, and the human is able to detect salient features without difficulty, it is essential to realize that the interpretation of such emergent features is simple only in the context of the powerful perceptual abilities of the human visual system.

For machine vision systems, the sole purpose of image processing is to produce images which make the subsequent analysis more simple and more reliable. We are not at all interested in how 'well' the image looks. In particular, the image processing phase should facilitate the extraction of information, it should compensate for non-uniform illumination, and, possibly, re-adjust the image to compensate for distortions introduced by the imaging system.

Historically, digital image processing had two main thrusts to its development. One was the natural extension of one-dimensional (temporal) digital signal processing to two (spatial) dimensions. Consequently, two-dimensional signal processing was approached from a mathematical basis, allowing a great deal of rigorous manipulation to be performed, using classical linear system theory. The second, more heuristic, thrust considers digital images as a set of discrete sample points, performing arithmetic operations on the individual points. This contrasts with the signal processing approach which treats images as a discrete representation of a continuous two-dimensional function. We will continue our discussion of digital image processing from the second viewpoint, addressing some simple but useful techniques, and drawing when appropriate from the signal processing approach.

There are, broadly speaking, three distinct classes of operations: point operations, neighbourhood operations, and geometric operations. We mentioned in the preceding chapter that there is a trend to perform as much image processing as possible in hardware, particularly in advanced frame-grabbers or in their sister boards which have access to the image data via a dedicated video bus. Point and neighbourhood operations are typically the type of operations that are performed by these frame-grabber sister boards, while very few systems offer any extensive operations for geometric image processing.

4.1 Point operations

A point operation is an operation in which each pixel in the output image is a function of the grey-level of the pixel at the corresponding position in the input image, and only of that pixel. Point operations are also referred to as grey-scale manipulation operations. They cannot alter the spatial relationships of the image. Typical uses of point operations include photometric decalibration, to remove the effects of spatial variations in the sensitivity of a camera system; contrast stretching

101	100	103	105	107	105	103	110
110	140	120	122	130	130	121	120
134	134	135	131	137	138	120	121
132	132	132	133	133	150	160	155
134	140	140	135	140	156	160	174
130	138	139	150	169	175	170	165
126	133	138	149	163	169	180	185
130	140	150	169	178	185	190	200

Figure 4.1 Digital image.

(e.g. if a feature or object occupies a relatively small section of the total grey-scale image, these point operations can manipulate the image so that it occupies the entire range); and thresholding, in which all pixels having grey-levels in specified ranges in the input image are assigned a single specific grey-level in the output image. As we shall see, these operations are most effectively accomplished using the hardware input look-up tables (LUTs) which are provided by most frame-grabbers.

4.1.1 Contrast stretching

Consider the contrived digital image shown in Figure 4.1. If we look at the distribution of the grey-levels in this image, we find that there are grey-levels in the ranges from 100 to 200. Obviously the complete range is not being used and the contrast of this image would be quite poor. The contrived grey-level histogram shown in Figure 4.2 illustrates graphically this poor use of the available grey-scale. We wish to enhance the contrast so that all grey-levels of the grey-scale are utilized. This contrast stretching is achieved by first shifting all the values so that the actual pixel grey-level range begins at 0, i.e. add to every pixel the difference between the final low value (0) and the initial low value (100): $0 - 100 = -100$. The effect of this is shown in Figure 4.3.

Next, we scale everything, reassigning values in the range 0–100 to the range 0–255, i.e. we scale by a factor $= (255 - 0)/(100 - 0) = 2.55$; see Figure 4.4.

Thus, in this instance, to stretch the contrast so that all grey-levels in the grey-scale are utilized, one must simply apply the following operation:

```
new pixel value:=(old pixel value-100)*2.55
```

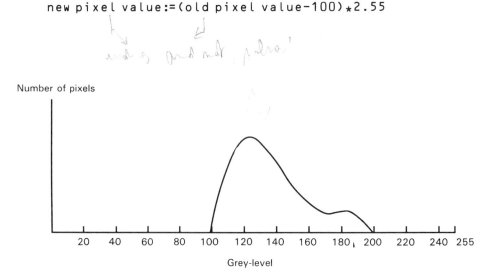

Figure 4.2 Grey-level histogram.

Number of pixels

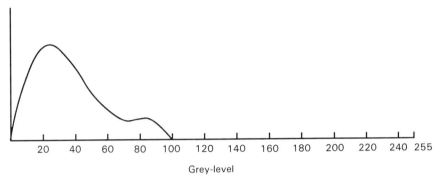

Grey-level

Figure 4.3 Shifted grey-level histogram.

Number of pixels

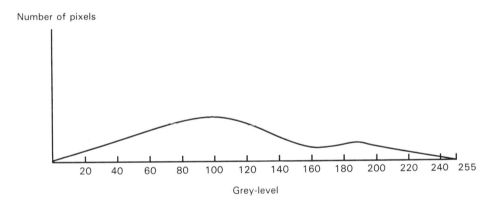

Grey-level

Figure 4.4 Stretched grey-level histogram.

By way of example, let us consider the application of this stretching to any pixel having either the lowest grey-level (100) in the original image or the highest grey-level (200) in the original image:

```
If old pixel value=100
   new pixel value:=(100-100)*2.55
                  =0

If old pixel value=200
   new pixel value:=(200-100)*2.55
                  =255
```

We can express the algorithm a little more formally in pseudo-code as follows:

```
/* contrast stretching in a 512×512 pixel image */

/* HIGH and LOW are assumed to be the highest and lowest
grey-levels, respectively, in the unstretched image */

scale_factor:=255 / (HIGH-LOW)

FOR i:=1 TO 512 DO
 FOR j:=1 to 512 DO

   IF image[i,j] < LOW
    THEN
      image[i,j]:=0
    ELSE
     IF image[i,j] > HIGH
      THEN
        image[i,j]:=255
      ELSE

       /* scale */

       image[i,j]:=(image[i,j] - LOW)
       *scale_factor
```

while the LUT formulation might be written as:

```
/* contrast stretching using LUT */

scale_factor:=255 / (HIGH-LOW)

/* initialise LUT */

FOR i:=0 TO LOW-1 DO
 LUT[i]:=0

FOR I:=LOW TO HIGH DO
 LUT[i]:=(i-LOW)*scale-factor

FOR i:=HIGH+1 TO 255 DO
 LUT[i]:=255

/* stretch using LUT */

FOR i:=1 TO 512 DO
 FOR j:=1 to 512 DO

   image[i,j]:=LUT[ image[i,j] ]
```

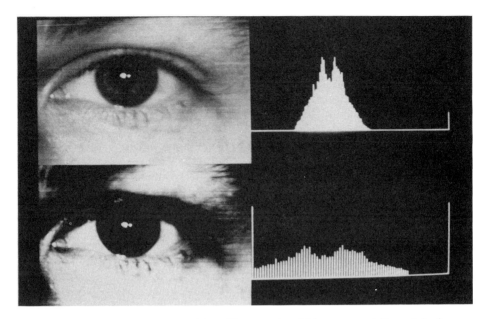

Figure 4.5 Contrast stretching. The grey-level histogram of the original image (top-left) is shown at the top-right; the stretched image with its histogram is shown below.

As an example, Figure 4.5 shows the results of applying this contrast stretching algorithm to a real digital image. The associated grey-level histograms are displayed to the right of the image.

There are many other approaches which can be used for contrast enhancement, e.g. histogram equalization is a technique which computes the histogram of the grey-level distribution in the image and reassigns grey-levels to pixels in an effort to generate a histogram where there are equally many pixels at every grey-level, thereby producing an image with a flat or uniform grey-level histogram.

4.1.2 Thresholding

Some scenes, e.g. those of bare printed circuit boards (PCBs), can be very simple, from a visual point of view, in that they comprise just one or two types of objects: in this case the solder tracks and the circuit board. Suppose we wish to process an image of such a scene so that it exhibits extremely high contrast and so that the solder tracks and circuit board are very easily distinguishable. If we stipulate that there are just two allowable grey-levels, black and white, then this would certainly result in the requisite contrast. The problem is to convert a grey-scale image (typically with 256 grey-levels) into an image with just two levels of grey. Consider again a contrived grey-scale histogram. In Figure 4.6 we can see that all the image pixels representing the circuit board *probably* have grey-levels in the range 0–160 while the solder tracks *probably* have grey-levels in the range 160–255. If we assign all the pixels in the range 0–160 to be black and all pixels in the range 160–255 to be white we will give effect to this extreme contrast stretching. Happily, we also now have an explicit labelling in our image: the circuit board pixels are labelled (identified) with a grey-level of 0 and the solder is labelled with a grey-level of 255. In effect we have nominated the grey-level 160 as the *threshold* and the reassignment of pixel values is known as *thresholding*. The effect of thresholding on the grey-scale histogram can be seen in Figure 4.7; the pseudo-code that follows summarizes the thresholding algorithm:

```
/* Threshold an image in place (i.e. without an */
/* explicit destination_image) */

FOR i:=1 TO 512 DO
 FOR j:=1 to 512 DO

  IF image[i,j] > threshold
    THEN
     image[i,j]:=255
    ELSE
     image[i,j]:=0
```

The algorithm may also be formulated using a LUT:

```
/* Threshold an image in place (i.e. without an */
/* explicit destination_image) using a LUT */

/* initialise LUT */

FOR i:=0 TO threshold DO
 LUT[i]:=0

FOR i:=threshold+1 TO 255 DO
 LUT[i]:=255

/* threshold using LUT */

FOR i:=1 TO 512 DO
 FOR j:=1 to 512 DO

  image[i,j]:=LUT[ image[i,j] ]
```

Note that the subject of thresholding is an important one to which we will return and will discuss in greater detail in Chapter 5, specifically with regard to the

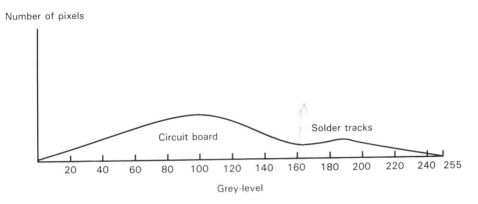

Figure 4.6 Grey-level histogram of a PCB.

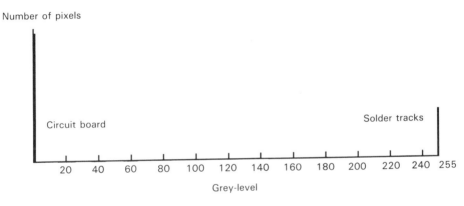

Figure 4.7 Grey-level histogram of a PCB after thresholding.

selection of the threshold point and to the incorporation of contextual information when applying the threshold.

An example of digital image thresholding is shown in Figure 4.8.

4.1.3 Noise suppression by image addition

If it is possible to obtain multiple images of a scene, each taken at a different time, and if the scene contains no moving objects, then the noise in the image can be reduced by averaging these images. The rationale is quite simple: in the averaging process the constant part of the image (that which is due to light reflected from stationary objects) is unchanged while the noise, which will in general change from image to image, will accumulate more slowly. The assumptions inherent in this

51

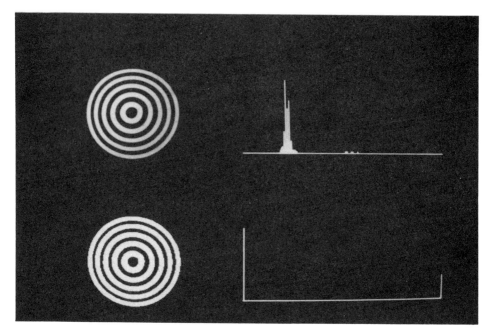

Figure 4.8 Thresholding. A grey-scale image (top-left) with its histogram (top-right) is thresholded at a grey-scale value of 128 (bottom-left); the resultant histogram is shown in the bottom-left quadrant.

approach are as follows:

1. The noise in each image is indeed uncorrelated.
2. The noise has a zero mean value, i.e. it averages out to an image with a grey-level of zero which contributes nothing to the real image.

With these assumptions, it is possible to show that averaging N images increases the signal-to-noise ratio by $\sqrt{N}$.

Many commercial framestores incorporate facilities to accomplish this averaging in real time (i.e. as the image is acquired) and, as such, it is worth bearing this technique in mind as it involves very little computational overhead. However, you should also bear in mind the assumptions upon which this technique is based; not all noise has these desirable properties.

4.1.4 Background subtraction

Digital image subtraction refers to an operation in which the pixel values of two images are subtracted on a point by point basis. It can be useful for the subtraction of a *known* pattern (or image) of superimposed noise or, indeed, for motion detection: stationary objects cancel each other out while moving objects are highlighted when two images of the same dynamic scene, which have been taken at slightly different times, are subtracted. This process of subtraction of an uninteresting background image from a foreground image containing information of interest is referred to, not surprisingly, as 'background subtraction'.

Photometric decalibration is one of the most important applications of background subtraction. In some circumstances, camera systems exhibit non-uniform response to light across the field of view. Quite often, this is caused by the lens and is manifested as an image centre which is somewhat brighter than the periphery. This can cause severe problems if one is using thresholding techniques to isolate objects. Since the grey-level which is assumed to correspond to the object may change (from point to point) depending on the position in the image, one solution (apart from replacing the lens) is to model this non-uniform response by, e.g. taking an image of a uniformly shaded surface, identifying the minimum grey-level of this image and subtracting this value from each pixel to generate an image which represents the effective response of the camera. Images which are subsequently acquired can then be processed by subtracting this calibration image from them.

4.2 Neighbourhood operations

A neighbourhood operation generates an 'output' pixel on the basis of the pixel at the corresponding position in the input image *and on the basis of its neighbouring pixels*. The size of the neighbourhood may vary: several techniques use 3×3 or 5×5 neighbourhoods centred at the input pixel, but many of the more advanced and useful techniques now use neighbourhoods which may be as large as 63×63 pixels. The neighbourhood operations are often referred to as 'filtering operations'. This is particularly true if they involve the *convolution* of an image with a filter kernel or mask. Such filtering often addresses the removal (or suppression) of noise or the enhancement of edges, and is most effectively accomplished using convolver (or filtering) hardware, available as sister boards for most frame-grabbers.

Other neighbourhood operations are concerned with modifying the image, not by filtering it in the strict sense, but by applying some logical test based on, e.g. the presence or absence of object pixels in the local neighbourhood surrounding the pixel in question. Object thinning, or skeletonizing, is a typical example of this type of operation, as are the related operations of erosion and dilation, which, respectively, seek to contract and enlarge an object in an orderly manner.

Since convolution is such an important part of digital image processing, we will discuss it in detail before proceeding.

4.2.1 Convolution

The convolution operation is much used in digital image processing and, though it can appear very inaccessible when presented in a formal manner for real continuous functions (signals and images), it is quite a simple operation when considered in a discrete domain.

Before discussing discrete convolution, let us consider why one is interested in the operation in the first place. The two-dimensional convolution integral, which is given by the equation:

$$g(i, j) = f * h = \int_{-\infty}^{\infty} \int_{-\infty}^{\infty} f(i - m, j - n) \, h(m, n) \, \mathrm{d}m \, \mathrm{d}n$$

embodies the fact that the output g of a shift-invariant linear system (i.e. most optical electronic and optoelectronic systems, to a good approximation, and most filtering techniques) is given by the 'convolution' or application of the input signal f with a function h which is characteristic of the system. Thus, the form of g depends on the input f (obviously) and on the form of the system h through which it is being passed. The relationship is given by the convolution integral. The function h is normally referred to as the filter, since it dictates what elements of the input image are allowed to pass through to the output image. By choosing an appropriate filter, we can enhance certain aspects of the output and attenuate

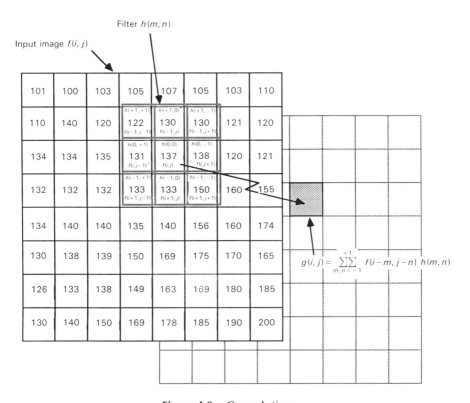

Figure 4.9. Convolution.

54

others. A particular filter h is often referred to as a 'filter kernel'. Attempts to form a conceptual model of this convolution operation in one's mind are often fruitless. However, it becomes a little easier if we transfer now to the discrete domain of digital images and replace the integral with the sigma (summation) operator. Now the convolution operation is given by:

$$g(i, j) = f * h = \sum_m \sum_n f(i - m, j - n) \, h(m, n)$$

The summation is taken only over the area where f and h overlap. This multiplication and summation is illustrated graphically in Figure 4.9. Here, a filter kernel h is a 3×3 pixel image, with the origin $h(0, 0)$ at the centre, representing a mask of nine distinct weights: $h(-1, -1)...h(+1, +1)$; see Figure 4.10. The kernel or mask is superimposed on the input image, the input image pixel values are multiplied by the corresponding weight, the nine results are summed, and the final value of the summation is the value of the output image pixel at a position corresponding to the position of the centre element of the kernel. Note that the convolution formula requires that the mask h be first rotated by $180°$ since, e.g., $f(i-1, j-1)$ must be multiplied by $h(1, 1)$, $f(i-1, j)$ must be multiplied by $h(1, 0)$, ..., and $f(i+1, j+1)$ must be multiplied by $h(1, 1)$. Quite often, the rotation by $180°$ is omitted if the mask is symmetric.

The algorithm to generate g is given by the following pseudo-code:

```
FOR i:=(low_limit_of_i + 1) TO (high_limit_of_i - 1) DO
 FOR j:=(low_limit_of_j + 1) TO (high_limit_of_j - 1) DO

  /* for each feasible point in the image
  ... form the convolution */

  temp:=0
  FOR m:= -1 TO +1 DO
   FOR n:=-1 TO +1 DO
    temp:=temp+F[i-m, j-n] * H[m, n]

  G[i,j]:=temp
```

Before returning to the discussion of neighbourhood operators, a short note about the relationship of the convolution operator to classical two-dimensional digital signal processing is appropriate. This can be safely skipped without any loss of continuity.

All image systems introduce some amount of distortion into an image, for example image blur due to camera shake. Since optical and electrical systems are (to an approximation) linear, the imaging system may also be assumed to be linear. This implies that, in the language of linear system theory, it has some transfer function $H(\omega_x, \omega_y)$. This is the frequency domain equivalent of the system impulse response $h(x, y)$ in the spatial domain; $h(x, y)$ typifies how the system would

$h(-1, -1)$	$h(-1, 0)$	$h(-1, +1)$
$h(0, -1)$	$h(0,0)$	$h(0, +1)$
$h(+1, -1)$	$h(+1, 0)$	$h(+1, +1)$

Figure 4.10 3×32 convolution filter h.

respond if a single unit spike were input to it. Thus, the transfer function describes how some input image is transformed into some output image. Since the output of this system is a distortion of the correct image we would expect that if we could model the system, i.e. define its transfer function, compute the inverse, and apply it to the distorted image, we would arrive at a much better approximation to the original. This is accomplished by convolving the inverse impulse response with the image: this operation is referred to as a 'deconvolution'. Alternatively, the image may be transformed to the frequency domain using the digital Fourier transform, multiplied by the inverse of the transfer function, and transformed back to the spatial domain by use of the inverse Fourier transform.

4.2.2 Noise suppression

If we define noise as any unwanted contamination of an image then the mechanism by which noise is removed depends on the assumption we make regarding the form of this unwanted contamination. One of the most common (and realistic) assumptions made about noise is that it has a high spatial frequency (refer back to Section 3.1.1). In this case, it is often adequate to apply a low-pass spatial filter which will attenuate the higher spatial frequencies and allow the low spatial frequency component to pass through to the resultant destination image. Of course if the image itself exhibits high spatial frequencies then it will be somewhat degraded after filtering.

These low-pass filters can be implemented by convolving the image with some simple mask; the mask values constitute the weighting factors which will be applied to the corresponding image point when the convolution is being performed. For example, each of the mask values might be equally weighted, in which case the operation we are performing is simply the evaluation of the local mean of the image in the vicinity of the mask.

Figure 4.11 shows this local neighbourhood average mask and Figure 4.12 illustrates the application of the mask to part of an image. Referring to Figure 4.12, we can see that the result of this filtering, i.e. the value of the output pixel which would be placed in the output image at the same position as the input pixel corresponding to the centre position of the mask, is:

$$101*1/9 + 100*1/9 + 103*1/9$$
$$+ 110*1/9 + 140*1/9 + 120*1/9$$
$$+ 134*1/9 + 134*1/9 + 135*1/9$$

1/9	1/9	1/9
1/9	1/9	1/9
1/9	1/9	1/9

Figure 4.11 Local average mask.

101 * 1/9	100 * 1/9	103 * 1/9	105	107	105	103	110
110 * 1/9	140 * 1/9	120 * 1/9	122	130	130	121	120
134 * 1/9	134 * 1/9	135 * 1/9	131	137	138	120	121
132	132	132	133	133	150	160	155
134	140	140	135	140	156	160	174
130	138	139	150	169	175	170	165
126	133	138	149	163	169	180	185
130	140	150	169	178	185	190	200

Figure 4.12 Image smoothing using local average mask.

which is equivalent to:

$$1/9*[101 + 100 + 103$$
$$+ 110 + 140 + 120$$
$$+ 134 + 134 + 135]$$

which is equal to 121.

Thus, the central point becomes 121 instead of 140 and the image will appear much smoother. This averaging or smoothing is, of course, applied at all points of the image.

Occasionally, it may be more useful to apply this smoothing subject to some condition, e.g. the centre pixel is only assigned if the difference between the average value and the original pixel value is greater than a previously set threshold. This goes some way towards removing noise without smoothing out too much of the detail in the original image.

The algorithm may be expressed in pseudo-code as follows:

```
/* For a 512×512 image, indexed from 0 to 511 */

FOR i :=1 TO 510 DO
  FOR j :=1 TO 510 DO

    /* for each feasible point in the image: compute
    average */

    average:=(source_image[i-1, j-1]   +
             source_image[i-1, j]      +
             source_image[i-1, j+1]    +
             source_image[i, j-1]      +
             source_image[i, j]        +
             source_image[i, j+1]      +
             source_image[i+1, j-1]    +
             source_image[i+1, j]      +
             source_image[i+1, j+1]    ) / 9

    /* destination image assumes the average value */

    destination_image[i, j]:=average
```

There are other noise-suppression techniques, of course. For example, median filtering is a noise-reducing technique whereby a pixel is assigned the value of the median of pixel values in some local neighbourhood. The size of the neighbourhood is arbitrary, but neighbourhoods in excess of 3×3 or 5×5 may be impractical from a computational point of view since the evaluation of the median requires that the image pixel values be first sorted. In general, the median filter is superior to the mean filter in that image blurring is minimized. Unfortunately, it is computationally complex and is not easily effected in hardware and thus tends not to be used much in machine vision.

Gaussian smoothing, whereby the image is convolved with a Gaussian function, is perhaps one of the most commonly used smoothing techniques in advanced computer vision since it possesses several useful properties. Unfortunately, it is not yet widely used in industrial machine vision because the sizes of the masks are very large and the processing is consequently computationally intensive. It should be noted, however, that some vendors do offer dedicated image processing boards for Gaussian filtering and, if such hardware is available, this type of smoothing should be considered. The Gaussian function $G(x, y)$ is defined by:

$$G(x, y) = \frac{1}{2\pi\sigma^2} \exp[-(x^2 + y^2)/2\sigma^2]$$

where σ defines the effective spread of the function: Gaussian functions with a small value for σ are narrow, whereas those with a large value for σ are broad. Figure 4.13 illustrates the shape of a Gaussian function with $\sigma = 1.5, 3.0,$ and 6.0 pixels respectively. The mask weights are included for reference. Note that, since the Gaussian function is defined over an infinite support, i.e. it has non-zero (but very small) values at $x, y = \pm \infty$, we must decide at what point to truncate the function. Normally, one chooses the quantization resolution of the function by deciding on the integer number which will represent the maximum amplitude at the centre point (e.g. 1000), and then one chooses the mask size which includes all non-zero values. Typically, a mask size of 23×23 pixels would be required to represent a two-dimensional Gaussian function with a value of 3.0 pixels for σ. Fortunately, there is no need to use two-dimensional Gaussian functions since the convolution of a two-dimensional Gaussian can be effected by two convolutions with one-dimensional Gaussian functions. Specifically:

$$G(x, y) * I(x, y) = G(x) * \{G(y) * I(x, y)\}$$

Thus, the image is first convolved with a 'vertical' Gaussian and then the resulting image is convolved with a 'horizontal' Gaussian.

Why is the Gaussian such a popular smoothing function? The reason is quite straightforward. While the primary purpose of a smoothing function is to reduce noise, it is often desirable to be able to choose the resolution at which intensity changes are manifested in the image, i.e. to choose the level of detail which is retained in the image. For example, an image which has been smoothed just a little (small σ) will retain a significant amount of detail, while one which has been smoothed a great deal (large σ) will retain only the gross structure (you can accomplish the same thing yourself by squinting). In more formal terms, we wish to sharply delimit the spatial frequencies (see Section 3.1.1) which are present in the image, i.e. to localize the spatial frequency bandwidth of the image. On the other hand, we also need to ensure that the smoothing function does not distort the image excessively by smearing the features. To allow for this, we need to ensure that

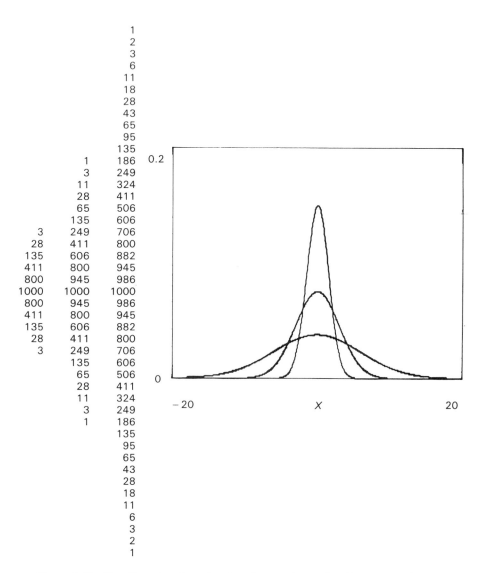

Figure 4.13 The Gaussian function for three values of σ (1.5, 3.0, and 6.0) together with their corresponding discrete one-dimensional masks; note that the result of convolution with these masks should be normalized by dividing by the sum of the mask weights.

the function has a limited support in space. The Gaussian function optimizes the trade-off between these two conflicting requirements.

4.2.3 Thinning, erosion, and dilation

Thinning is an iterative neighbourhood operation which generates a skeletal representation of an object. It assumes, of course, that you know exactly what constitutes the object in the image and what constitutes the background (i.e. everything which is not part of the object). Such an image is said to have been *segmented* into its component parts: the topic of segmentation is extremely important and will be discussed in detail in the next chapter.

The skeleton of an object may be thought of as a generalized axis of symmetry of the object and hence it is a suitable representation for objects which display obvious axial symmetry. The medial axis transform (MAT) proposed by Blum is one of the earliest and most widely studied techniques for generating the skeleton. More recently, Brady has introduced the related (but extended) concept of smoothed local symmetries (SLS) which we will discuss in the last section of Chapter 7.

The skeleton is frequently used as a shape descriptor which exhibits three topological properties: connectedness (one object generates one skeleton); invariance to scaling and rotation; and information preservation in the sense that the object can be reconstructed from the medial axis. The concept of thinning a binary image – an image comprising just two grey-levels: black and white – of an object is related to such medial axis transformations in that it generates a representation of an *approximate* axis of symmetry of a shape by successive deletion of pixels from the boundary of the object. In general, this thinned representation is not formally related to the original object shape and it is not possible to reconstruct the original boundary from the object.

Thinning can be viewed as a logical neighbourhood operation where object pixels are removed from an image. Obviously, the removal must be constrained somewhat so that we have a set of conditions for pixel removal. *The first restriction is that the pixel must lie on the border of the object. This implies that it has at least one 4-connected neighbouring pixel which is a background pixel.* The removal of pixels from all borders simultaneously would cause difficulties: for example, an object two pixels thick will vanish if all border pixels are removed simultaneously. A solution to this is to remove pixels of one border orientation only on each pass of the image by the thinning operator. Opposite border orientations are used alternately to ensure that the resultant skeleton is as close to the medial axis as possible.

The second restriction is that the deletion of a pixel should not destroy the object's connectedness, i.e. the number of skeletons after thinning should be the same as the number of objects in the image before thinning. This problem depends on the manner in which each pixel in the object is connected to every other pixel. A pixel can be considered to be connected to, and a component of, an object if it has

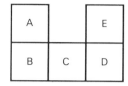

Figure 4.14 A critically connected object.

a grey-level of 255 and at least one adjacent object pixel (note that we are assuming object pixels have a grey-level of 255 – white – and background pixels have a grey-level of 0 – black). Consider now the 5 pixel object shown in Figure 4.14. The pixel C 'connects' the two object segments AB and ED, that is, if C were removed then this would break the object in two; this pixel is 'critically connected'. Obviously, this property may occur in many more cases than this, and critical-connectivity may be characterized as follows:

> Given a pixel, labelled 9 and its eight adjacent neighbours, labelled 0–7 (see Figure 3.6), and assume that writing the pixel number (e.g. 7) indicates presence, i.e. it is an object pixel, whereas writing it with an overbar (e.g. $\bar{7}$) indicates absence, i.e. it is a background pixel. Assume, also, normal Boolean logic sign conventions (+ indicates logical OR, and . indicates logical AND). Then pixel 8 is critically connected if the following expression is true.

$$8.\{[(1 + 2 + 3).(5 + 6 + 7).\bar{4}.\bar{0}]$$
$$+ [(1 + 0 + 7).(3 + 4 + 5).\bar{2}.\bar{6}]$$
$$+ [3.(5 + 6 + 7 + 0 + 1).\bar{2}.\bar{4}]$$
$$+ [1.(3 + 4 + 5 + 6 + 7).\bar{2}.\bar{0}]$$
$$+ [7.(1 + 2 + 3 + 4 + 5).\bar{0}.\bar{6}]$$
$$+ [5.(7 + 0 + 1 + 2 + 3).\bar{4}.\bar{6}]\}$$

Figure 4.15 depicts these six neighbourhood conditions which correspond to the presence of critical connectivity. *Hence, the second restriction implies that if a pixel is critically connected then it should not be deleted.*

A thinning algorithm should also preserve an object's length. To facilitate this, a third restriction must be imposed such that arc-ends, i.e. object pixels which are adjacent to just one other pixel, must not be deleted.

Note that a thinned image should be invariant under the thinning operator, i.e. the application of the thinning algorithm to a fully thinned image should produce no changes. This is also important as it provides us with a condition for stopping the thinning algorithm. Since the pixels of a fully thinned image are either critically connected or are arc-ends, imposing the second and third restrictions allows this property to be fulfilled. The final thinning algorithm, then, is to scan the image in a raster fashion, removing all object pixels according to these three restrictions, varying border from pass to pass. The image is thinned until four successive passes (corresponding to the four border orientations) producing no changes to the image are made, at which stage thinning ceases. Figure 4.16 illustrates the result of thinning an object in a binary image.

The concepts of *erosion* and *dilation* are related to thinning in the sense that erosion can be considered as a single pass of a thinning operator (stripping object pixels of all four border orientations). However, there is one significant difference in that, for most applications, one does not mind if the object breaks in two and, hence, the complex check for critical connectivity is no longer required. In fact, it

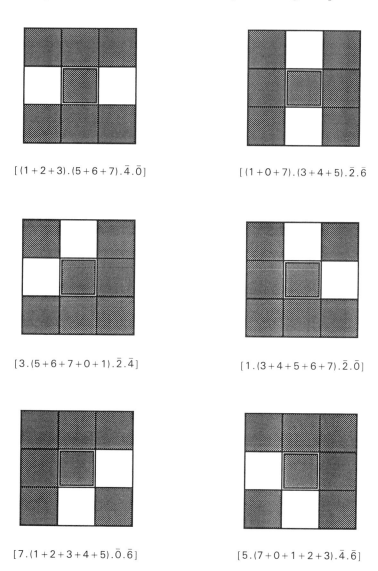

$[(1+2+3).(5+6+7).\bar{4}.\bar{0}]$

$[(1+0+7).(3+4+5).\bar{2}.\bar{6}$

$[3.(5+6+7+0+1).\bar{2}.\bar{4}]$

$[1.(3+4+5+6+7).\bar{2}.\bar{0}]$

$[7.(1+2+3+4+5).\bar{0}.\bar{6}]$

$[5.(7+0+1+2+3).\bar{4}.\bar{6}]$

Figure 4.15 Neighbourhoods exhibiting critical connectivity.

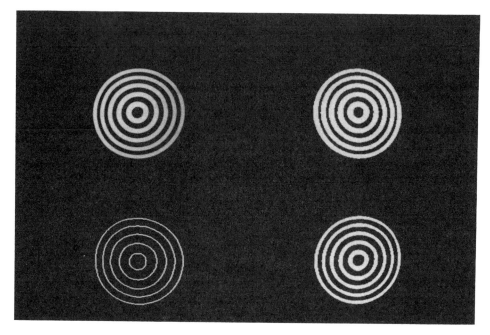

Figure 4.16 A grey-scale image (top-left) is thresholded to produce a binary image (top-right) which is then thinned (bottom-right). The image at the bottom-left is an intermediate partially thinned version.

is this property of object splitting that makes the erosion operation particularly useful. The dilation operation effects the reverse of erosion, i.e. an expansion of the object into all those background pixel cells which border the object. Thus, erosion 'shrinks' an object while dilation 'enlarges' it. This interpretation of erosion and dilation, although common, is quite a loose one. The operations of erosion and dilation do have a much more formal meaning in the context of a branch of image processing referred to as *mathematical morphology*. We will return to mathematical morphology in Section 4.4 but, for the present, we will continue with the informal treatment.

   To see the usefulness of erosion and dilation operations, consider the following common printed circuit board inspection problem. Typically, in PCB manufacturing, a film negative depicting the appropriate pattern of electrical contacts (pads) and conductors (tracks) is contact-printed on a copper-clad board which has been covered with a photoresistive solution. The board is then etched, leaving just the copper circuit patterns. Such a process can lead to many problems with the final circuit pattern, e.g. the track may be broken, it may be too wide or too thin, or there may be spurious copper remaining on the PCB. These potential faults (shorts and breaks) are impossible for conventional functional (electrical) testing to detect and it is for this reason that these visual techniques are so useful.

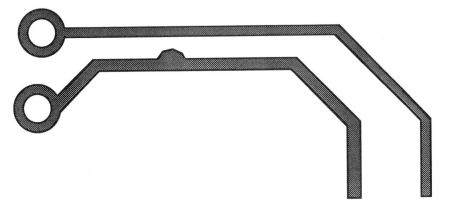

Figure 4.17 PCB track with extraneous copper.

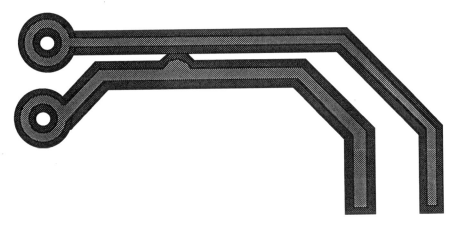

Figure 4.18 Dilated PCB track.

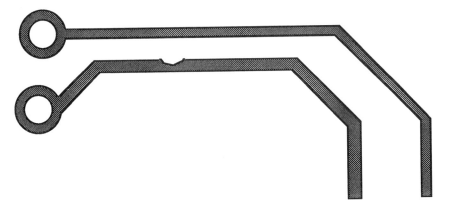

Figure 4.19 PCB track with a neck.

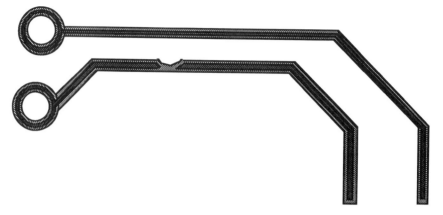

Figure 4.20 Eroded PCB track.

If the tracks (and/or pads) are too large or have extraneous copper attached (see Figure 4.17), then dilating the image a number of times will cause the two tracks to merge (see Figure 4.18) and a subsequent analysis of the track connectivity will identify this potential fault. Conversely, a track which is too thin or has a neck (see Figure 4.19) will break when eroded (Figure 4.20). Similar connectivity analysis will identify this potential circuit break.

A pseudo-coded algorithm for erosion can be formulated as follows:

```
/* erosion */

FOR all pixels in the image
  IF the pixel is an object pixel AND all its
  neighbours are
    object pixels
    copy it to the destination image
```

while a dilation algorithm can be formulated as:

```
/* dilation */

FOR all pixels in the image
  IF the pixel is an object pixel
    make it and its eight neighbours object pixels
    in the destination image
```

Figure 4.21 illustrates the effect of several applications of these erosion and dilation algorithms to an object in a binary image.

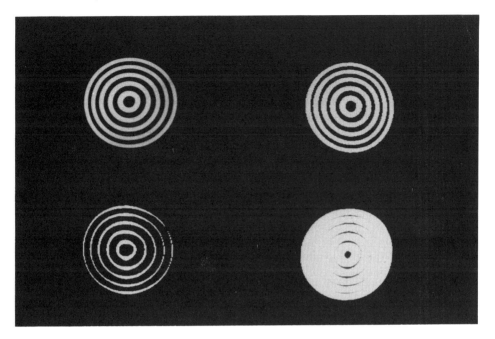

Figure 4.21 A grey-scale image (top-left) is thresholded to produce a binary image (top-right) which is then eroded twice (bottom-left). The application of two passes of the dilation algorithm is shown at bottom-right.

4.3 Geometric operations

Geometric operations change the spatial relationships between objects in an image, i.e. the relative distances between points a, b and c will typically be different after a geometric operation or 'warping'. The applications of such warping include geometric decalibration, i.e. the correction of geometric distortion introduced by the imaging system (most people are familiar with the barrel distortion that arises in photography when using a very short focal length 'fish-eye' lens), and image registration, i.e. the intentional distortion of one image with respect to another so that the objects in each image superimpose on one another. The techniques used in both these applications are identical and will be discussed in detail before describing actual usage.

4.3.1 Spatial warping

The approach to geometric image manipulation described here is called *spatial warping* and involves the computation of a mathematical model for the required distortion, its application to the image, and the creation of a new corrected (decalibrated or registered) image.

The distortion may be specified by locating control points (also called fiducial points) in the input image (the image to be warped) and identifying their corresponding control points in an ideal (undistorted or registered) image. The distortion model is then computed in terms of the transformation between these control points generating a spatial warping function which will allow one to build the output image pixel by pixel, by identifying the corresponding point in the input image.

Since, in general, the estimates of the coordinates of input pixels yielded by the warping function will not correspond to exact (integer) pixel locations, we also require some method of estimating the grey-level of the output pixel when the 'corresponding' pixel falls 'between the integer coordinates' (see Figure 4.22). The question is: how do the four pixels surrounding the computed point contribute to our estimate of its grey-level, i.e. how do we interpolate between the four? We will return to this question later; suffice it at present to summarize the two requirements of geometric operations:

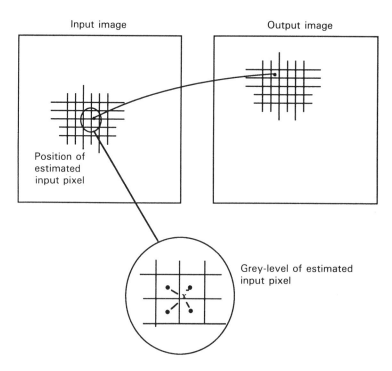

Figure 4.22 Spatial transformation and grey-level interpolation.

(a)   a spatial transformation which allows one to derive the position of a pixel in the input which corresponds to the pixel being 'filled' or generated in the output;

(b)   an interpolation scheme to estimate the grey-level of this input pixel.

Note that the grey-level interpolation algorithm may be permanently established in the software whereas the spatial transformation will change as the environment changes (e.g. camera, lens, registration requirements).

4.3.1.1   The spatial transformation

The spatial transformation is expressed in general form as a mapping from a point (x, y) in the output image to its corresponding (warped) position (i, j) in the input image:

$$(i, j) = (W_x(x, y), W_y(x, y))$$

That is, the first coordinate, i, of the warped point is a function of the current position in the output; likewise for the second coordinate, j. Thus, given any point (x, y) in the output image, the coordinates of the corresponding point in the input image may be generated using the warping functions W_x and W_y respectively. It would, of course, be ideal if we had some analytic expression for W_x and W_y but this is rarely the case. Instead, we normally model each spatial warping function by a polynomial function. So, we assume that, for example, the warping functions are given by the following equations:

$$W_x(x, y) = \sum_p^n \sum_q^n a_{pq} x^p y^q$$

$$W_y(x, y) = \sum_p^n \sum_q^n b_{pq} x^p y^q$$

For example, if $n = 2$ (which is adequate to correct for most distortions):

$$\begin{aligned}
W_x(x, y) = {} & a_{00} x^0 y^0 + a_{10} x^1 y^0 + a_{20} x^2 y^0 \\
& + a_{01} x^0 y^1 + a_{11} x^1 y^1 + a_{21} x^2 y^1 \\
& + a_{02} x^0 y^2 + a_{12} x^1 y^2 + a_{22} x^2 y^2
\end{aligned}$$

$$\begin{aligned}
W_y(x, y) = {} & b_{00} x^0 y^0 + b_{10} x^1 y^0 + b_{20} x^2 y^0 \\
& + b_{01} x^0 y^1 + b_{11} x^1 y^1 + b_{21} x^2 y^1 \\
& + b_{02} x^0 y^2 + b_{12} x^1 y^2 + b_{22} x^2 y^2
\end{aligned}$$

Now, the only thing that remains to complete the specification of the spatial warping function is to determine the values of these coefficients, i.e. to compute $a_{00}-a_{22}$ and $b_{00}-b_{22}$.

To do this, we have to assume that we know the transformation exactly for a number of points (at least as many as the number of coefficients; nine in this case), that is, to assume that we know the values of x and y and their corresponding i

and j values. We then write the relationships explicitly in the form of the two equations above. We then solve these equations simultaneously to determine the value of the coefficients. Remember that we have two sets of simultaneous equations to set up: one for the 'a' coefficients and one for the 'b' coefficients. However, the same values relating x, y to i, j can be used in each case. This is now where the control points come in as we are going to use these to provide us with the (known) relationships between (x, y) and (i, j).

If we have nine unknown coefficients, as in the example above, then in order to obtain a solution we require at least nine such observations, $\{(x_1, y_1), (i_1, j_1)\} \dots \{(x_9, y_9), (i_9, j_9)\}$, say. Such a system is said to be exactly determined. However, the solution of these exact systems is often ill-conditioned (numerically unstable) and it is usually good practice to overdetermine the system by specifying more control points than you need (and hence generate more simultaneous equations). These equations can then be solved, yielding the coefficients and hence the warping functions, using standard personal computer based maths packages such as MATLAB$^{©}$.

For the sake of completeness, we include here details of how to solve such an overdetermined system. The reader can safely skip this section if (s)he so wishes.

The first point to note is that an overdetermined system (where the number of equations is greater than the number of unknown values) does not have an exact solution and there are going to be some errors for some points. The idea, then, is to minimize these errors. We will use the common approach of minimizing the sum of the square of each error (i.e. to generate the so-called least-square-error solution).

Consider, again, a single control point and assume we are attempting to compute the a_{pq} coefficients:

$$
\begin{aligned}
i_1 = {} & a_{00}x_1{}^0 y_1{}^0 + a_{10}x_1{}^1 y_1{}^0 + a_{20}x^2{}_1 y_1{}^0 \\
& + a_{01}x_1{}^0 y_1{}^1 + a_{11}x_1{}^1 y_1{}^1 + a_{21}x_1{}^2 y_1{}^1 \\
& + a_{02}x_1{}^0 y_1{}^1 + a_{12}x_1{}^1 y_1{}^2 + a_{22}x_1{}^2 y_1{}^2
\end{aligned}
$$

If we use m control points in total we will have m such equations which (noting that x^0 and y^0 are both equal to 1) we may write in matrix form as:

$$
\begin{bmatrix} i_1 \\ i_2 \\ \vdots \\ i_m \end{bmatrix} = \begin{bmatrix} 1\,x_1{}^1\,x_1{}^2\,y_1{}^1\,x_1{}^1\,y_1{}^1\,x_1{}^2\,y_1{}^1\,y_1{}^2\,x_1{}^1\,y_1{}^2\,x_1{}^2\,y_1{}^2 \\ 1\,x_2{}^1\,x_2{}^2\,y_2{}^1\,x_2{}^1\,y_2{}^1\,x_2{}^2\,y_2{}^1\,y_2{}^2\,x_2{}^1\,y_2{}^2\,x_2{}^2\,y_2{}^2 \\ \vdots \\ 1\,x_m{}^1\,x_m{}^2\,y_m{}^1\,x_m{}^1\,y_m{}^1\,x_m{}^2\,y_m{}^1\,y_m{}^2\,x_m{}^1\,y_m{}^2\,x_m{}^2\,y_m{}^2 \end{bmatrix} * \begin{bmatrix} a_{00} \\ a_{10} \\ \vdots \\ a_{22} \end{bmatrix} + \begin{bmatrix} e_1 \\ e_2 \\ \vdots \\ e_m \end{bmatrix}
$$

We have to include the errors since there will not be a set of $a_{00}-a_{22}$ which will simultaneously provide us with exactly i_1-i_m, in the overdetermined case.

Let us abbreviate this matrix equation to:

$$
\boldsymbol{i} = \boldsymbol{Xa} + \boldsymbol{e}
$$

Similarly:

$$j = Xb + e$$

We require a, so we might think of multiplying across by X^{-1} to obtain an appropriate expression. Unfortunately, X is non-square (number of equations is greater than the number of coefficients) and one cannot invert a non-square matrix. However, we can indulge in a little algebra and calculus to derive an expression for a in terms of X and i:

$$i = Xa + e$$
$$e = i - Xa$$

We form the sum of the square of each error by computing $e^{\mathrm{T}}e$:

$$e^{\mathrm{T}}e = (i - Xa)^{\mathrm{T}}(i - Xa)$$

Differentiating $e^{\mathrm{T}}e$ with respect to a, to find out how the errors change as the coefficients change:

$$\frac{\mathrm{d}(e^{\mathrm{T}}e)}{\mathrm{d}(a)} = (0 - XI)^{\mathrm{T}}(i - Xa) + (i - Xa)^{\mathrm{T}}(0 - XI)$$

$$= (-XI)^{\mathrm{T}}(i - Xa) + (i^{\mathrm{T}} - (Xa)^{\mathrm{T}})(-XI)$$
$$= -IX^{\mathrm{T}}(i - Xa) + (i^{\mathrm{T}} - a^{\mathrm{T}}X^{\mathrm{T}})(-XI)$$
$$= -IX^{\mathrm{T}}i + IX^{\mathrm{T}}Xa - i^{\mathrm{T}}XI + a^{\mathrm{T}}X^{\mathrm{T}}XI$$

But noting that $i^{\mathrm{T}}XI$ and $a^{\mathrm{T}}X^{\mathrm{T}}XI$ are 1×1 matrices and that the transpose of a 1×1 matrix is equal to itself, we transpose these two sub-expressions:

$$= -IX^{\mathrm{T}}i + IX^{\mathrm{T}}Xa - IX^{\mathrm{T}}i + IX^{\mathrm{T}}Xa$$
$$= 2(I)(X^{\mathrm{T}}Xa - X^{\mathrm{T}}i)$$

The sum of the square of each error is minimized when $\mathrm{d}(e^{\mathrm{T}}e)/\mathrm{d}(a)$ is equal to zero, thus:

$$0 = 2(I)(X^{\mathrm{T}}Xa - X^{\mathrm{T}}i)$$
$$(X^{\mathrm{T}}X)^{-1}X^{\mathrm{T}}Xa = (X^{\mathrm{T}}X)^{-1}X^{\mathrm{T}}i$$
$$a = (X^{\mathrm{T}}X)^{-1}X^{\mathrm{T}}i$$

$(X^{\mathrm{T}}X)^{-1}X^{\mathrm{T}}$ is commonly referred to as the 'pseudo-inverse' of X and is written $X^{\dagger}$.

When this has been computed, the coefficient matrix a may be computed by simply multiplying $X^{\dagger}$ by i; b is obtained in a like manner.

4.3.1.2 Grey-level interpolation

Once the spatial mapping function has been found, the output image can be built, pixel by pixel and line by line. The coordinates given by the warping function, denoting the corresponding points in the input image, will not in general be integer values and the grey-level must be interpolated from the grey-levels of the surrounding pixels.

The simplest interpolation function is *nearest-neighbour* interpolation (zero-order interpolation) whereby the grey-level of the output pixel (which is what we are trying to estimate) is given by the grey-level of the input pixel which is nearest to the calculated point in the input image (see Figure 4.23). The computation involved in this interpolation function is quite trivial but the function generally yields quite adequate results. If the image exhibits very fine detail in which adjacent pixel grey-level varies significantly, i.e. the image exhibits high spatial frequencies, some of this detail may be lost. In such cases, *bi-linear* (i.e. first-order) interpolation should be considered since the estimate is made on the basis of four neighbouring input pixels. Consider the case shown in Figure 4.24 where we need to estimate the grey-level of a point somewhere between image pixels (i, j), $(i, j + 1)$, $(i + 1, j)$, and $(i + 1, j + 1)$. Let the position of this point relative to pixel (i, j) be given by coordinates (p, q); $0 \leqslant p, q \leqslant 1$. The grey-level at point (p, q) is constrained by the grey-level at the four neighbouring pixels and is a function of its position between these neighbours. To estimate the grey-level, $f(p, q)$, we fit a surface through the four neighbours' grey-levels, the equation of which will in general identify the grey-level at any point between the neighbours. The surface we fit is a hyperbolic paraboloid and is defined by the bilinear equation:

$$f(p, q) = ap + bq + cpq + d$$

There are four coefficients, a, b, c, and d, which we must determine to identify this

101	100	103	105	107	105	103	110
110	140	120	122	130	130	121	120
134	134	135	131	137	138	120	121
132	132	132	133	133	150	160	155
134	140	140	135	140	156	160	174
130	138	139	150	169	175	170	165
126	133	138	149	163	169	180	185
130	140	150	169	178	185	190	200

Nearest neighbour

Computed point

Figure 4.23 Nearest-neighbour interpolation.

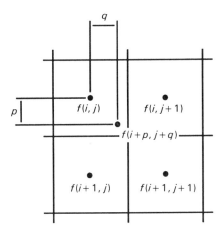

Figure 4.24 Bilinear interpolation.

function for any given 2×2 neighbourhood in which we wish to interpolate. Thus we require four simultaneous equations in a, b, c, and d; these are supplied from our knowledge of the grey-level at the four neighbours given by relative coordinates $(0, 0)$, $(0, 1)$, $(1, 0)$, $(1, 1)$. Specifically, we know that:

$$a \times 0 + b \times 0 + c \times 0 \times 0 + d = f(i, j) \tag{4.1}$$

$$a \times 0 + b \times 1 + c \times 0 \times 1 + d = f(i, j + 1) \tag{4.2}$$

$$a \times 1 + b \times 0 + c \times 1 \times 0 + d = f(i + 1, j) \tag{4.3}$$

$$a \times 1 + b \times 1 + c \times 1 \times 1 + d = f(i + 1, j + 1) \tag{4.4}$$

Directly from (4.1), we have:

$$d = f(i, j) \tag{4.5}$$

Rearranging (4.2) and substituting for d, we have:

$$b = f(i, j + 1) - f(i, j) \tag{4.6}$$

Rearranging (4.3) and substituting for d, we have:

$$a = f(i + 1, j) - f(i, j) \tag{4.7}$$

Rearranging (4.4) and substituting for a, b, and d, we have:

$$c = f(i + 1, j + 1) + f(i, j) - f(i + 1, j) - f(i, j + 1) \tag{4.8}$$

Equations (4.5)–(4.8) allow us to compute the coefficients a, b, c, and d, which define the bilinear interpolation for a given 2×2 neighbourhood with known pixel grey-levels.

For example, if the coordinates of the point at which we wish to estimate the grey-level are $(60.4, 128.1)$ and the grey-level at pixels $(60, 128)$, $(60, 129)$, $(61, 128)$, and (61, 129) are 10, 12, 14, and 15, respectively, then the grey-level at this point, in relative coordinates, is given by:

$$f(0.4, 0.1) = (14 - 10) \times 0.4$$
$$+ (12 - 10) \times 0.1$$
$$+ (15 + 10 - 14 - 12) \times 0.4 \times 0.1$$
$$+ 10$$
$$= 11.76$$

4.3.2 Registration and geometric decalibration

This technique for spatial warping can be used directly to effect either registration of two images or to correct the geometric distortion which may have been introduced by the imaging system. In the former case, one merely needs to identify several corresponding points in the two images and use these as the control points when generating the polynomial coefficients. In the latter case, one might use the imaging system to generate an image of a test card (e.g. a square grid) and superimpose an undistorted copy of this pattern on the distorted image. The corresponding control points can then be explicitly identified in each version of the pattern. For example, in the case of the grid pattern, the control points might be the points of intersection of the grid lines.

4.4 Mathematical morphology

4.4.1 Basic set theory

Mathematical morphology is a methodology for image processing and image analysis which is based on set theory and topology. As such, it is a formal and rigorous mathematical technique and we need to establish a basic 'language' before proceeding. For the most part, this is the language of set theory. In the following, points and vectors will be denoted by latin lowercase letters: x, y, z; sets will be denoted by latin uppercase letters: X, Y, Z; and the symbol ϕ denotes the empty set. The more common set operations we will encounter in this brief treatment of morphology include the following:

- *Set inclusion.* This is written: $Y \subset X$, i.e. Y is a subset of (is included in) the set X. This is defined as $y \in Y \Rightarrow y \in X$: if y is an element of Y, then y is also an element of X.
- *Complement.* For any set X, the complement of X is written X^c. This is the set of all elements which are *not* elements of X.
- *Union.* The union of two sets X and Y, written $X \cup Y$, is defined:

$$X \cup Y = \{x \mid x \in X \text{ or } x \in Y\}$$

This should be read: the set X union Y is the set of all x such that x is an element of X or x is an element of Y.

● *Intersection.* The intersection of two sets X and Y, written $X \cap Y$, is defined:

$$X \cap Y = (X^c \cup Y^c)^c$$

In effect, the intersection of two sets is the complement of the union of their respective complements. Thus, the intersection of X and Y is the complement of the set of elements which are not in X or not in Y, i.e. *the set of elements which is common to both sets X and Y.*

Let us now consider two further concepts. The first is translation. The translation of a set X by h is denoted X_h. This is a set where each element (point) is translated by a vector h. Second, we need to introduce a general symbolism for set transformation. A transformation of a set X is denoted by $\Psi(X)$. $\Psi(\ )$ is the set transformation and in an expression such as $Y = \Psi(X)$, Y is the transformed set.

Finally, we require the concept of *duality* of set transformations. Given some transformation Ψ, we define the dual of the transformation Ψ^*:

$$\Psi^*(X) \rightarrow (\Psi(X^c))^c$$

For example, intersection is the dual of union since $X \cap Y = (X^c \cup Y^c)^c$.

4.4.2 Structuring elements and hit or miss transformations

We are now in a position to continue with the discussion of mathematical morphology. Let us begin with the concept of a *structuring element.*

A structuring element B_x, centred at x, is a set of points which is used to 'extract' structure in a set, X, say. For example, the structuring element might be a square or a disk, as shown in Figure 4.25, or any other appropriate shape.

Now we define a *hit or miss transformation* as the 'point by point' transformation of a set X, working as follows. We choose, and fix, a structuring element B. Define B_x^1 to be that subset of B_x (recall B_x is the translate of B to a position x) whose elements belong to the 'foreground' and B_x^2 to be the subset of B_x whose elements belong to the 'background' (i.e. $B^1 \cap B^2 = \phi$).

Figure 4.25 Square and circular structuring elements.

A point x belongs to the hit or miss transform, denoted $X \otimes B$, if and only if $B_x{}^1$ is included in X and $B_x{}^2$ is included in X^c the complement of X:

$$X \otimes B = \{x \mid B_x{}^1 \subset X; B_x{}^2 \subset X^c\}$$

Thus, $X \otimes B$ defines the points where the structuring element B exactly matches (hits) the set X, i.e. the image.

For example, let B be the structuring element shown in Figure 4.26(a) and let X be the set shown in Figure 4.26(b). Then $X \otimes B$ is the set shown in Figure 4.26(c).

4.4.3 Erosion and dilation

In Section 4.2.3, we informally introduced the concepts of erosion and dilation. We will now define them formally. Let $\breve{B}$ be the transposed set of B, i.e. the

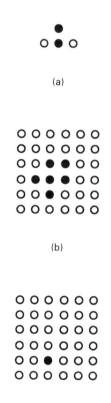

(a)

(b)

(c)

Figure 4.26 (a) Structuring element B; (b) image set X; (c) B 'hit or miss' $X: X \otimes B$.

symmetrical set of B with respect to its origin. Then, the erosion operation is denoted $\ominus$ and the erosion of a set X with $\check{B}$ is defined:

$$X \ominus \check{B} = \{x \mid B_x \subset X\}$$

Note that this is equivalent to a hit or miss transformation of X with B, where $B^2 = \phi$, i.e. where there are *no* background points. Note also that $X \ominus B$ is not an erosion – it is the *Minkowski subtraction* of B from X.

Intuitively, the erosion of a set by a structuring element amounts to the generation of a new (transformed/eroded) set where each element in the transformed set is a point where the structuring element is included in the original set X.

For example, let B and X be the structuring element and set shown in Figure 4.27(a) and (b), respectively; then $X \ominus \check{B}$ is depicted in Figure 4.27(c).

In a more complex case, if B is a circular structuring element, Figure 4.28 schematically illustrates the effect of erosion.

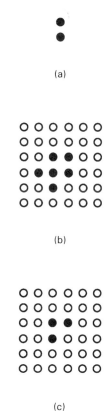

(a)

(b)

(c)

Figure 4.27 (a) Structuring element B; (b) image set X; (c) the erosion of X with B: $X \ominus \check{B}$.

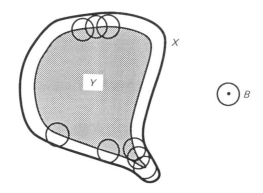

Figure 4.28 Erosion of X by a circular structuring element B.

Dilation is a closely related operation. In fact, dilation is the dual of erosion. The dilation operation is denoted by the symbol $\oplus$. Thus:

$$X \oplus \breve{B} = X^c \ominus \breve{B}$$

That is, the dilation of X is the erosion of X^c. This amounts to saying that the erosion of a set (e.g. an object) with a given structuring element is equivalent to the dilation of its complement (i.e. its background) with the same structuring element, and *vice versa*.

4.4.4 Opening and closing

After having eroded X by B, it is not possible in general to recover the initial set by dilating the eroded set $X \ominus B$ by the same B. This dilate reconstitutes only a part of X, which is simpler and has fewer details, but may be considered as that part which is most essential to the structure of X. This new set (i.e. the results of erosion followed by dilation) filters out (i.e. generates) a new subset of X which is extremely rich in morphological and size distribution properties. This transformation is called an *opening*.

The opening of a set X with a structuring element B, denoted X_B, is defined:

$$X_B = (X \ominus \breve{B}) \oplus B$$

The *closing* of X with respect to B, denoted X^B, is defined:

$$X^B = (X \oplus \breve{B}) \ominus B$$

Opening is the dual of closing, i.e.:

$$(X^c)_B = (X^B)^c$$

and

$$(X_B)^c = (X^c)^B$$

The opening is the domain swept out by all the translates of B which are included in X. This effects a smoothing of the contours of X, cuts narrow isthmuses, suppresses small islands and sharp edges in X.

4.4.5 Thinning and the extraction of endpoints

As we have seen in Section 4.2.3, an approximation to the skeleton can be achieved by an iterative transformation known as thinning. From the perspective of mathematical morphology, the thinning of a set X by a sequence of structuring elements L, is denoted

$$X \bigcirc \{L^i\}$$

that is

$$(((...(X \bigcirc L^1) \bigcirc L^2) \bigcirc L^3)... \bigcirc L^i)$$

$X \bigcirc L$ is defined:

$$X \bigcirc L = X/X \otimes L$$

That is, the set X less the set of points in X which hit L. Thus, if $X \otimes L$ identified border points, and L is appropriately structured to maintain connectivity of a set, then repeated application of the thinning process successively removes border points from a set until the skeleton is achieved. At this point, further application of the thinning transform yields no change in the skeletal set. This, of course, should be reminiscent of the thinning algorithm discussed in Section 4.2.3.

Recalling the definition of a hit and miss transformation:

$$X \otimes L = \{x \mid {}^1L_x \subset X; {}^2L_x \subset X^c\}$$

$${}^1L_x \cap {}^2L_x = \phi$$

We can now proceed to develop a thinning algorithm by defining L. The sequence $\{L\}$ which is used for thinning is based on a single structuring element and is generated by rotating the structuring element (through $360°$ in increments of $45°$ for a square lattice). This sequence $\{L\}$ is shown in Figure 4.29. The thinning algorithm then amounts to the repeated transformation of a set $X_i \rightarrow X_{i+1}$ defined:

$$X_{i+1} = (((...(X_i \bigcirc L_1) \bigcirc L_2) \bigcirc L_3)... \bigcirc L_8)$$

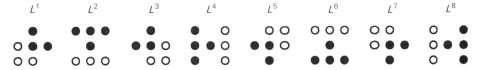

Figure 4.29 Sequence of structuring elements used in the thinning operation.

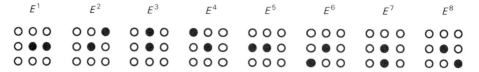

Figure 4.30 Structuring elements used to identify end-points.

The skeleton is achieved when $X_i = X_{i+1}$. Initially $X_0 = X$, i.e. the original (unthinned) image.

Given a skeleton set X, we can identify the endpoints, i.e. points which are connected to just one other point, using the hit or miss transform and an appropriate set of structuring elements $\{E\}$, shown in Figure 4.30. Thus, the endpoints of the skeleton are given by:

$$Y = \bigcup_{i=0}^{8} X \otimes E^i$$

That is, the union of all those points which *hit* with one of these endpoint structuring elements.

4.4.6 Application: identification of endpoints of electrical wires

In Chapter 8, we will be considering a complete vision and robotics case study: automated crimping of electrical wires. Part of this application is concerned with the identification of the positions of the ends of these electrical wires lying on a flat surface. In Chapter 8, we will be employing conventional techniques, but for the sake of illustration we will briefly consider a morphological approach here. Assuming that we are dealing with a grey-scale image of long thin wires (see Figures 8.18 and 8.19), then there are just three simple steps in achieving our objective:

Step 1. Threshold the grey-level image to obtain a binary image. Call this set X_1.
Step 2. Generate the skeleton X_2:

$$X_2 = X_1 \bigcirc \{L\}$$

Step 3. Identify endpoints of skeleton X_3:

$$X_3 = \bigcup_{i=0}^{8} X_2 \otimes E^i$$

X_3 is the set of all endpoints of these electrical wires.

4.4.7 A brief introduction to grey-scale mathematical morphology

So far, all of the mathematical morphology has assumed that we are dealing with

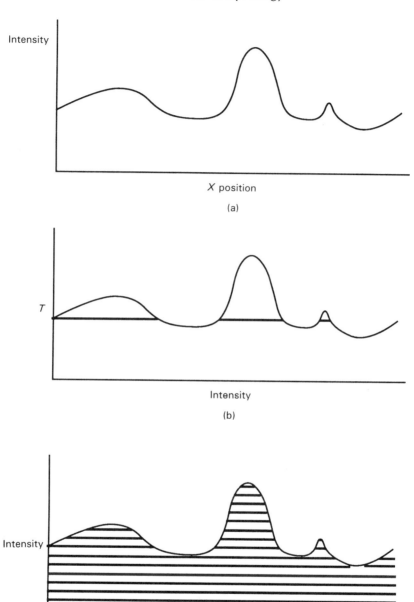

Figure 4.31 (a) A one-dimensional slice of a two-dimensional image function. (b) Thresholding this one-dimensional function at a value T generates a set $x_\lambda = \{x \mid x \geqslant T\}$ depicted by the bold line. (c) Representation of an image by a sequence of such sets.

a set X and its complement X^c, i.e. that we have been dealing with binary images comprising a foreground (the set of object points X) and a background (the set of all other points X^c). Unfortunately, grey-scale mathematical morphology is considerably more difficult to understand than binary morphology and this section is just intended to serve as an introduction to the manner in which we approach grey-level images from a morphological point of view.

For the following, we will consider one-dimensional slices of a two-dimensional image function. This makes it easier to represent in diagrams and it is somewhat easier to follow. Thus, a slice along the X-axis (i.e. a line of) a grey-scale image can be viewed as shown in Figure 4.31(a). If we threshold this function choosing values $\geqslant x_\lambda$, that is, generate a set x_λ:

$$x_\lambda = \{x \mid x \geqslant T\}$$

where T is the threshold value, we generate the set of points shown in a bold horizontal line in Figure 4.31(b). A grey-scale image, then, is considered to be a function f and is a sequence of sets:

$$f \Leftrightarrow \{x_\lambda(f)\}$$

and the grey-scale image is effectively the entire sequence of sets generated by successively decreasing the threshold level, as shown in Figure 4.31(c).

Grey-level erosion is defined:

$$f \to f \ominus \breve{B})$$

and equivalently:

$$\{x_\lambda(f)\} \to \{x_\lambda(f) \ominus \breve{B})\}$$

This grey-level erosion is the function, or sequence of sets, which are individually the erosion of sets generated at successive thresholds. Figure 4.32 illustrates the erosion of a (one-dimensional) function with a flat structuring element.

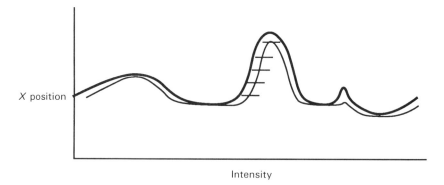

Figure 4.32 Erosion of a one-dimensional function with a flat structuring element; the eroded function is depicted by the thin curve.

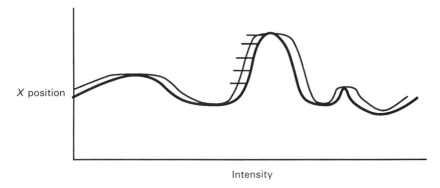

X position

Intensity

Figure 4.33 Dilation of a one-dimensional function with a flat structuring element; the dilated function is depicted by the thin curve.

Similarly, *grey-level dilation* is defined:

$$f \rightarrow f \oplus \check{B})$$
$$\{x_\lambda(f)\} \rightarrow \{x_\lambda(f) \oplus \check{B})\}$$

and Figure 4.33 illustrates the dilation of a (one-dimensional) function with a flat structuring element.

Exercises

1. Why is convolution a useful operation in image processing? Be specific in your answer by identifying the relationship between convolution and filtering.
2. Identify and annotate two simple techniques for noise removal in digital images; detail any assumptions upon which the techniques are based.
3. What is the essential difference between erosion and thinning? What is the relationship between thinning and the medial axis transform?
4. Why are look-up table (LUT) formulations of algorithms computationally efficient?
5. If two images can be registered by translation and rotation operations, is it necessary to use spatial warping techniques? Will grey-level interpolation be an issue?

References and further reading

Arcelli, C. 1979 'A condition for digital points removal', *Signal Processing*, Vol. 1, pp. 283–5.

Blum, H. 1967 'A transformation for extracting new descriptors of shape', in *Models for the Perception of Speech and Visual Form*, W. Wathen-Dunn (ed.), MIT Press Cambridge, Massachusetts, pp. 153–71.

Brady, M. and Asada, H. 1984 'Smoothed local symmetries and their implementation', *The International Journal of Robotics Research*, Vol. 3, No. 3, pp. 36–61.

Castleman, K.R. 1979 *Digital Image Processing*, Prentice Hall, New York.

Gonzalez, R.C. and Wintz, P. 1977 *Digital Image Processing*, Addison-Wesley, Reading, Massachusetts.

Hall, E.L. 1979 *Computer Image Processing and Recognition*, Academic Press, New York.

Hilditch, C.J. 1983 'Comparison of thinning algorithms on a parallel processor', *Image and Vision Computing*, Vol. 1, No. 3, pp. 115–32.

Kenny, P.A., Dowsett, D.J., Vernon, D. and Ennis J.T. 1990 'The application of spatial warping to produce aerosol ventilation images of the lung immediately after perfusion with the same labelled isotope', *Physics in Medicine and Biology*, Vol. 35, No. 5, 679–85.

Motzkin, Th. 1935 'Sur Quelques Proprietes Caracteristiques des Ensembles Bornes Non Convexes', *Atti. Acad. Naz. Lincei*, 21, pp. 773–9.

Nackman, L.R. and Pizer, S.M. 1985 'Three dimensional shape description using the symmetric axis transform 1: Theory', *IEEE Transactions on Pattern Analysis and Machine Intelligence*, Vol. PAMI-7, No. 2, pp. 187–202.

Pratt, W.K. 1978 *Digital Image Processing*, Wiley, New York.

Rosenfeld, A. and Kak, A. 1982 *Digital Picture Processing*, Academic Press, New York.

Rosenfeld, A. 1975 'A characterization of parallel thinning algorithms', *Information and Control*, Vol. 29, pp. 286–91.

Serra, J. 1982 *Image Analysis and Mathematical Morphology*, Academic Press, London.

Tamura, H. 1978 'A comparison of line-thinning algorithms from a digital geometry viewpoint', *Proceedings 4th International Joint Conference on Pattern Recognition*, pp. 715–19.

Zhang, T.Y. and Suen, C.Y. 1984 'A fast parallel algorithm for thinning digital patterns', *Communications of the ACM*, Vol. 27, No. 3, pp. 236–9.

5

The segmentation problem

5.1 Introduction: region- and boundary-based approaches

Segmentation is a word used to describe a grouping process in which the components of a group are similar with respect to some feature or set of features. The inference is that this grouping will identify regions in the image which correspond to unique and distinct objects in the visual environment.

There are two complementary approaches to the problem of segmenting images and isolating objects: boundary detection and region growing. Region growing effects the segmentation process by grouping elemental areas (in simple cases, individual image pixels) sharing a common feature into connected two-dimensional areas called regions. Such features might be pixel grey-level or some elementary textural pattern, e.g. the short thin bars present in a herringbone texture.

Boundary-based segmentation is concerned with detecting or enhancing the boundary pixels of objects within the image and subsequently isolating them from the rest of the image. The boundary of the object, once extracted, may easily be used to define the location and shape of the object, effectively completing the isolation.

An image comprising boundaries alone is a much higher level representation of the scene than is the original grey-scale image, in that it represents important information explicitly. In cases where the boundary shape is complicated, the gap between these two representations is wide and it may be necessary to introduce an intermediate representation which is independent of the shape. Since boundaries of objects are often manifested as intensity discontinuities, a natural intermediate representation is composed of local object-independent discontinuities in image intensity, normally referred to as 'edges'. The many definitions of the term *edge* can be summarized by the observation (or premise) that an edge occurs in an image if some image attribute (normally image intensity) changes its value dis-continuously. In particular, edges are seen as local intensity discontinuities while boundaries are global ones. The usual approach to segmentation by boundary detection is to first construct an edge image from the original grey-scale image, and then to use this edge to construct the boundary image without reference to the original grey-scale data by edge linking to generate short-curve segments, edge-thinning, gap-filling, and curve segment linking, frequently with the use of domain-dependent knowledge. This association of local edges is normally referred to as *boundary detection* and the generation of the local edge image is referred to as *edge detection*.

Boundary detection algorithms vary in the amount of domain-dependent information or knowledge which they incorporate in associating or linking the edges, and their effectiveness is obviously dependent on the quality of the edge image. The more reliable the edge elements in terms of their position, orientation and, indeed, authenticity, the more effective the boundary detector will be. However, for relatively simple, well-defined shapes, boundary detection may become redundant, or at least trivial, as edge detection performance improves. Since computational complexity for the segmentation process as a whole is a function of the complexity of both the edge detection and boundary detection then minimal segmentation complexity may be achieved by a trade-off between the sophistication of the edge detector and the boundary detector.

It is worth noting, however, that since edge detection is essentially a filtering process and can often be effected in hardware, while boundary detection will require more sophisticated software, the current (and, probably, correct) trend is to deploy the most effective and sophisticated edge detector (e.g. the Canny operator or the Marr–Hildreth operator) and to simplify the boundary detection process.

The remainder of this chapter is devoted to a discussion of a region-based segmentation technique (thresholding), edge detection, region growing and, finally, boundary detection.

5.2   *Thresholding*

Grey-level thresholding, which we covered briefly in Chapter 4, is a simple region-based technique. However, we include it in a section on its own here because it is a very commonly used and popular technique. As we saw in Chapter 4, in situations where an object exhibits a uniform grey-level and rests against a background of a different grey-level, thresholding will assign a value of 0 to all pixels with a grey-level less than the threshold level and a value of 255 (say) to all pixels with a grey-level greater than the threshold level. Thus, the image is segmented into two disjoint regions, one corresponding to the background, and the other to the object.

5.2.1 *Global, local, and dynamic approaches*

In a more general sense, a threshold operation may be viewed as a test involving some function of the grey-level at a point, some local property of the point, e.g. the average grey-level over some neighbourhood, and the position of the point in the image. Thus, a threshold operation may be viewed as a test involving a function T of the form:

$$T(x, y, N(x, y), g(x, y))$$

where $g(x, y)$ is the grey-level at the point (x, y) and $N(x, y)$ denotes some local property of the point (x, y). If $g(x, y) > T(x, y, N(x, y), g(x, y))$ then (x, y) is labelled an object point, otherwise it is labelled a background point, or conversely. This is the most general form of the function T, however, and three classes of thresholding (global, local, and dynamic) may be distinguished on the basis of restrictions placed on this function (see Weszka, 1978). These are:

$T = T(g(x, y))$ — Global thresholding: the test is dependent only on the grey-level of the point.

$T = T(N(x, y), g(x, y))$ — Local thresholding: the test is dependent on a neighbourhood property of the point and on the grey-level of the point.

$T = T(x, y, N(x, y), g(x, y))$ — Dynamic thresholding: the test is dependent on the point coordinates, a neighbourhood property of the point and on the grey-level of the point.

It is pertinent to note, however, that most systems utilize the simplest of these three approaches, global thresholding: the threshold test is based exclusively on the global threshold value and on the grey-level of a test-point, irrespective of its position in the image or of any local context. The approach is facilitated either by constraining the scene to ensure that there is no uneven illumination or by photometrically decalibrating the image before thresholding. The advantage of this approach is that the thresholding can be accomplished by commonly available hardware using a look-up table, as described in Chapter 4.

5.2.2 *Threshold selection*

The selection of an appropriate threshold is the single major problem for reliable segmentation. Of the several techniques which have been proposed, most are based on the analysis of the grey-level histogram, selecting thresholds which lie in the region between the two modes of the (bi-modal) histogram. The assumption that the histogram is indeed bi-modal, with one mode corresponding to the grey-level representing the object and the other to the grey-level representing the background, is often not valid; histograms are frequently noisy and the two modes may be difficult to detect (see Figure 5.1). Just as often, the object will generate a single mode while the background will comprise a wide range of grey-level, giving rise to a uni-modal histogram (see Figure 5.2). While several applications of a simple smoothing (or local averaging) operator to a noisy histogram will help with noisy bi-modal histograms, it will be of little use with uni-modal histograms. Figure 5.3

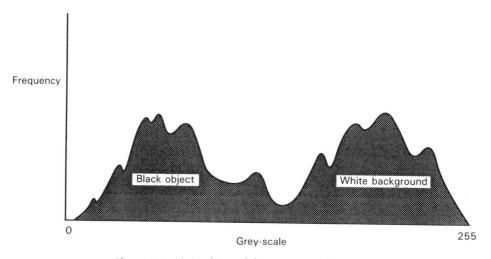

Figure 5.1 Noisy bi-modal grey-scale histogram.

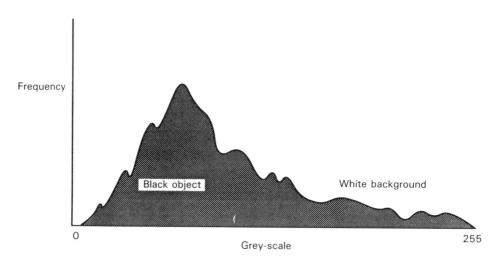

Figure 5.2 Uni-modal grey-scale histogram.

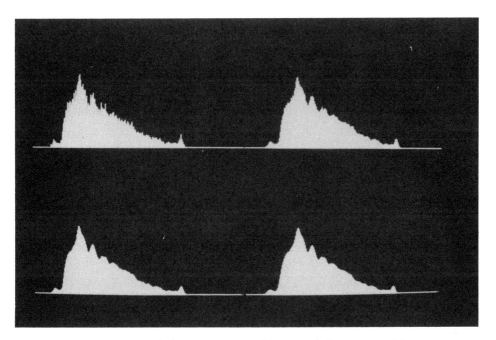

Figure 5.3 Grey-scale histogram smoothing: top-left: no smoothing; top-right: one application of a 3 × 1 neighbourhood average operator; bottom-left: two applications; bottom-right: three applications.

illustrates the effect of smoothing a grey-scale histogram by iterative application of a local 3 × 1 neighbourhood averaging operator.

Another useful approach to thresholding selection is to use the average grey-level of those pixels which are on the boundary between the object and the background as an estimate of the threshold value. As the grey-level of this boundary pixel will typically lie between those of the object and the background, it provides a good indication of the threshold value (see Figure 5.4). The difficulty, of course, lies in deciding which pixels *are* on the boundary.

One of the best approaches is to use a reliable edge detector, such as the Marr–Hildreth operator described in the next section, to identify these boundary points. The threshold selection procedure first uses a Marr–Hildreth operator to locate edges in the image and the mean grey-level of the image pixels at these edge locations is computed. This mean represents the global threshold value. To illustrate this approach, Figure 5.5 shows the binary image generated by thresholding the original grey-scale image at a threshold equal to the mean grey-level of the boundary points generated using the Marr–Hildreth operator. It should be noted that, although this threshold selection technique is computationally complex and may take a significant amount of time to compute, it is only a calibration exercise and need not be performed before every threshold operation.

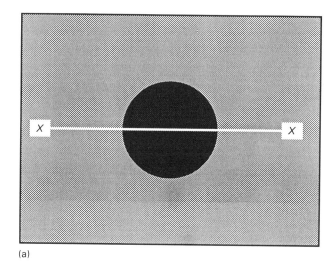

(a)

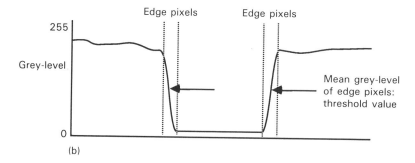

(b)

Figure 5.4 Using edge pixels to select a threshold: (a) image of dark, round object on a light background with section $X-X$ shown; (b) profile of image intensity along section $X-X$.

5.3 An overview of edge detection techniques

As might be expected when dealing with a process which is fundamental to image segmentation, the literature concerning edge detection is large. This section will not attempt to review all detectors in detail; rather it will survey and describe the different approaches to edge detection and illustrate the approach with specific algorithms.

There are four distinct approaches to the problem of edge detection:

(a) gradient- and difference-based operators;
(b) template matching;

(a)

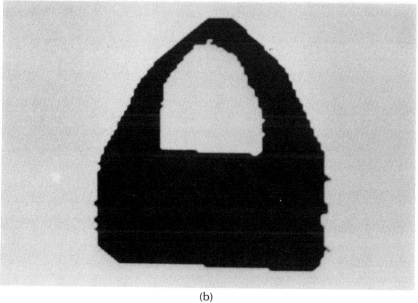

(b)

Figure 5.5 Automatic threshold selection using the Marr–Hildreth theory of edge detection: (a) original grey-scale image; (b) automatically thresholded binary image.

(c) edge fitting;
(d) statistical edge detection.

Each of these four approaches will be considered in turn.

5.3.1 Gradient- and difference-based operators

If we define a local edge in an image to be a transition between two regions of significantly different intensities, then the gradient function of the image, which measures the rate of change, will have large values in these transitional boundary areas. Thus gradient-based, or first-derivative-based, edge detectors enhance the image by estimating its gradient function and then signal that an edge is present if the gradient value is greater than some defined threshold.

In more detail, if $\partial/\partial x$ and $\partial/\partial y$ represent the rates of change of a two-dimensional function $f(x, y)$ in the x- and y-directions, respectively, then the rate of change in a direction θ (measured in the positive sense from the X-axis) is given by:

$$\frac{\partial f}{\partial x} \cos \theta + \frac{\partial f}{\partial y} \sin \theta$$

The direction θ, at which this rate of change has the greatest magnitude is given by:

$$\arctan \left[\frac{\partial f}{\partial y} \middle| \frac{\partial f}{\partial x} \right]$$

with magnitude:

$$\sqrt{\left[\left(\frac{\partial f}{\partial x}\right)^2 + \left(\frac{\partial f}{\partial y}\right)^2 \right]}$$

The gradient of $f(x, y)$ is a vector at (x, y) with this magnitude and direction. Thus the gradient may be estimated if the directional derivatives of the function are known along (any) two orthogonal directions. The essential differences between all gradient-based edge detectors are the directions which the operators use, the manner in which they approximate the one-dimensional derivatives of the image function in these directions, and the manner in which they combine these approximations to form the gradient magnitude.

These gradient functions are intuitively easy to understand when we confine ourselves to the discrete domain of digital images where partial derivatives become simple first differences. For example, the first difference of a two-dimensional function in the x-direction is simply:

$$f(x + 1, y) - f(x, y)$$

Similarly, the first difference of a two-dimensional function in the y-direction is simply:

$$f(x, y + 1) - f(x, y)$$

An operator due to Roberts estimates the derivatives diagonally over a 2×2 neighbourhood. The magnitude of the gradient $g(x, y)$, at an image point (x, y), is approximated by taking the RMS of the directional differences:

$$g(x, y) \approx R(x, y) = \sqrt{[\{f(x, y) - f(x + 1, y + 1)\}^2 + \{f(x, y + 1) - f(x + 1, y)\}^2]}$$

$R(x, y)$ is usually referred to as the Roberts cross operator. The differences may be combined in a way other than the RMS to provide a computationally simpler version, the Roberts absolute value estimate of the gradient function, given by:

$$g(x, y) \approx R(x, y) = |f(x, y) - f(x + 1, y + 1)| + |f(x, y + 1) - f(x + 1, y)|$$

Rosenfeld and Kak have argued that a third version, the Roberts max operator, given by:

$$g(x, y) \approx R(x, y) = \text{Max} \, (|f(x, y) - f(x + 1, y + 1)|, |f(x, y + 1) - f(x + 1, y)|)$$

affords better invariance to edge orientation. Applying the Roberts max operator to edges of equal strength, but of different orientation, produces less variation in the resultant magnitude value than if the cross operator were used.

To illustrate these edge detectors, a test image with fairly fine structure (a tray of electrical wires) was acquired: see Figure 5.6. The Roberts RMS, absolute value, and Roberts max operators are shown in Figures 5.7, 5.8, and 5.9 respectively.

One of the main problems with the Roberts operator is its susceptibility to noise because of the manner in which it estimates the directional derivatives, i.e. the first differences, of the image function $f(x, y)$. This has prompted an alternative estimation of the gradient by combining the differencing process with local averaging. For example, the Sobel operator estimates the partial derivative in the

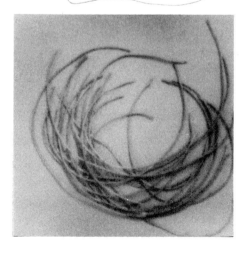

Figure 5.6 A tray of wires.

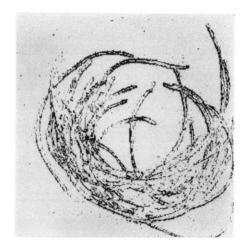

Figure 5.7 Roberts RMS edge detection operator.

Figure 5.8 Roberts absolute value edge detection operator.

x-direction over a 3×3 region centred at $f(x, y)$ by:

$$S_x = \{f(x+1, y-1) + 2f(x+1, y) + f(x+1, y+1)\}$$
$$- \{f(x-1, y-1) + 2f(x-1, y) + f(x-1, y+1)\}$$

This essentially takes the difference of a weighted average of the image intensity on either side of $f(x, y)$. Similarly:

$$S_y = \{f(x-1, y+1) + 2f(x, y+1) + f(x+1, y+1)\}$$
$$- \{f(x-1, y-1) + 2f(x, y-1) + f(x+1, y-1)\}$$

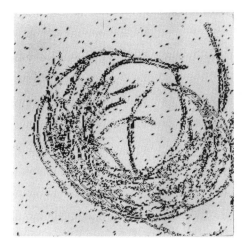

Figure 5.9 Roberts max edge detection operator.

Figure 5.10 Sobel RMS edge detection operator.

The gradient may then be estimated as before by either calculating the RMS (see Figure 5.10):

$$g(x, y) \approx S = \sqrt{(S_x^2 + S_y^2)}$$

or by taking the absolute values (see Figure 5.11):

$$g(x, y) \approx S = |S_x| + |S_y|$$

In an analogous manner Prewitt suggests an approximation of the partial

95

derivatives by:

$$P_x = \{f(x+1, y-1) + f(x+1, y) + f(x+1, y+1)\}$$
$$- \{f(x-1, y-1) + f(x-1, y) + f(x-1, y+1)\}$$

$$P_y = \{f(x-1, y+1) + f(x, y+1) + f(x+1, y+1)\}$$
$$- \{f(x-1, y-1) + f(x, y-1) + f(x+1, y-1)\}$$

and the gradient may be estimated as before (see Figures 5.12 and 5.13).

Quite often, the directional differences are estimated using simple convolution

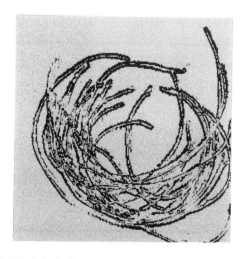

Figure 5.11 Sobel absolute value edge detection operator.

Figure 5.12 Prewitt RMS edge detection operator.

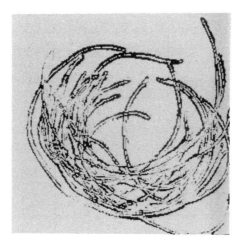

Figure 5.13 Prewitt absolute value edge detection operator.

kernels, one kernel for each different operator. These yield two partial derivative images, which are then combined on a point by point basis, either as the RMS or as the sum of absolute values, to produce the final gradient estimate. Figure 5.14 illustrates the convolution kernels for the Roberts, Sobel, and Prewitt operators. Strictly speaking, the kernel should first be rotated by $180°$ before the convolution is performed (see Section 4.2.1). However, this is normally omitted since the resultant error of $180°$ in the gradient direction can be ignored.

Once the gradient magnitude has been estimated, a decision as to whether or not an edge exists is made by comparing it to some predefined value; an edge is deemed to be present if the magnitude is greater than this threshold. Obviously the choice of threshold is important and in noisy images threshold selection involves a trade-off between missing valid edges and including noise-induced false edges.

So far, edge detection has been discussed on the basis of first-derivative directional operators. However, an alternative method uses an approximation to the Laplacian:

$$\nabla^2 = \frac{\partial^2}{\partial x^2} + \frac{\partial^2}{\partial y^2}$$

i.e. the sum of second-order, unmixed, partial derivatives. The standard approximation is given by:

$$L(x, y) = f(x, y) - 1/4\{f(x, y + 1) + f(x, y - 1) + f(x + 1, y) + f(x - 1, y)\}$$

The digital Laplacian has zero response to linear ramps (and thus gradual changes in intensity) but it does respond on either side of the edge, once with a positive sign and once with a negative sign. Thus in order to detect edges, the image is enhanced by evaluating the digital Laplacian and isolating the points at which the resultant

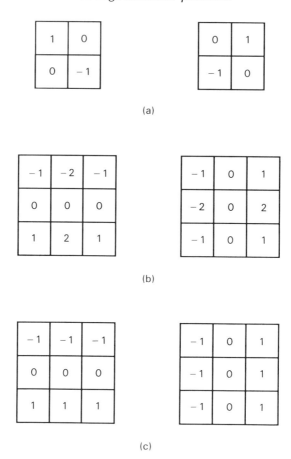

(a)

(b)

(c)

Figure 5.14 Convolution kernels for estimation of the partial derivatives with (a) Roberts; (b) Sobel; and (c) Prewitt edge detection operators.

image goes from positive to negative, i.e. at which it crosses zero. The Laplacian has one significant disadvantage: it responds very strongly to noise.

A different and much more successful application of the Laplacian to edge detection was proposed by Marr and Hildreth in 1980. This approach first smooths the image by convolving it with a two-dimensional Gaussian function, and subsequently isolating the zero-crossings of the Laplacian of this image:

$$\nabla^2\{I(x, y) * G(x, y)\}$$

where $I(x, y)$ represents the image intensity at a point (x, y) and $G(x, y)$ is the two-dimensional Gaussian function, of a given standard deviation σ, defined by:

$$G(x, y) = \frac{1}{2\pi\sigma^2} \exp[-(x^2 + y^2)/2\sigma^2]$$

Despite some criticism of this technique, it is very widely used. The operator possesses a number of useful properties: for example: the evaluation of the Laplacian and the convolution commute so that, for a Gaussian with a given standard deviation, we can derive a single filter: *the Laplacian of Gaussian*:

$$\nabla^2\{I(x, y) * G(x, y)\} = \nabla^2 G(x, y) * I(x, y)$$

Furthermore, this two-dimensional convolution is separable into four one-dimensional convolutions (see Appendix I for a derivation):

$$\nabla^2\{I(x, y) * G(x, y)\} = G(x) * \left\{I(x, y) * \frac{\partial^2}{\partial y^2} G(y)\right\}$$

$$+ G(y) * \left\{I(x, y) * \frac{\partial^2}{\partial x^2} G(x)\right\}$$

Bearing in mind that an implementation of the operator requires an extensive support, e.g. 63×63 pixels for a Gaussian with standard deviation of 9.0, this separability facilitates significant computational savings, reducing the required number of multiplications from n^2 to $4n$ for a filter kernel size of n pixels. The Laplacian of Gaussian operator also yields thin continuous closed contours of zero-crossing points. This property is most useful in subsequent processing, such as when characterizing the intensity discontinuities or edges as object boundaries.

The location of the zero-crossings in space is not the only information that can be extracted from the convolved image: the amplitude (which is related to the slope) and orientation of the gradient of the convolved image at the zero-crossing point provide important information about edge contrast and orientation. The slope of a zero-crossing is the rate at which the convolution output changes as it crosses zero and is related to the contrast and width of the intensity change.

Since the Gaussian is used to smooth the image and since different standard deviations yield edges detected at different scales within the image (successively smoothing out image detail), Marr's theory also requires the correlation of edge segments derived using Gaussians of different standard deviation. However, the edges detected by one operator alone are often sufficiently reliable for many industrial applications: see Figure 5.15. In any event, we will return to this issue of multi-scale or multi-resolution edge detection when we discuss image understanding in Chapter 9.

5.3.2 Template matching

Since an ideal edge is essentially a step-like pattern, one straightforward approach to edge detection is to try to match templates of these ideal step edges with regions of the same size at every point in the image. Several edge templates are used, each template representing an ideal step at a different orientation. The degree of match can, for example, be determined by evaluating the cross-correlation between the

Figure 5.15 Marr–Hildreth edge detection operator.

template and the image.* The template producing the highest correlation determines the edge magnitude at that point and the edge orientation is assumed to be that of the corresponding template. Detection is accomplished by thresholding in the same manner as discussed for gradient approaches. These templates are often referred to as edge masks.

Such a set of masks, due to Kirsch, is:

```
 1  1  1    1  1  1   -1  1  1   -1 -1  1
 1 -2  1   -1 -2  1   -1 -2  1   -1 -2  1
-1 -1 -1   -1 -1  1   -1  1  1    1  1  1

-1 -1 -1    1 -1 -1    1  1 -1    1  1  1
 1 -2  1    1 -2 -1    1 -2 -1    1 -2 -1
 1  1  1    1  1  1    1  1 -1    1 -1 -1
```

Figure 5.16 illustrates the effect of the application of this set of masks.
Another set, due to Prewitt, is:

```
 5  5  5   -3  5  5   -3 -3  5   -3 -3 -3
-3  0 -3   -3  0  5   -3  0  5   -3  0  5
-3 -3 -3   -3 -3 -3   -3 -3  5   -3  5  5

-3 -3 -3   -3 -3 -3    5 -3 -3    5  5 -3
-3  0 -3    5  0 -3    5  0 -3    5  0 -3
 5  5  5    5  5 -3    5 -3 -3   -3 -3 -3
```

This edge detection technique is shown in Figure 5.17.

---

* Cross-correlation is discussed in Chapter 6 on image analysis.

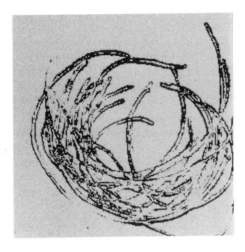

Figure 5.16 Kirsch template edge detection operator.

Figure 5.17 Prewitt template edge detection operator.

All the masks discussed so far, with the exception of the Laplacian of Gaussian, when convolved with the image, will produce an enhanced image with large values, not only at the centre of the edge, but also at points close to that edge. Subsequent thresholding of such an enhanced image will generate an edge map with thick edges. Nevatia and Babu suggested a template-matching algorithm (see Figure 5.18) which produces a thin edge. In this case, six 5×5 masks (corresponding to edges at $0°$, $30°$, $60°$, $90°$, $120°$, and $150°$ orientations) are correlated with the image. An edge is deemed present at a particular orientation if:

(a) the response at that orientation exceeds a set threshold; and
(b) it is not dominated by responses at neighbouring points in a direction that is normal to the candidate edge.

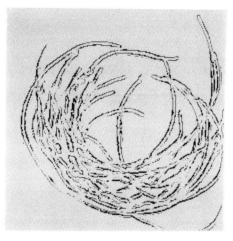

Figure 5.18 Nevatia–Babu template edge detection operator.

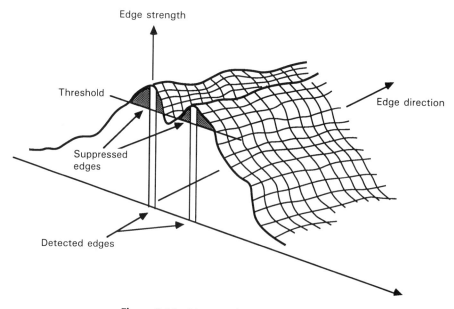

Figure 5.19 Non-maxima suppression.

In particular, the edge magnitude must be higher than the edge magnitude of the pixels on either side of it, in a direction normal to the edge orientation (see Figure 5.19), and the neighbouring pixels are also required to have edge orientations similar to (within thirty degrees) that of the central point. This general technique is referred to as 'non-maxima suppression' and was originally proposed by Rosenfeld and Thurston in 1971.

5.3.3 Edge fitting

As mentioned above, an ideal edge can be modelled as a step discontinuity in intensity at a particular location in the image. A step function can be defined in a circular region by a function $S(x, y)$ defined as follows (refer to Figure 5.20):

$$S(x, y) = \begin{cases} b & (x \cos \theta + y \sin \theta) < \rho \\ b + h & (x \cos \theta + y \sin \theta) \geqslant \rho \end{cases}$$

where

> h is the step height (intensity difference);
> b is the base intensity;
> ρ and θ define the position and orientation of the edge line with respect to the origin of this circular region.

The approach to edge detection in this case is to determine how closely this model fits a given image neighbourhood and to identify the values of b, h, ρ, and θ that minimize some measure of the distance between this circular step function and a corresponding area in the image. This is the basis of Hueckel's operator. The error, $\mathscr{E}$ between the ideal step $S(x, y, b, h, \rho, \theta)$, defined over a circular region C

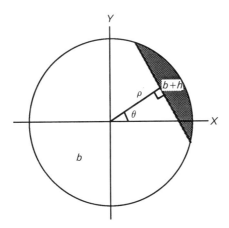

Figure 5.20 Parameters defining a step function in a circular region.

and (some) circular sub-image $f(x, y)$ of the same size can be given by:

$$\mathscr{E}^2 = \sum_{x,y \in C} (f(x, y) - S(x, y, b, h, \rho, \theta))$$

Note that $f(x, y)$ is the image intensity at a point (x, y) and $S(x, y, b, h, \rho, \theta)$ is the ideal step edge for chosen values of b, h, ρ, and θ at a point (x, y). The summation is to be performed over the entire region C and b, h, ρ, and θ are to be chosen so that $\mathscr{E}^2$ is minimized. This minimization process is simplified by expanding both $f(x, y)$ and $S(x, y, b, h, \rho, \theta)$ in terms of a set of orthogonal (Fourier) basis functions and using the corresponding coefficients (f_i and s_i, say) in the error measure given above instead of $f(x, y)$ and $S(x, y, b, h, \rho, \theta)$. In practice, only the first eight terms of the expansion are used. The operator was designed to detect the presence of two edge elements in the circular neighbourhood simultaneously, reporting only the more dominant edge. Each edge requires four parameters to describe it and it was for this reason that the eighth term was chosen as the cut-off.

Thus, the problem is now to minimize:

$$E^2 = \sum_{i=0}^{7} (f_i - s_i)$$

Hueckel then presents and proves a theorem which, in effect, reduces this problem to one of extremization of a function in θ and he derives subsequent expressions for ρ, b, and h. The decision as to whether an edge is present or not is based on the amplitude of the computed step as well as the degree of fit. Bearing in mind the computational complexity of the Hueckel edge fitting technique, the results are, in general, quite disappointing (see Figure 5.21).

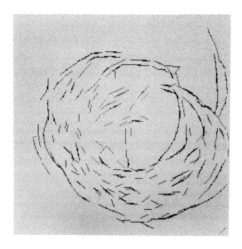

Figure 5.21 Hueckel edge detection operator.

5.3.4 Statistical techniques

If you consider a small region or window in an image (e.g. a 7×7 pixel area), you can view an edge as a boundary between two inhomogeneous sub-regions. On the other hand, if the entire region is homogeneous, then no edge exists. This is the basis of an edge detection technique due to Yakimovsky (see Figure 5.22) who treated edge detection as an exercise in hypothesis testing, choosing between the two following hypotheses:

H0: The image values on two sides of a line through the window are taken from the same region.

H1: The image values on one side are from one region and on the other side from a different region.

Assuming that each region comprises pixels having normally distributed grey-levels and each pixel in the region is mutually independent, Yakimovsky argued that the choice can be made by considering the ratio of (a) the grey-level standard deviation of the combined region (raised to the power of the number of pixels in the region) to (b) the product of the grey-level standard deviations of both individual regions, each with standard deviation raised to the power of the number of pixels in the respective region.

To decide whether an edge of a given orientation exists in a window, one can bisect the window at that orientation, thus creating two sub-regions, calculate the appropriate standard deviations and decide as to the presence of an edge based on some selected threshold. This may be done for several orientations, for example $0°$, $30°$, $60°$, $90°$, $120°$, and $150°$. There are several other statistical edge detectors but this one serves to illustrate the approach.

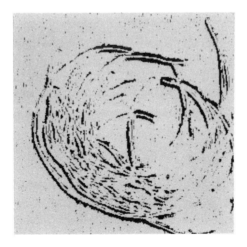

Figure 5.22 Yakimovsky edge detection operator.

5.3.5 Assessment of edge detection

One point on which there is a definite consensus in the computer vision community is that it is difficult quantitatively to evaluate and compare edge detector performance. Reasons for this include the fact that there are a large number of detectors and each detector incorporates its own inherent edge model. Thus, certain edge detectors may be more appropriate or more successful in certain circumstances. Also, edge detectors will display differing degrees of noise immunity: some may be too sensitive to noise; others will cater for (certain types of) noise but possibly at the cost of missing valid edges. A generic mathematical analysis of detectors is difficult, even for simple images, due to the frequent complexity and non-linearity of the detectors (but see Hildreth, 1985, and Torre and Poggio, 1986, for discussions of the topic). It is also worth noting that many of the detectors which can claim some degree of optimality (e.g. Canny, Marr–Hildreth, Fleck) are optimal only with respect to the criteria they choose as relevant. To coin a phrase: 'You pick your optimality criteria and you take your choice.'

In spite of these difficulties, a quantitative evaluation is clearly desirable even if only to provide a very rough guide to the relative performance of detectors in limited circumstances. If a clear-cut objective analytic measure is difficult to establish (but, again, see Torre and Poggio, 1986), an empirical assessment may often suffice. It cannot be stressed too much, however, that empirical tests are only relevant in the application domain in which they are carried out. One figure of measure that can be used in such tests was suggested by Pratt (Pratt, 1978; Abdou and Pratt, 1979) and provides a way of assessing the performance of edge detectors in localizing the position of edges. Specifically, a figure of merit R, yielding a value in the interval 0.0–1.0, is defined:

$$R = \frac{1}{\max(I_A, I_I)} \sum_{i=1}^{I_A} \frac{1}{1 + \alpha d^2}$$

where I_I and I_A represent the number of ideal and actual edge map points, d is the separation distance of an actual edge point normal to a line of ideal edge points. The value α is a scaling constant and is adjusted to penalize edges offset from their true location. It is typically set at 0.111. Normalizing the figure of merit by the maximum of the number of actual and ideal edgepoints ensures that fragmented and smeared edges are penalized.

5.4 Region growing

As we noted at the beginning of this section, region growing effects the segmentation process by grouping elemental areas which share a common feature into large connected two-dimensional areas called 'regions', with the implicit assumption that these resultant regions correspond to some real-world surface or object. Thus, the central idea underlying region-growing techniques is to merge initially small regions (e.g. individual pixels) into large ones. This merging process must then address two questions: upon what criterion will two regions be merged and at what point will merging cease? To answer the first question, we must define more rigorously what we understand by the term *region*. A region is an aggregate (collection) of pixels all of which satisfy some *uniformity predicate* $U(p)$, such that the value of $U(p)$ is true if some local property of the neighbourhood of pixel p satisfies the uniformity predicate and false otherwise. Most region-growing techniques base the test for uniformity on some feature of the grey-level. The answer to the question: 'what is the criteria for merging two regions?' is thus, quite simply, the uniformity predicate. Two *adjacent* regions are merged if the merged region satisfies the uniformity predicate. The answer to the second question: 'at what point does merging cease?' is now clear. Merging (or growing) ceases when no two adjacent regions satisfy the uniformity predicate. Thus, the region-growing procedure is an iterative one: small regions are merged to form larger ones; these are then merged (if appropriate) to form still larger ones, and so on until no more regions can be merged. A natural consequence of this approach is that sophisticated data structures are required to keep track of the intermediate regions and their features.

In the trivial global thresholding technique, the uniformity predicate is simply that the grey-level of the pixel (region) in question should lie within a pre-set range of grey-levels; the final regions are grown in one step as only one test is needed for each pixel and there are no intermediate regions.

5.4.1 The split and merge procedure using quad-trees

This region-growing algorithm, developed by Horowitz and Pavlidis in 1976, makes use of an image representation called the quad-tree. A quad-tree is a tree (a collection of nodes organized in a hierarchical manner) in which each node has either four sons or no sons.

The root of the quad-tree is a node which represents the average grey-level of the entire image. The leaves of a full quad-tree, i.e. the nodes which do not have any offspring, correspond to the individual pixels of the image. The parent of a group of four nodes corresponds to the average grey-level of a 2×2 neighbourhood of the image: if each of these four pixels/nodes have the same grey-level, then, obviously, there is no need to represent them explicitly as the parent node can do the job just as well and they can be deleted. Similarly, the parent of each of these nodes corresponds to a further 2×2 grouping of these 2×2 neighbourhoods; again, the off-spring are present in the quad-tree if and only if they have different grey-levels. The hierarchical aggregation continues until one reaches the root of the tree which clearly represents the average grey-level of its sons, and hence the average grey-level of the entire image. Thus, one can see that the quad-tree is a useful method of image compression if there are large regions of uniform grey-level since much of these regions can be represented by nodes close to the root, without the need to have nodes for the individual pixels; see Figure 5.23.

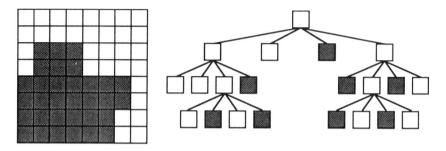

Figure 5.23 A quad-tree representation of an 8×8 binary image.

The split and merge procedure begins with a quad-tree of a given depth, typically where the depth is such that the leaves correspond not to pixels but to larger blocks. Leaves are then merged: if four leaves from a parent satisfy the uniformity predicate then the leaves are deleted and the parent inherits their average grey-level (assuming that we are going to use grey-level as a way of labelling a region). This merging continues at the next highest level, and then at subsequent levels, until no more merging is possible. At this stage a splitting procedure is initiated. Here, the quad-tree is traversed and at each leaf the uniformity predicate of the corresponding group is evaluated; if the value is false then the block is split and the four corresponding nodes are added to the node. This process continues until all leaves satisfy the uniformity predicate. At this stage, the quad-tree is traversed horizontally. The neighbours of each leaf are examined and adjacent leaves from different parents which satisfy the uniformity predicate are linked together to form a region.

It is worth noting that, for industrial applications, region-growing techniques are considered too computationally complex (and hence too slow) to be of much use and should only be considered when thresholding or edge detection techniques are incapable of yielding satisfactory results.

5.5 Boundary detection

As we discussed previously, edge detection is only the first stage of the boundary-based segmentation process. We also need to aggregate these local edge elements, which are a relatively featureless representation, into structures better suited to the process of interpretation. This is normally achieved using processes such as edge thinning (recall that gradient-based template matching edge detectors produce thick edges), edge linking, gap-filling, and curve-segment linking in order to generate a distinct, explicit, and unambiguous representation of the boundary. There are several techniques for boundary detection and they vary in the amount of knowledge or domain-dependent information that is used in the grouping process. These approaches include, in order of decreasing use of domain-dependent information, boundary refining, the Hough transform, graph searching, dynamic programming, and contour following. Since the Hough transform will be described in detail in the next chapter, we will confine ourselves here to the other four techniques, placing emphasis on contour following. However, the reader can, if he/she likes, skip ahead and preview the Hough transform section without any difficulty.

5.5.1 Boundary refining

Boundary refining methods use an initial *a priori* estimate of the position of the boundary to guide a search for the actual, or real, boundary and subsequently to refine this initial estimate. The estimate may have been generated by the analysis of lower-resolution images or, alternatively, explicit high-level knowledge can be utilized, for example knowledge that the boundary lies on, or close to, a given curve. For example, Bolles incorporated this technique in an algorithm which builds boundaries by searching in a direction at right-angles to the *a priori* boundary for local edges and selects the element with the highest gradient value, provided its direction is (almost) parallel to the boundary direction (Bolles, 1977). This is repeated at regular intervals along the approximate *a priori* boundary and, if sufficient edge elements are extracted, then these locations are fitted with some analytic function, e.g. a low-degree polynomial. This parameterized curve then represents the actual boundary.

Another approach, referred to as *divide-and-conquer* or *iterative end-point fit* boundary detection, is often applicable where a low curvature boundary is known to exist between two edge elements. The general idea here is to fit an initial line between the two points; if the normal distance from the line to the point of maximum gradient magnitude is less than some pre-set tolerance, the approximation is complete, otherwise the point of greatest normal distance from the line becomes a break-point on the boundary, forming two new line segments. All new segments are then subjected, in an iterative manner, to this same process.

5.5.2 Graph-theoretic techniques

A second approach to boundary detection, which need not depend significantly on the existence of *a priori* knowledge, treats the aggregation or association of edge points into boundaries as a (low-cost) graph traversal. In particular, edge points are viewed as nodes in a graph and there is a cost function or weight associated with connecting two neighbouring points or nodes; the desired boundary may be interpreted as the minimal cost (or any low-cost) path through the graph. The cost function or weight associated with connecting two edge points is normally defined to be a function of the distance between them, the difference in their directions, and edge strength.

5.5.3 *Dynamic programming*

This approach formulates the boundary-following procedure as a dynamic programming problem by defining a cost function which embodies a notion of the 'best boundary'. This is not dissimilar to the idea of the graph-theoretic technique in that the path specified by the boundary minimizes the cost function. For example, suppose that a local edge detection operator is applied to a grey-level image to produce edge magnitude and direction information at points $x_1, ..., x_n$. One possible criterion for a good boundary is a weighted sum of high cumulative edge strength and low cumulative curvature, that is, for a curve with n segments:

$$H(x_1, ..., x_n) = \sum_{k=1}^{n} s(x_k) + c \sum_{k=1}^{n-1} q(x_k, x_{k+1})$$

with the implicit constraint that consecutive points must be grid neighbours:

$$\| x_{k+1} - x_k \| < 2$$

The function $q(x_k, x_{k+1})$ embodies the difference in direction between edge element x_k and element x_{k+1}. Note that c is a negative constant. The function $s(x_k)$ is the edge strength (or gradient magnitude). The evaluation function $H(x_1, ..., x_n)$ is in the form of a serial optimization problem where not all variables in the evaluation function are simultaneously inter-related, and can be solved by a multi-stage optimization process referred to as *serial dynamic programming* (Bellman and Dreyfus, 1962).

5.5.4 *Contour following*

Contour following is a simple approach which uses no domain-dependent information and 'follows' the boundary or contour exclusively on the basis of locally derived data. The basis of the technique is, essentially, to start with a point that is believed to be on the boundary (some local edge point, say) and to extend the boundary by adding a neighbouring point in the contour direction (i.e. the direction which is normal to the gradient direction). This process of extension is reiterated, starting at this new boundary pixel. In this way a contour is followed around the boundary (see Figure 5.24). The basis for selecting a candidate varies from task to task and from algorithm to algorithm but normally is dependent at least on the gradient direction and on the gradient magnitude. Since contour following techniques are often based on gradient edge detectors, these techniques are normally most successful with images in which there is little noise. For the purpose of illustration, the following section details a simple contour following algorithm.

To begin with, contour following algorithms cannot assume that the boundary constitutes a closed curve. Thus, the boundary is followed in two directions: first in the forward boundary direction and then in the reverse direction. The forward boundary direction is arbitrarily designated the direction equal to the

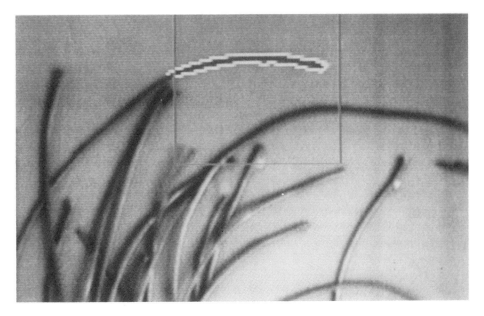

Figure 5.24 Contour following.

edge normal (or gradient) direction $+90°$ and the reverse direction corresponds to the edge normal direction $-90°$. The boundary following algorithm proceeds on a pixel to pixel basis, tracing the local maximum gradient given by the gradient direction at that point on the boundary to the next pixel.

Tracing continues as long as the difference between the current and candidate pixel gradient directions is not too large; this helps to avoid following boundaries into noisy areas which are characterized by frequent changes in edge direction. If no acceptable edge is encountered when tracing, a search is made in two zones ahead of the boundary: the first zone separated by a gap of one pixel from the current boundary point, the second by two pixels. If a suitable edge is found, the intervening gap pixels are filled in and the trace is restarted from this point. If none is found then the boundary is traced in the reverse direction from the original start point, provided this has not already been done.

The boundary following algorithm terminates when the boundary can be followed no further: that is, if neither the tracing nor the searching algorithms yield a valid boundary point. Boundary following also terminates if the original start point is re-encountered during tracing, signifying that a boundary is represented by a closed curve. Thus, the extraction of both open and closed contours is facilitated.

As the algorithm traces around the boundary, it builds a boundary chain code (BCC) representation of the contour. The BCC is defined and discussed in detail in Chapter 7. For the purposes of this section it is sufficient to summarize its essential structure and properties. A boundary chain code comprises an integer pair, denoting the coordinates of an origin point on the contour, and a sequence (or chain) of integer values representing the direction of the next pixel on the contour. The range of possible directions is coarsely quantized and there are just eight possible directions corresponding to each of the eight pixels which are adjacent to the centre pixel in a 3×3 neighbourhood. The boundary following algorithm adheres to the Freeman chain code convention: the pixel to the right of centre (east neighbour) is given by the direction 0, the north-east pixel is given by the direction 1. Continuing anti-clockwise around the neighbourhood, the south-east neighbour is given by the direction 7. Figure 5.25 illustrates these direction codes.

To avoid following multiple close parallel boundaries caused by the presence of 'thick' edge responses, pixels in directions normal to the boundaries extracted by the following algorithm are suppressed, i.e they are labelled, so as to exclude them from later consideration by either the trace or search modules.

The next two sections discuss the component trace and search modules of the contour following algorithm in more detail.

☐ *The trace algorithm*
The purpose of the trace algorithm is to follow a sequence of boundary pixels and to generate a model of the boundary, i.e. the BCC, by recording all the boundary pixels visited. It is assumed that the boundary pixels correspond to the pixels exhibiting the local maximum gradient magnitude and that the gradient direction indicates, approximately at least, the neighbouring boundary pixel. The boundary direction, D, of an (edge) point is given by the edge gradient direction G as $D = G + 2$ for the forward direction and as $D = G - 2$ for the reverse direction ($+90°$ and $-90°$ respectively). All directional additions and subtractions are modulo 8 operations. The tracing algorithm chooses as candidates for inclusion in the boundary those pixels given by directions $D, D + 1$, and $D - 1$, that is, the pixel directly ahead of the current pixel and one pixel on either side of it. For example,

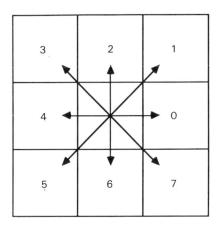

Figure 5.25 Freeman direction codes.

if $D = 1$ (boundary direction is $45°$), then pixels 0, 1, and 2 are chosen as candidates (pixel labels adhere to the convention described in Chapter 3: see Figure 3.6, i.e. they are labelled sequentially from 0 to 7 in an anti-clockwise rotation from the middle right-hand pixel in a 3×3 neighbourhood).

The potential of each of these candidates to be a boundary point is evaluated as the difference between the points gradient magnitude and the predefined gradient magnitude threshold. If the pixel has been visited previously, either by the tracing or searching algorithms, or if the pixel overlaps the image boundary, then it is assumed to have a negative potential. The candidate with the highest positive potential is selected as the next boundary point from which to continue the trace and is implicitly included in the list of boundary points by updating the BCC. If no candidate satisfies this condition, tracing is suspended and the search algorithm is invoked.

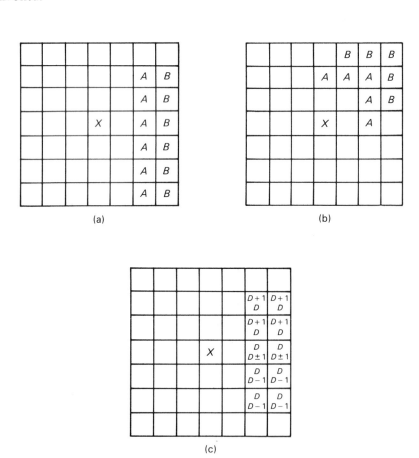

Figure 5.26 (a) Zone-of-influence A. (b) Zone-of-influence B. (c) Allowable directional variation of zones A and B.

☐   *The search algorithm*

If all three neighbouring candidate boundary pixels selected by the trace algorithm fail to satisfy the criteria for inclusion in the boundary, then the boundary follower searches for other potential boundary pixels which are not immediate neighbours of the current boundary pixel. The position and direction of this search is dependent on the direction of the current boundary point; the associated region for searching is termed the 'zone of influence' of the current boundary pixel. Two zones of influence, labelled A and B, of a boundary pixel are defined, based on the boundary direction D. Zone A comprises those pixels ahead of the boundary direction, separated from the current point by a one-pixel gap. Pixels in zone B are separated by a two-pixel gap. Figure 5.26(a) shows the pixels in zones A and B with $D = 0$. Figure 5.26(b) shows these zones when $D = 1$. The zone A configuration for directions $D = 2, 4$, and 6 is simply a rotation of the configuration where $D = 0$; similarly, simple rotations of zones A and B corresponding for direction $D = 1$ define the configurations for directions $D = 3, 5$, and 7.

A pixel in a particular zone of influence is selected for inclusion in the boundary if it satisfies the following two criteria:

(a)   the gradient magnitude is greater than the given threshold;
(b)   the gradient direction is within a certain directional range.

This directional range is based on the orientation of the current boundary point and the position of this candidate pixel relative to the current boundary point. Figure 5.26(c) defines the allowable directional variations for zones A and B, with the boundary direction equal to zero. The directional variations corresponding to other orientations may be determined simply by substituting the new direction for D in the diagram.

The order in which the individual pixels are tested within a zone is important. In general, they are searched in the following order:

$$
\begin{array}{c}
3 \\
1 \\
\text{Direction of boundary} \rightarrow \quad 0 \\
2 \\
4
\end{array}
$$

Since searching terminates as soon as an acceptable edge point is encountered, this ordering favours the extraction of a point that coincides with the boundary direction. In addition, zone A is searched before zone B; thus, the bridging of short boundary gaps is favoured over larger gaps. If a search is successful the BCC is updated to include the selected pixel and the intermediate gap pixel(s). If the search is not successful, boundary following in the current bias (forward or reverse) is terminated.

Figure 5.24 illustrates the operating of this contour following algorithm.

Exercises

1. Discuss thresholding as a segmentation process. Describe three possible methods for automatic threshold selection.

2. Gradient-based edge detection operators require some method for approximating the partial derivatives of an intensity function (i.e. an image) in two orthogonal directions. Why? How can the gradient direction and magnitude be estimated from these partial derivatives? Identify one simple gradient operator and explain how it affects each of the above components of edge detection.

3. What is the relationship of the Laplacian operator and the gradient operator? Identify a significant shortcoming of the Laplacian operator and state how it is ameliorated by the Marr–Hildreth operator.

4. Describe how the Marr–Hildreth theory of edge detection might be used to facilitate automatic threshold selection for binary image segmentation.

5. How would the contour following algorithm described in this chapter fare in a noisy image?

References and further reading

Abdou, I.E. and Pratt, W.K. 1979 'Quantitative design and evaluation of enhancement/ thresholding edge detectors', *Proceedings of the IEEE*, Vol. 67, No. 5, (May), pp. 753–63.

Argyle, E. 1971 'Techniques for edge detection', *Proc. IEEE*, Vol. 59, pp. 285–7.

Bellman, R. and Dreyfus, S. 1962 *Applied Dynamic Programming*, Princeton University Press, Princeton, New Jersey.

Canny, J. 1986 'A computational approach to edge detection', *IEEE Transactions on Pattern Analysis and Machine Intelligence*, Vol. PAMI-8, No. 6, pp. 679–98.

Cooper, D. and Sung, F. 1983 'Multiple-window parallel adaptive boundary finding in computer vision', *IEEE Transactions on Pattern Analysis and Machine Intelligence*, Vol. PAMI-5, No. 3, pp. 299–316.

Davis, L.S. 1975 'A survey of edge detection techniques', *Computer Graphics and Image Processing*, Vol. 4, No. 3, pp. 248–70.

Fischler, M.A. and Bolles, R.C. 1986 'Perceptual organisation and curve partitioning', *IEEE Transactions of Pattern Analysis and Machine Intelligence*, Vol. PAMI-8, No. 1, pp. 100–5.

Fram, J.R. and Deutsch, E.S. 1975 'On the quantitative evaluation of edge detection schemes and their comparison with human performance', *IEEE Transactions of Computers*, Vol. C-24, No. 6, pp. 616–28.

Frei, W. and Chen, C-C. 1977 'Fast boundary detection: a generalization and a new algorithm', *IEEE Transactions on Computers*, pp. 988–98.

Giordano, A., Maresca, M., Sandini, G., Vernazza, T. and Ferrari, D. 1985 *A Systolic*

Convolver for Parallel Multiresolution Edge Detection, Internal Report, DIST – University of Genoa.

Giordano, A., Maresca, M., Sandini, G., Vernazza, T. and Ferrari, D. 1987 'VLSI-based systolic architecture for fast Gaussian convolution', *Optical Engineering*, Vol. 26, No. 1, pp. 63–8.

Griffith, A.K. 1973 'Edge detection in simple scenes using *a priori* information', *IEEE Transactions on Computers*, Vol. 22, No. 4, pp. 371–80.

Grimson, W.F.L. and Hildreth, E.C. 1985 'Comments on digital step edges from zero crossings of second directional derivatives', *IEEE Trans. on Pattern Analysis and Machine Intelligence*, Vol. PAMI-7, No. 1, pp. 121–7.

Guari, E. and Wechsler, H. 1982 'On the difficulties involved in the segmentation of pictures', *IEEE Transactions on Pattern Analysis and Machine Intelligence*, Vol. PAMI-4, No. 3.

Haralick, R.M. 1984 'Digital step edges from zero-crossing of second directional derivatives', *IEEE Transactions on Pattern Analysis and Machine Intelligence*, Vol. PAMI-6, No. 1, pp. 58–68.

Hildreth, E.C. 1981 'Edge detection in man and machine', *Robotics Age*, Sept/Oct, pp. 8–14.

Hildreth, E.C. 1985 *Edge Detection*, AI Memo No. 858, MIT AI Lab.

Hueckel, M. 1971 'An operator which locates edges and digitises pictures', *JACM*, Vol. 18, No. 1, pp. 113–25.

Hueckel, M. 1973 'A local visual operator which recognises edges and lines', *JACM*, Vol. 20, No. 4, pp. 643–7.

Hueckel, M. 1973 'Erratum to "a local visual operator which recognizes edges and lines"', *JACM*, Vol. 21, No. 2, p. 350.

Huertas, A. and Medioni, G. 1986 'Detection of intensity changes with subpixel accuracy using Laplacian–Gaussian masks', *IEEE Transactions on Pattern Analysis and Machine Intelligence*, Vol. PAMI-8, No. 5, pp. 651–64.

Jacobus, C. and Chien, R. 1981 'Two new edge detectors', *IEEE Transactions on Pattern Analysis and Machine Intelligence*, Vol. PAMI-3, No. 5, pp. 581–92.

Juvin, D. and de Cosnac, B. 1984 'ANIMA 2: Un Systeme Generale de Vision Pour la Robotique', *Proceedings of the Premier Colloque Image*, CESTA, Biarritz, pp. 165–9.

Kasvand, T. 1975 'Iterative edge detection', *Computer Graphics and Image Processing*, Vol. 4, pp. 279–86.

Kelly, M.D. 1971 'Edge detection in pictures by computer using planning', *Machine Intelligence*, B. Meltzer and D. Michie (eds.), Vol. 6, pp. 397–409, Edinburgh, Edinburgh University Press.

Kirsch, R. 1971 'Computer determination of the constituent structure of biological images', *Computers and Biomedical Research*, Vol. 4, No. 3, pp. 315–28.

Lee, C.C. 1983 'Elimination of redundant operations for a fast Sobel operator', *IEEE Transactions on Systems, Man, and Cybernetics*, Vol. SMC-13, No. 3, pp. 242–5.

Lunscher, W.F. and Beddoes, M.P. 1986 'Optimal edge detector design I: Parameter selection and noise effects', *IEEE Transactions on Pattern Analysis and Machine Intelligence*, Vol. PAMI-8, No. 2, pp. 164–77.

Lunscher, W.F. and Beddoes, M.P. 1986 'Optimal edge detector design II: Coefficient quantisation', *IEEE Transactions on Pattern Analysis and Machine Intelligence*, Vol. PAMI-8, No. 2, pp. 178–87.

Marr, D. 1976 'Early processing of visual information', *Philosophical Transactions of the Royal Society of London*, **B275**, pp. 483–524.

Marr, D. and Hildreth, E. 1980 'Theory of edge detection', *Proceedings of the Royal Society of London*, **B207**, pp. 187–217.

Mero, L. and Vassy, Z. 1975 'A simplified and fast version of the Hueckel operator for finding optimal edges in pictures', *Proceedings of the International Joint Conference on Artificial Intelligence, Tbilisi, Georgia, USSR*, pp. 650–5.

Nalwa, V.S. and Binford, T.O. 1986 'On detecting edges', *IEEE Transactions on Pattern Analysis and Machine Intelligence*, Vol. PAMI-8, No. 6, pp. 699–714.

Nazif, A.M. and Levine M.D. 1984 'Low level segmentation: an expert system', *IEEE Transactions on Pattern Analysis and Machine Intelligence*, Vol. PAMI-6, No. 5, pp. 555–77.

Nevatia, R. 1977 'Note: Evaluation of a simplified Hueckel edge-line detector', *Journal of Computer Graphics and Image Processing*, pp. 582–8.

Nevatia, R. and Babu, K. 1980 'Linear feature extraction and description', *Computer Graphics and Image Processing*, Vol. 13, pp. 257–69.

Perkins, W.A. 1980 'Area segmentation of images using edge points', *IEEE Transactions on Pattern Analysis and Machine Intelligence*, Vol. PAMI-2, No. 1, pp. 8–15.

Prewitt, J.M.S. 1970 'Object enhancement and extraction' in *Picture Processing and Psychopictorics*, B. Lipkin and A. Rosenfeld (eds.), Academic Press, New York, pp. 75–149.

Roberts, L.G. 1965 'Machine perception of three-dimensional solids' in *Optical and Electro-Optical Information Processing*, J.T. Tippett *et al.* (eds.), MIT Press, Cambridge, Massachusetts, pp. 159–97.

Rosenfeld, A. and Thurston, M. 1971 'Edge and curve detection for visual scene analysis', *IEEE Transactions on Computers*, Vol. C-20, No. 5, pp. 562–9.

Sandini, G. and Torre, V. 1985 'Thresholding techniques for zero-crossings', *Proceedings of 'Winter '85 Topical Meeting on Machine Vision', Incline Village, Nevada*.

Torre, V. and Poggio, T.A. 1986 'On edge detection', *IEEE Transactions on Pattern Analysis and Machine Intelligence*, Vol. PAMI-8, No. 2, pp. 147–63.

Weszka, J.S. 1978 'A survey of threshold selection techniques', *Computer Graphics and Image Processing*, Vol. 7, pp. 259–65.

Weszka, J.S., Nagel, R.N. and Rosenfield, A. 1974 'A threshold selection technique', *IEEE Transactions on Computers*, Vol. C-23, No. 12, pp. 1322–7.

Wiejak, J.S. 1983 'Regions estimation and boundary estimation', *Image and Vision Computing*, Vol. 1, No. 2, May 1983, pp. 99–102.

Yakimovsky, Y. 1976 'Boundary and object detection in real world images', *JACM*, Vol. 23, No. 4, pp. 599–618.

6

Image analysis

6.1 Introduction: inspection, location, and identification

Image analysis is the term that is used to embody the idea of automatically extracting useful information from an image of a scene. The important point regarding image analysis is that this information is explicit and can be used in subsequent decision making processes. Techniques vary across a broad spectrum, depending on the complexity of the image and, indeed, on the complexity of the information to be extracted from it. The more commonly used image analysis techniques include template matching, statistical pattern recognition, and the Hough transform. Unfortunately, this classification is not particularly useful when one is trying to identify a technique for a potential application. However, we can also classify the types of analysis we wish to perform according to function. There are essentially three types of things we would wish to know about the scene in an image. First, we might wish to ascertain whether or not the visual appearance of objects is as it should be, i.e. we might wish to inspect the objects. The implicit assumption here is, of course, that we know what objects are in the image in the first place and approximately where they are. If we don't know where they are, we might wish to find out. This is the second function of image analysis: location. Note that the location of an object requires the specification of both position and orientation (in either two dimensions or three dimensions). Also, the coordinates might be specified in terms of the image frame of reference (where distance is specified in terms of pixels) or in the real world where distances correspond to millimetres, say. The latter obviously necessitates some form of calibration, since initial measurements will be made in the image frame of reference. Finally, if we do not know what the objects in the image are, we might have to perform a third type of analysis: identification.

Generally speaking, inspection applications utilize the template matching paradigm, location problems utilize the template matching paradigm and the

Hough transform, while the problem of identification can be addressed using all three techniques, depending on the complexity of the image and the objects. From time to time, all of them make use of some of the more advanced techniques to be described in later chapters. For example, if we are interested in the local shape or three-dimensional structure, we might exploit the structured-light techniques described in Chapter 8.

6.2 *Template matching*

Many of the applications of computer vision simply need to know whether an image contains some previously defined object or, in particular, whether a pre-defined sub-image is contained within a test image. The sub-image is called a *template* and should be an ideal representation of the pattern or object which is being sought in the image. The template matching technique involves the translation of the template to every possible position in the image and the evaluation of a measure of the match between the template and the image at that position. If the similarity measure is large enough then the object can be assumed to be present. If the template does represent the complete object for which you wish to check the image, then the technique is sometimes referred to as 'global template matching', since the template is in effect a global representation of the object. On the other hand, local template matching utilizes several templates of local features of the object, e.g. corners in the boundary or characteristic marks, to represent the object.

6.2.1 *Measures of similarity*

Apart from this distinction between global and local template matching, the only other aspect which requires detailed consideration is the measure of similarity between template and image. Several similarity measures are possible, some based on the summation of differences between the image and template, others based on cross-correlation techniques. Since similarity measures are widely used, not just in this image template matching situation, but also for evaluation of the similarity between any two signatures (i.e. characteristic signals), such as when comparing shape descriptors, it is worth discussing these similarity measures in more detail. We will look at measures based on Euclidean distance and cross-correlation.

A common measure employed when comparing the similarity of two images (e.g. the template $t(i, j)$ and the test image $g(i, j)$) is the metric based on the standard Euclidean distance between two sectors, defined by:

$$E(m, n) = \sqrt{\left\{ \sum_i \sum_j \left[g(i, j) - t(i - m, j - n) \right]^2 \right\}}$$

The summation is evaluated for all i, such that $(i - m)$ is a valid coordinate of the template sub-image. This definition amounts to translating the template $t(i, j)$ to a position (m, n) along the test image and evaluating the similarity measure at that point. Thus, when searching for a template shape, the template is effectively moved along the test image and the above template match is evaluated at each position. The position (m, n) at which the smallest value of $E(m, n)$ is obtained corresponds to the best match for the template.

The similarity measure based on the Euclidean distance is quite an appealing method, from an intuitive point of view. To see why, consider a complete one-dimensional entity, e.g. size (represented by, say, length). To compare the difference in size of two objects, we just subtract the values, square the difference and take the square root of the result, leaving us with the absolute difference in size:

$$d = \sqrt{[(s_1 - s_2)^2]}$$

Extending this to the two-dimensional case, we might wish to see how far apart two objects are on a table, i.e. to compute the distance between them. The difference in position is simply:

$$d = \sqrt{[(x_1 - x_2)^2 + (y_1 - y_2)^2]}$$

Similarly, in three dimensions

$$d = \sqrt{[(x_1 - x_2)^2 + (y_1 - y_2)^2 + (z_1 - z_2)^2]}$$

We can easily extend this to n dimensions (although we lose the intuitive concept of 'distance') by just making each coordinate an independent variable which characterizes the entities we are comparing. For example, a 10×10 image template comprises 100 independent pixels, each of which specifies the template sub-image. Thus, we are now dealing with a $10 \times 10 = 100$-dimensional comparison and the difference between the two sub-images is:

$$d = \sqrt{\{ [\text{image}(1,1) - \text{template}(1,1)]^2 + \cdots + [\text{image}(10,10) - \text{template}(10,10)]^2 \}}$$

which is identical to our definition of the Euclidean metric.

A frequently used and simpler template matching metric is based on the absolute difference of $g(i, j)$ and $t(i - m, j - n)$ rather than the square of the difference. It is defined by:

$$S(m, n) = \sum_i \sum_j | g(i, j) - t(i - m, j - n) |$$

Alternatively, the square root in the Euclidean definition can be removed by squaring both sides of the equation and letting the similarity measure be $E^2(m, n)$. Hence:

$$E^2(m, n) = \sum_i \sum_j [g(i, j)^2 - 2g(i, j) \, t(i - m, j - n) + t(i - m, j - n)^2]$$

As before, the summation is evaluated for all i and j, such that $(i - m, j - n)$ is a valid coordinate of the template sub-image. Note that the summation of the last term is constant since it is a function of the template only and is evaluated over the complete domain of the template. If it is assumed that the first term is also constant, or that the variation is small enough to be ignored, then $E^2(m, n)$ is small when the summation of the middle term is large. Thus, a new similarity measure might be $R(m, n)$, given by:

$$R(m, n) = \sum_i \sum_j g(i, j) \, t(i - m, j - n)$$

again summing over the usual range of i and j; $R(m, n)$ is the familiar cross-correlation function. The template $t(i - m, j - n)$ and the section of $g(i, j)$ in the vicinity of (m, n) are similar when the cross-correlation is large.

If the assumption that the summation of $g(i, j)$ is independent of m and n is not valid, an alternative to computing R is to compute the normalized cross-correlation $N(m, n)$ given by:

$$N(m, n) = R(m, n) \Big/ \sqrt{\left[\sum_i \sum_j g(i, j)^2 \right]}$$

summing over the usual range of i and j. Note that, by the Cauchy–Schwarz inequality:

$$N(m, n) \leqslant \sqrt{\left[\sum_i \sum_j t(i - m, j - n)^2 \right]}$$

Hence, the normalized cross-correlation may be scaled so that it lies in the range 0 to 1 by dividing it by the above expression. Thus, the normalized cross-correlation may be redefined:

$$N(m, n) = R(m, n) \Big/ \left\{ \sqrt{\left[\sum_i \sum_j g(i, j)^2 \right]} \sqrt{\left[\sum_i \sum_j t(i - m, j - n)^2 \right]} \right\}$$

Figure 6.1 illustrates the use of cross-correlation in which a template of a human eye was recorded and subsequently located in a series of images. The cross-hair denotes the position at which the maximum cross-correlation between template and image occurred.

6.2.2 *Local template matching*

One of the problems of template matching is that each template represents the object or part of it as we expect to find it in the image. No cognizance is taken of variations in scale or in orientation. If the expected orientation can vary, then we will require a separate template for each orientation and each one must be matched with the image. Thus template matching can become computationally expensive, especially if the templates are large. One popular way of alleviating this computational overhead is to use much smaller local templates to detect salient features in the image which characterize the object we are looking for. The spatial relationships between occurrences of these features are then analysed. We can infer the presence of the object if valid distances between these features occur.

In summary, template matching techniques are useful in applications that can

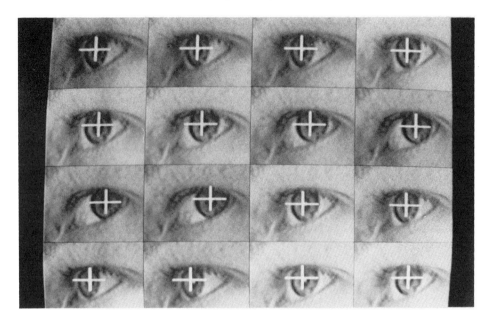

Figure 6.1 Eye-tracking using normalized cross-correlation.

be severely restricted and where the number of objects, and the variability of these objects, is small; it is not an approach that is applicable in general situations.

6.3   Decision-theoretic approaches

If the objective of the image analysis is to find objects within the image and identify, or classify, those objects then an approach based on statistical decision theory may be the most appropriate route to take. The central assumption in this approach is that the image depicts one or more objects and that each object belongs to one of several distinct and exclusive pre-determined classes, i.e. we know what objects exist and an object can only have one particular type or label.

6.3.1 Components of a statistical pattern recognition process

There are effectively three components of this type of pattern recognition process: an object isolation module, a feature extraction module, and a classification module. Each of these modules is invoked in turn and in the order given, the output of one module forming the input of the next. Thus, the object isolation module operates on a digital image and produces a representation of the object. The feature extraction module then abstracts one or more characteristic features and produces a (so-called) feature vector. This feature vector is then used by the classification module to identify and label each object.

Since we will be covering some of these topics again in more detail later on, e.g. methods for object isolation and description, we will just give a brief overview of the representative techniques at this stage.

Object isolation, often referred to as 'segmentation', is in effect the grouping process which we discussed in the preceding chapter. The similarity measure upon which the grouping process is based in this instance is the grey-level of the region.

Once we have segmented the image, we have essentially identified the objects which we wish to classify or identify. The next phase of the recognition scheme is the extraction of features which are characteristic of the object and which will be used in the classification module. The selection of the features to be used is an extremely important task, since all subsequent decisions will be based on them, and frequently it is intuition and experience which guides the selection process. Normally, we will identify a number of reasonable feasible potential features, test these to check their performance, and then select the final set of features to be used in the actual application. When selecting features, you should bear in mind the desirability of each feature being *independent* (a change in one feature should not change the value of another feature significantly), *discriminatory* (each feature should have a significantly different value for each different object), *reliable* (features should have the same value for all objects in the same class/group). Finally, it is worth noting that the computational complexity of the pattern recognition exercise increases very rapidly as the number of features increases and hence it is desirable to use the fewest number of features possible, while ensuring a minimal number of errors.

6.3.2 Simple feature extraction

Before proceeding to discuss the mechanism by which we can classify the objects, let us first take a look at some representative features that we might use to describe that object.

Most features are either based on the size of the object or on its shape. The most obvious feature which is based on size is the area of the object: this is simply the number of pixels comprising the object multiplied by the area of a single pixel (frequently assumed to be a single unit). If we are dealing with grey-scale images, then the integrated optical density (IOD) is sometimes used: it is equivalent to the area multiplied by the average grey-level of the object and essentially provides a measure of the 'weight' of the object, where the pixel grey-level encodes the weight per unit area.

The length and the width of an object also describe its size. However, since we will not know its orientation in general, we may have to first compute its orientation before evaluating the minimum and maximum extent of its boundary, providing us with a measure of its length and width. Thus, these measures should always be made with respect to some rotation-invariant datum line in the object, e.g. its major or minor axis. The *minimum bounding rectangle* is a feature which is related to this idea of length and width. This is the smallest rectangle which can completely enclose the object. The main axis of this rectangle is in fact the principal axis of the object itself and, hence, the dimensions of the minimum bounding rectangle correspond to the features of length and width.

Quite often, the distance around the perimeter of the object can be useful for discriminating between two objects (quite apart from the fact that one can compute the area of the object from the perimeter shape). Depending on how the object is represented, and this in turn depends on the type of segmentation used, it can be quite trivial to compute the length of the perimeter and this makes it an attractive feature for industrial vision applications.

Features which encode the shape of an object are usually very useful for the purposes of classification and because of this, Chapter 7 has been entirely given over to them. For the present, we will content ourselves by mentioning two very simple shape measures: rectangularity and circularity. There are two popular measures of rectangularity, both of which are easy to compute. The first is the ratio of the area of the object to the area of the minimum bounding rectangle:

$$R = \frac{A_{\text{object}}}{A_{\text{min. bound. rectangle}}}$$

This feature takes on a maximum value of 1 for a perfect rectangular shape and tends toward zero for thin curvy objects.

The second measure is the aspect ratio and is simply the ratio of the width of the minimum bounding rectangle to its length:

$$Aspect\ ratio = \frac{W_{\text{min. bound. rectangle}}}{L_{\text{min. bound. rectangle}}}$$

The most commonly used circularity measure is the ratio of the square of the perimeter length to the area:

$$C = \frac{A_{\text{object}}}{P_{\text{object}}^2}$$

This assumes a maximum value for discs and tends towards zero for irregular shapes with ragged boundaries.

6.3.3 Classification

The final stage of the statistical pattern recognition exercise is the classification of the objects on the basis of the set of features we have just computed, i.e. on the basis of the feature vector. If one views the feature values as 'coordinates' of a point in n-dimensional space (one feature value implies a one-dimensional space, two features imply a two-dimensional space, and so on), then one may view the object of classification as being the determination of the sub-space of the feature space to which the feature vector belongs. Since each sub-space corresponds to a distinct object, the classification essentially accomplishes the object identification.

For example, consider a pattern recognition application which requires us to discriminate between nuts, bolts, and washers on a conveyor belt. Assuming that we can segment these objects adequately, we might choose to use two features on which to base the classification: washers and nuts are almost circular in shape, while bolts are quite long in comparison, so we decide to use a circularity measure as one feature. Furthermore, washers have a larger diameter than nuts, and bolts have an even larger maximum dimension. Thus, we decide to use the maximum length of the object (its diameter in the case of the nuts and washers) as the second feature. If we then proceed to measure these feature values for a fairly large set of these objects, called the training set, and plot the results on a piece of graph paper (representing the two-dimensional feature space, since there are two features) we will probably observe the clustering pattern shown in Figure 6.2 where nuts, bolts, and washers are all grouped in distinct sub-spaces.

At this stage, we are now ready to classify an unknown object (assuming, as always, that it is either a nut, a bolt or a washer). We generate the feature vector for this unknown object (i.e. compute the maximum dimension and its circularity measure A/P^2) and see where this takes us in the feature space (see Figure 6.3). The question is now: to which sub-space does the vector belong, i.e. to which class does the object belong? One of the most popular and simple techniques, the nearest-neighbour classification technique, classifies the object on the basis of the distance of the unknown object vector position from the centre of the three clusters, choosing the closest cluster as the one to which it belongs. In this instance, the

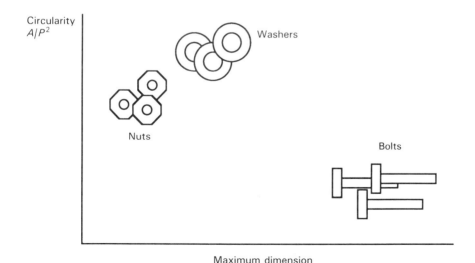

Figure 6.2 Feature space.

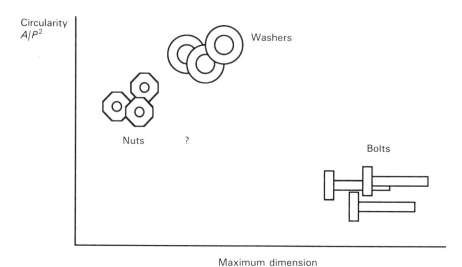

Figure 6.3 Coordinates of an unknown object in the feature space.

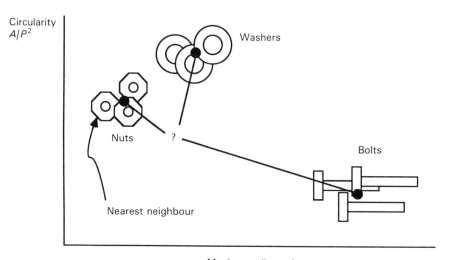

Figure 6.4 Nearest neighbour classification.

object is a nut (see Figure 6.4). This technique is called, not surprisingly, the nearest-neighbour classifier. Incidentally, the position of the centre of each cluster is simply the average of each of the individual training vector positions.

6.3.3.1 A synopsis of classification using Bayes' rule

There are, however, more sophisticated approaches to classification. The one which we are going to describe here utilizes Bayes' theorem from statistical decision theory and is called the *maximum-likelihood classifier*. We will develop the discussion using an example which requires only one feature to discriminate between two objects; we do this because it is easier to visualize (and draw!) the concepts being discussed.

Suppose that in a situation similar to that described in the preceding example, we wish to distinguish between nuts and bolts (no washers this time). In this instance, the circularity measure will suffice and we now have just one feature and one-dimensional feature space with two classes of object: nuts and bolts. Let us refer to these classes as C_n and C_b. Let us also refer, for brevity, to the circularity feature value as x. The first thing that is required is the probability density functions (PDFs) for each of these two classes, i.e. a measure of the probabilities that an object from a particular class will have a given feature value. Since it is not likely that we will know these *a priori*, we will probably have to estimate them. The PDF for nuts can be estimated in a relatively simple manner by measuring the value of x for a large number of nuts, plotting the histogram of these values, smoothing the histogram, and normalizing the values so that the total area under the histogram equals one. The normalization step is necessary since probability values have values between zero and one and the sum of all the probabilities (for all the possible circularity measures) must necessarily be equal to a certainty of encountering that object, i.e. a probability value of one. The PDF for the bolts can be estimated in a similar manner.

Let us now continue to discuss in a little more detail the probability of each class occurring and the probability of objects in each class having a particular value of x. We may know, for instance, that the class of nuts is, in general, likely to occur twice as often as the class of bolts. In this case we say that the *a priori* probabilities of the two classes are:

$$P(C_n) = 0.666 \text{ and } P(C_b) = 0.333$$

In fact, in this case it is more likely that they will have the same *a priori* probabilities (0.5) since we usually have a nut for each bolt.

The PDFs tell us the probability that the circularity x will occur, given that the object belongs to the class of nuts C_n in the first instance and to the class of bolts C_b in the second instance. This is termed the 'conditional probability' of an object having a certain feature value, given that we know that it belongs to a particular class. Thus, the conditional probability:

$$P(x \mid C_b)$$

enumerates the probability that a circularity x will occur, given that the object is a bolt. The two conditional probabilities $P(x \mid C_b)$ and $P(x \mid C_n)$ are shown in Figure 6.5. Of course, this is not what we are interested in at all. We want to determine the probability that an object belongs to a particular class, given that a particular value of x has occurred (i.e. been measured), allowing us to establish its identity. This is called the *a posteriori* probability $P(C_i \mid x)$ that the object belongs to a

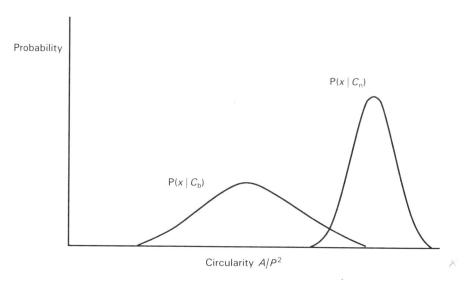

Figure 6.5 Conditional probabilities.

particular class i and is given by Bayes' theorem:

$$P(C_i \mid x) = \frac{P(x \mid C_i)\ P(C_i)}{P(x)}$$

where:

$$P(x) = \sum_{i=1}^{2} P(x \mid C_i)\ P(C_i)$$

$P(x)$ is a normalization factor which is used to ensure that the sum of the *a posteriori* probabilities sums to one, for the same reasons as mentioned above.

In effect, this Bayes' theorem allows us to use the *a priori* probability of objects occurring in the first place, the conditional probability of an object having a particular feature value given that it belongs to a particular class, and actual measurement of a feature value (to be used as the parameter in the conditional probability) to estimate the probability that the measured object belongs to a given class.

Once we can estimate the probability that, for a given measurement, the object is a nut and the probability that it is a bolt, we can make a decision as to its identity, choosing the class with the higher probability. This is why it is called the maximum likelihood classifier. Thus, we classify the object as a bolt if:

$$P(C_b \mid x) > P(C_n \mid x)$$

Using Bayes' theorem again, and noting that the normalizing factor $P(x)$ is the same for both expressions, we can rewrite this test as:

$$P(x \mid C_b)P(C_b) > P(x \mid C_n)\ P(C_n)$$

Figure 6.6 illustrates the advantage of the maximum-likelihood classifier over the nearest-neighbour classifier: if we assume that the chances of an unknown object being either a nut or a bolt are equally likely (i.e. $P(C_b) = P(C_n)$), then we classify the unknown object as a bolt if:

$$P(x \mid C_b) > P(x \mid C_n)$$

For the example shown in Figure 6.6, $P(x \mid C_b)$ is indeed greater than $P(x \mid C_n)$ for the measured value of circularity and we classify the object as a bolt. If, on the other hand, we were to use the nearest-neighbour classification technique, we would choose the class whose mean value 'is closer to' the measured value. In this case,

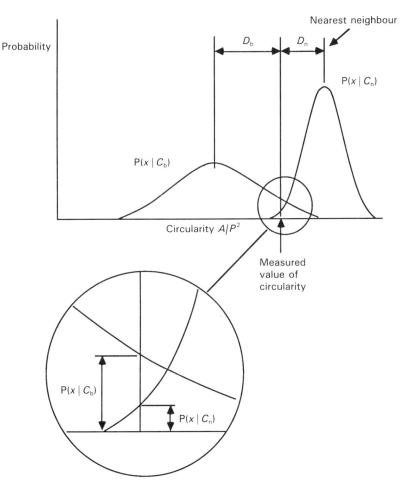

Figure 6.6 Advantage of using maximum likelihood classifier over nearest neighbour classifier.

the distance D_n from the measured value to the mean of the PDF for nuts is less than D_b, the distance from the measured value to the mean of the PDF for bolts; we would erroneously classify the object as a nut.

We have restricted ourselves to a simple example with just one feature and a one-dimensional feature space. However, the argument generalizes directly to an n-dimensional case, where we have n features, in which case the conditional probability density functions are also n-dimensional. In the two-dimensional case, the PDFs can be represented by grey-scale images: the grey-level encoding the probability.

6.4 The Hough transform

The Hough transform is a technique which is used to isolate curves of a given shape in an image. The classical Hough transform requires that the curve be specified in some parametric form and, hence, is most commonly used in the detection of regular curves such as lines, circles, and ellipses. Fortunately, this is not as restrictive as it might first seem since most manufactured parts do, in fact, have boundaries which are defined by such curves. However, the Hough transform has been generalized so that it is capable of detecting arbitrary curved shapes. The main advantage of this transform technique is that it is very tolerant of gaps in the actual object boundaries or curves and it is relatively unaffected by noise. We will begin by describing the classical Hough transform for the detection of lines; we will indicate how it can be applied to the detection of circles; and then we will discuss the generalized Hough transform and the detection of arbitrary shapes.

6.4.1 Hough transform for line detection and circle detection

We wish to detect a set of points lying on a straight line. The equation of a straight line is given in parametric form by the equation:

$$x \cos \phi + y \sin \phi = r$$

where r is the length of a normal to the line from the origin and ϕ is the angle this normal makes with the X-axis (refer to Figure 6.7).

If we have a point (x_i, y_i) on this line, then:

$$x_i \cos \phi + y_i \sin \phi = r$$

For a given line, r and ϕ are constant. Suppose, however, that we do not know which line we require (i.e. r and ϕ are unknown) but we do know the coordinates of the point(s) on the line. Now we can consider r and ϕ to be variable and x_i and y_i to be constants. In this case, the equation:

$$x_i \cos \phi + y_i \sin \phi = r$$

defines the values of r and ϕ such that the line passes through the point (x_i, y_i). If

130

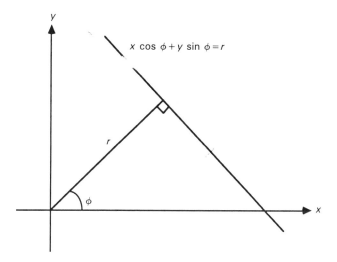

Figure 6.7 Parametric representation of a straight line.

we plot these values of r and ϕ, for a given point (x_i, y_i), on a graph (see Figure 6.8) we see that we get a sinusoidal curve in the $(r - \phi)$ space, i.e. in a space where r and ϕ are the variables. The transformation between the image plane (x- and y-coordinates) and the parameter space (r- and ϕ-coordinates) is known as the Hough transform. Thus, the Hough transform of a point in the image plane is a sinusoidal curve in the Hough ($r - \phi$) space. However, collinear points in the image plane will give rise to transform curves which all intersect in one point since they share common r_i and ϕ_i and they all belong to the line given by:

$$x \cos \phi_i + y \sin \phi_i = r_i$$

This, then, provides us with the means to detect collinear points, i.e. lines. First of all we must sample the Hough transform space, i.e. we require a discrete representation of $(r - \phi)$ space. Since ϕ varies between 0 and 2π radians, we need only decide on the required angular resolution to define the sampling. For example, a $6°$ resolution on the angle of the line might suffice, in which case we will have $360°/6° = 60$ discrete values of ϕ. Similarly, we can limit r by deciding on the maximum distance from the origin (which is effectively going to be the maximum size of the image, 256 pixels in length, say). Our representation of $(r - \phi)$ space is now simply a two-dimensional array of size 256×60, each element corresponding to a particular value of r and ϕ: see Figure 6.9. This is called an accumulator since we are going to use it to collect or accumulate evidence of curves given by particular boundary points (x, y) in the image plane. For each boundary point (x_i, y_i) in the image we increment all accumulator cells such that the cell coordinates (r, ϕ) satisfy the equation:

$$x_i \cos \phi + y \sin \phi = r$$

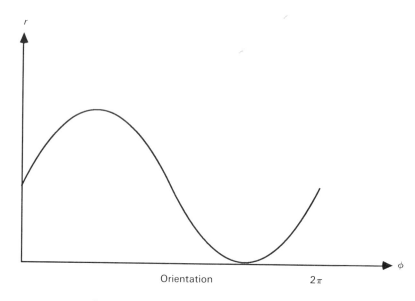

Figure 6.8 Hough transform of a point (x_i, y_i).

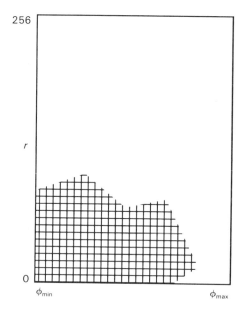

Figure 6.9 Hough transform accumulator array.

When we have done this for all available (x_i, y_i) points we can scan the accumulator searching for cells which have a high count since these will correspond to lines for which there are main points in the image plane. In fact, because there are likely to be some errors in the actual position of the x- and y-coordinates, giving rise to errors in r and ϕ, we search for clusters of points in the accumulator having high counts, rather than searching for isolated points.

Since edge detection processes are often employed in generating the candidate boundary points in the image and, in general, these yield not only the position of the edge (x_i, y_i) but also its orientation θ, where $\theta = \phi + 90°$.* We can use this information to simplify the Hough transform and, knowing x_i, y_i, and ϕ, use:

$$x_i \cos \phi + y_i \sin \phi = r$$

to compute r giving the coordinates of the appropriate accumulator cell to be incremented. The following pseudo-code summarizes this procedure:

```
/* Pseudo-code for Hough Transform: Line Detection */

● Quantize the Hough transform space: identify maximum
  and minimum values of r and φ and the total number of
  r and φ values.

● Generate an accumulator array A(r,φ); set all values
  to 0.

● For all edge points (xi, yi) in the image
  Do
    compute the normal direction φ (gradient direction
    or orientation -90°)†
    compute r from xi cos φ+yi sin φ=r
    increment A(r,φ)

● For all cells in the accumulator array
  Do
    search for maximum values
    the coordinates r and φ give the equation of the
      corresponding line in the image.
```

Just as a straight line can be defined parametrically, so can a circle. The equation of a circle is given by:

$$(x - a)^2 + (y - b)^2 = r^2$$

---

* Some edge detectors, e.g. the Sobel operator, are usually formulated such that they directly yield the gradient direction which is equivalent to ϕ.

† Remember to normalize the result so that it lies in the interval $0-2\pi$.

where (a, b) are the coordinates of the centre of the circle and r is its radius. In this case, we have three coordinates in the parameter space: a, b, and r. Hence, we require a three-dimensional accumulator with an attendant increase in the computational complexity of the algorithm. Figure 6.10 illustrates the use of the Hough transform to detect the boundary between the cornea and iris of a human eye.

One further point is worth noting: the Hough transform identifies the parameter of the curve (or line) which best fits the data (the set of edge points). However, the circles that are generated are complete circles and the lines are infinite. If one wishes to identify the actual *line segments* or *curve segments* which generated these transform parameters, further image analysis will be required.

6.4.2 The generalized Hough transform

In the preceding formulation of the classical Hough transform, we used the parametric equation of the shape to effect the transform from image space to transform space. In the case where the shape we wish to isolate does not have a simple analytic equation describing its boundary, we can still use a generalized form of the Hough transform. The essential idea is that, instead of using the parametric equation of the curve, we use a look-up table to define the relationship between the boundary coordinates and orientation, and the Hough parameters. Obviously, the look-up table values must be computed during a training phase using a prototype shape.

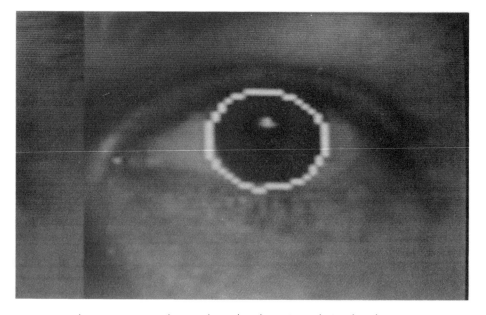

Figure 6.10 Hough transform for detection of circular shapes.

Suppose we know the shape and orientation of the required object, e.g. see Figure 6.11, the first step is to select an arbitrary reference point (x_{ref}, y_{ref}) in the object; we now define the shape in terms of the distance and angle of lines from the boundary to this reference point. For all points of the boundary, we draw a line to the reference point. We then compute the orientation of the boundary, Ω_i say, and make a note in the look-up table of the distance and direction from the boundary point to the reference point at a location in the look-up table indexed by the boundary orientation Ω_i. Since it is probable that there will be more than one occurrence of a particular orientation as we travel around the boundary, we have to make provision for more than one pair of distance and angle values. This look-up table is called an *R*-table.

The Hough transform space is now defined in terms of the possible positions of the shape in the image, i.e. the possible ranges of x_{ref} and y_{ref} (instead of r and ϕ in the case of the Hough transform for line detection). To perform the transform on an image we compute the point (x_{ref}, y_{ref}) from the coordinates of the boundary point, the distance r and the angle β:

$$x_{ref} = x + r \cos \beta$$
$$y_{ref} = y + r \sin \beta$$

The question is: what values of r and β do we use? These are derived from the *R*-table by computing the boundary orientation Ω at that point and using it as an index to the *R*-table, reading off all the (r, β) pairs. The accumulator array cell (x_{ref}, y_{ref}) is then incremented. We reiterate this process for all edge points in the image. As before, we infer the presence of the shape by identifying local maxima in the accumulator array.

There is just one problem: we have assumed that we know the orientation of the shape. If this is not the case, we have to extend the accumulator by incorporating an extra parameter ϕ to take changes in orientation into consideration. Thus, we now have a three-dimensional accumulator indexed by

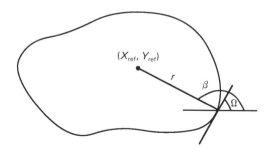

Figure 6.11 Generalized Hough transform – definition of *R*-table components.

(x_{ref}, y_{ref}, ϕ) and we compute:

$$x_{ref} = x + r \cos (\beta + \phi)$$
$$y_{ref} = y + r \sin (\beta + \phi)$$

for all values of ϕ and update each accumulator cell for each value of ϕ. The following pseudo-code again summarizes this procedure:

```
/* Pseudo-code for Generalized Hough Transform

• Train the shape by building the R-table:
    For all points on the boundary
       compute orientation Ω (gradient direction +90°)
       compute r and β
       add an (r,β) entry into the R-table
       at a location indexed by Ω

• Quantize the Hough transform space: identify maximum
  and minimum values of xref, yref, and φ and identify
  the total number of xref, yref, and φ values.

• Generate an accumulator array A(xref, yref, φ);
  set all values to 0.

• For all edge points (xi, yi) in the image
  Do
     compute the orientation Ω (gradient direction
  +90°)
     compute possible reference points Xref, yref
     For each table entry, indexed by Ω
        For each possible shape orientation φ
           compute xref=xi+r cos (β+φ)
                   yref=yi+r sin (β+φ)
           increment A(xref, yref, φ)

• For all cells in the accumulator array
  Do
     search for maximum values
  the coordinates xref, yref, and φ give the position and
  orientation of the shape in the image.
```

6.5 *Histogram analysis*

We began this chapter with a function classification of image analysis, noting that there are essentially three common objectives: inspection, location, and identification. As we have seen, each of these can be tackled using various combinations of the techniques which have been discussed in Sections 6.2–6.4. It would be wrong, however, if the impression was given that this is all there is to image analysis. Indeed, in the introduction we did note that some of the more advanced techniques to be dealt with in the remaining chapters are often brought to bear. In certain circumstances, however, there are other simpler approaches which can be taken and often it is the very simplicity which makes them attractive. Such analysis techniques are often heuristic in nature, but no less useful for that. The following material on histogram analysis is intended to give a feel for this type of simple and practical approach.

The grey-level histogram of an image often contains sufficient information to allow analysis of the image content and, in particular, to discriminate between objects and to distinguish objects with defects. It has the distinct advantage that it is not necessary to segment the image first and it is not dependent on the location of the object in the image. The analysis is based exclusively on the visual appearance of the scene or image as a whole. As a simple example, consider the case where one is inspecting a bright shiny object, i.e. one which exhibits specular reflectivity. In bright field illumination, where the camera and the light source are approximately aligned, a great deal of light will be reflected and the histogram of the imaged object will be biased towards the bright end of the scale. Blemishes, or unwanted surface distortions, will tend to diffuse the light and less bright specular reflections will be imaged. In this case, the histogram will be biased more towards the dark end of the spectrum. In effect, the two cases can be distinguished by considering the distribution of grey-levels in the image, i.e. by analysis of the histogram.

There are two ways to consider histogram analysis:

(a) by extracting features which are descriptive of the shape of the histogram;
(b) by matching two histogram signatures.

In the former case, discrimination can be achieved using the classification techniques we discussed in Section 6.3, whereas in the latter case, the template matching paradigm of Section 6.2 is more appropriate.

The following (statistical) features are frequently used as a means of describing the shape of histograms:

Mean: $$\bar{b} = \sum_{b=0}^{L-1} bP(b)$$

Variance: $$\sigma_b{}^2 = \sum_{b=0}^{L-1} (b - \bar{b})^2 P(b)$$

Skewness: $$b_S = \frac{1}{\sigma_b{}^3} \sum_{b=0}^{L-1} (b - \bar{b})^3 P(b)$$

Kurtosis: $b_K = \dfrac{1}{\sigma_b^4} \displaystyle\sum_{b=0}^{L-1} (b - \bar{b})^4 P(b) - 3$

Energy: $b_N = \displaystyle\sum_{b=0}^{L-1} [P(b)]^2$

These features are based on 'normalized' histograms, $P(b)$, defined as:

$$P(b) = \frac{N(b)}{M}$$

where M represents the total number of pixels in the image, $N(b)$ is the conventional histogram (i.e. a function which represents the number of pixels of a given grey-level b). Note that L is the number of grey-levels in the grey-scale.

Exercises

1. Statistical pattern recognition is sometimes used in industrial vision systems, but it is not always an appropriate technique. Identify the characteristics of an application for which the approach would be suitable. Detail the component processes of the statistical pattern recognition procedure. Given that one wishes to distinguish between integrated circuit chips and other discrete components on a printed circuit board during an inspection phase of an integrated FMS (Flexible Manufacturing System), identify an appropriate feature space and describe, in detail, how the classification might be effected.
2. Two types of defects commonly occur during the manufacture of 6 cm wide strips of metal foil. They are circular (or near circular) pin-holes of various sizes and longitudinal hairline cracks. Describe how an automated visual inspection system would distinguish between these flaws, given that the metal foil is bright silver in colour.
3. Explain with the use of diagrams, how the use of Bayes' rule facilitates improved classification *vis-à-vis* the nearest-neighbour classification scheme.
4. Show how the Hough transform can be generalized to cater for arbitrary two-dimensional shapes. What are the limitations of such a generalization?

References and further reading

Dessimoz, J-D., Birk, J.R., Kelley, R.B., Martins, A.S. and Chi Lin, I. 1984 'Matched filters for bin-picking', *IEEE Transactions on Pattern Analysis and Machine Intelligence*, Vol. PAMI-6, No. 6, pp. 686–97.

References and further reading

Duda, R.O. and Hart, P.E. 1973 *Pattern Classification and Scene Analysis*, New York, Wiley.

Fu, K. 1982 'Pattern recognition for automatic visual inspection', *Computer*, Vol. 15, No. 12, pp. 34–40.

Hough, P.V.C. 1962 *Methods and Measures for Recognising Complex Patterns*, US Patent 3069654, 18 December.

Illingworth, J. and Kittler, J. 1987 'The adaptive Hough transform', *IEEE Transactions on Pattern Analysis and Machine Intelligence*, Vol. PAMI-9, No. 5, pp. 690–8.

Sklansky, J. 1978 'On the Hough technique for curve detection', Vol. C-27, No. 10, pp. 923–6.

Turney, J.L., Mudge, T.N. and Volz, R.A. 1985 'Recognizing partially occluded parts', *IEEE Transactions on Pattern Analysis and Machine Intelligence*, Vol. PAMI-7, No. 4, pp. 410–21.

7

An overview of techniques for shape description

Many machine vision applications, and robot vision applications in particular, require the analysis and identification of relatively simple objects which may have to be manipulated. While it is very desirable that a vision system should be able to deal with random three-dimensional presentation of objects, it is also, in general, beyond the current capabilities of most commercial systems. If, however, the objects are (to an approximation) two-dimensional, the problem is more tractable, requiring the description and classification of planar shapes which may, or may not, be partially occluded. In Chapter 9, we will return to the more complex issues of three-dimensional object description and representation when we discuss image understanding. For the present, however, we will stay with the simpler two-dimensional approaches and this chapter introduces some of the more common techniques in shape description. Note well, though, that this chapter is *not* intended to be a complete and rigorous survey of the area of shape description. It is, rather, intended to provide a useful overview of some popular techniques and to identify a taxonomy, or classification, to facilitate the discussion of shape descriptors.

Before proceeding, a brief digression is in order. As we saw in the section on edge detection, topics of fundamental importance in computer vision typically give rise to a very large number of widely differing techniques. Unlike edge detection, however, the issue of shape description and representation is very far from being resolved; although edge detection is not a closed subject by any means, it is a much more mature topic than that of shape. The difficulty with shape is that it is not clear exactly what we are trying to abstract or represent: it seems to depend strongly on the use to which we intend putting the resulting representation (see, for example, Brady, 1983). Practitioners in some areas (e.g. mathematical morphology) go a little further and put forward the idea that shape is not an objective entity, in the sense of having an independent existence, and depends both on the observed and observer. Although these issues are important, it would not be wise to get locked into a deep discussion of them in a book such as this. It is sufficient to note here that *shape* as an issue in computer vision is both ubiquitous and ill-defined; the solution to the riddle of a general understanding of shape will probably shed light on many other areas in advanced computer vision, if only because it epitomizes the stone wall with which we are currently presented when we wish to develop truly adaptive robust visual systems.

7.1 A taxonomy of shape descriptors

Perhaps the most useful and general taxonomy of shape description is that introduced by Pavlidis in 1978 in which he classifies shape descriptors according to whether they are based on external or internal properties of the shape and according to whether they are based on scalar transform techniques or on space domain techniques. External descriptors are typically concerned with properties based on the boundary of the shape, while internal descriptors, as you would expect, take cognizance of the complete region comprising the shape. Scalar transform techniques generate vectors of scalar features while space domain techniques generate spatial or relational descriptions of certain characteristics of features of the shape. Thus, Pavlidis identifies the following four distinct types of shape descriptor:

(a) external scalar transform techniques utilizing features of the shape boundary;
(b) internal scalar transform techniques utilizing features of the shape region;
(c) external space domain techniques utilizing the spatial organization of the shape boundary;
(d) internal space domain techniques utilizing the spatial organization of the shape region.

7.2 External scalar transform descriptors: features of the boundary

External scalar transform descriptors are based on scalar features derived from the boundary of an object. Simple examples of such features include the following:

- the perimeter length;
- the ratio of the major to minor axis of the minimal bounding rectangle of the shape (see Figure 7.1);
- the number and size of residual concavities lying within the bounds of the shape's convex hull (see Figure 7.2);
- the ratio of the area of a shape to the square of the length of its perimeter (A/P^2): this is a measure of circularity which is maximized by circular shapes;
- the ratio of the area of a shape to the area of the minimal bounding rectangle: this is a measure of rectangularity and is maximized for perfectly rectangular shapes.

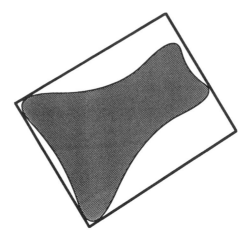

Figure 7.1 Bounding rectangle of a simple two-dimensional shape.

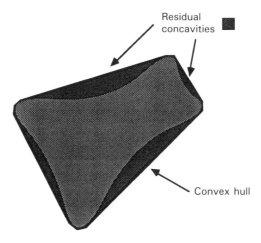

Figure 7.2 Residual concavities within the convex hull of a simple two-dimensional shape.

More sophisticated scalar transform techniques are often based on the Fourier series expansion of a periodic function derived from the boundary. For example, consider the shape depicted in Figure 7.3. The rotation θ of the tangent at the boundary of the object will vary between 0 and 2π radians as the boundary is traversed. In particular, θ will vary with the distance, s, around the perimeter and can be expressed as a function $\theta(s)$. If L is the length of the boundary of the shape, $\theta(0) = 0$ and $\theta(L) = -2\pi$. Unfortunately, this is obviously not a periodic function and so we cannot express it in terms of a Fourier series expansion. However, an

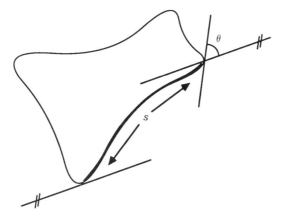

Figure 7.3 Rotation of tangent to a boundary of a shape.

alternative formulation, suggested by Zahn and Roskies, can be. Let $t = (2\pi/L)s$ (thus: $0 \leqslant t \leqslant 2\pi$) and define a new function $\phi(t)$:

$$\phi(t) = \theta\left(\frac{Lt}{2\pi}\right) + t$$

Now, $\phi(0) = \phi(2\pi) = 0$. This function is not dependent on the size, position, and orientation of a shape and, hence, the low-order coefficients of its Fourier series expansion can be used as features for translation, rotation, and scale invariant shape recognition. Unfortunately, it suffers from the disadvantage, common to all transform techniques, of difficulty in describing local shape information, e.g. it would have difficulty in discriminating between two shapes where the only dissimilarity is a small notch in the perimeter.

7.3   *Internal scalar transform descriptors: features of the region*

Internal scalar transform techniques generate shape descriptors based on the entire shape. One of the most popular is the method of moments. The standard two-dimensional moments m_{uv} of an image intensity function $g(x, y)$ are defined:

$$m_{uv} = \int_{-\infty}^{\infty} \int_{-\infty}^{\infty} g(x, y)\, x^u y^v \, dx \, dy \qquad u, v = 0, 1, 2, 3 \dots$$

which, in the discrete domain of digital images becomes:

$$m_{uv} = \sum_{x} \sum_{y} g(x, y)\, x^u y^v \qquad u, v = 0, 1, 2, 3 \dots$$

summed over the entire sub-image within which the shape lies.

143

Unfortunately, these moments will vary for a given shape depending on where the shape is positioned, i.e. they are computed on the basis of the absolute position of the shape. To overcome this, we can use the central moments:

$$\mu_{uv} = \sum_x \sum_y g(x, y)(x - \bar{x})^u (y - \bar{y})^v \qquad u, v = 0, 1, 2, 3 \ldots$$

where:

$$\bar{x} = \frac{m_{10}}{m_{00}} \text{ and } \bar{y} = \frac{m_{01}}{m_{00}}$$

That is, $\bar{x}$ and $\bar{y}$ are the coordinates of the centroid of the shape. Thus, these moments take the centroid of a shape as their reference point and hence are position invariant.

Assuming that the intensity function $g(x, y)$ has a value of one everywhere in the object (i.e. one is dealing with a simple segmented binary image), the computation of m_{00} is simply a summation yielding the total number of pixels within the shape, since the terms in x and y, when raised to the power of zero, become unity. If one also assumes that a pixel is one unit area, then m_{00} is equivalent to the area of the shape. Similarly, m_{10} is effectively the summation of all the x-coordinates of pixels in the shape and m_{01} is the summation of all the y-coordinates of pixels in the shape; hence m_{10}/m_{00} is the average x-coordinate and m_{01}/m_{00} is the average y-coordinate, i.e. the coordinates of the centroid.

The central moments up to order three are:

$$\mu_{00} = m_{00}$$
$$\mu_{10} = 0$$
$$\mu_{01} = 0$$
$$\mu_{20} = m_{20} - \bar{x}m_{10}$$
$$\mu_{02} = m_{02} - \bar{y}m_{01}$$
$$\mu_{11} = m_{11} - \bar{y}m_{10}$$
$$\mu_{30} = m_{30} - 3\bar{x}m_{20} + 2\bar{x}^2 m_{10}$$
$$\mu_{03} = m_{03} - 3\bar{y}m_{02} + 2\bar{y}^2 m_{01}$$
$$\mu_{12} = m_{12} - 2\bar{y}m_{11} - \bar{x}m_{02} + 2\bar{y}^2 m_{10}$$
$$\mu_{21} = m_{21} - 2\bar{x}m_{11} - \bar{y}m_{20} + 2\bar{x}^2 m_{01}$$

These central moments can be normalized, defining a set of normalized central moments η_{ij}:

$$\eta_{ij} = \frac{\mu_{ij}}{(\mu_{00})^k}$$

where:

$$k = ((i + j)/2) + 1 \qquad i + j \geqslant 2$$

However, moment invariants (linear combinations of the normalized central moments) are more frequently used for shape description as they generate values

144

which are invariant with position, orientation, and scale changes. These seven invariant moments are defined as:

$$\phi_1 = \eta_{20} + \eta_{02}$$
$$\phi_2 = (\eta_{20} - \eta_{02})^2 + 4\eta_{11}{}^2$$
$$\phi_3 = (\eta_{30} - 3\eta_{12})^2 + (3\eta_{21} - \eta_{03})^2$$
$$\phi_4 = (\eta_{30} + \eta_{12})^2 + (\eta_{21} + \eta_{03})^2$$
$$\phi_5 = (\eta_{30} - 3\eta_{12})(\eta_{30} + \eta_{12})\{(\eta_{30} + \eta_{12})^2 - 3(\eta_{21} + \eta_{03})^2\}$$
$$\qquad + (3\eta_{21} - \eta_{03})(\eta_{21} + \eta_{03})\{3(\eta_{30} + \eta_{12})^2 - (\eta_{21} + \eta_{03})^2\}$$
$$\phi_6 = (\eta_{20} - \eta_{02})\{(\eta_{30} + \eta_{12}) - (\eta_{21} + \eta_{03})^2\}$$
$$\qquad + 4\eta_{11}(\eta_{30} + \eta_{12})(\eta_{21} + \eta_{03})$$
$$\phi_7 = (3\eta_{21} - \eta_{03})(\eta_{30} + \eta_{12})\{(\eta_{30} + \eta_{12})^2 - 3(\eta_{21} + \eta_{03})^2\}$$
$$\qquad - (3\eta_{12} - \eta_{30})(\eta_{21} + \eta_{03})\{3(\eta_{30} + \eta_{12})^2 - (\eta_{21} + \eta_{03})^2\}$$

The logarithm of ϕ_1 to ϕ_7 is normally used to reduce the dynamic range of the values when using these moment invariants as features in a feature classification (i.e. shape recognition) scheme.

Shape descriptors based on moment invariants convey significant information for simple objects but fail to do so for complicated ones. Since we are discussing internal scalar transform descriptors, it would seem that these moment invariants can only be generated from the entire region. However, they can also be generated from the boundary of the object by exploiting Stokes' theorem or Green's theorem, both of which relate the integral over an area to an integral around its boundary. We will return to this in the next section on external space domain shape descriptors when describing the BCC (boundary chain code).

7.4 External space domain descriptors: spatial organization of the boundary

One popular technique is the use of syntactic descriptors of boundary primitives, e.g., short curves, line segments, and corners. Thus, the shape descriptor is a list or string of primitive shapes and the formation of the list or string must adhere to given rules: the shape syntax or grammar. A polar radii signature, encoding the distance from the shape centroid to the shape boundary as a function of ray angle, is another much simpler external space domain descriptor (see Figure 7.4).

Descriptors based on external space domain techniques are generally efficient, require minimal storage requirements, and, in the case of the more sophisticated syntactic techniques expounded by Fu *et al.* are based on well-developed general methodologies such as the theory of formal languages: syntactic patterns are recognized by parsing the string of primitive patterns in a manner somewhat similar to the way a compiler parses a computer program to check its syntax (see Fu, 1982). In the case of the simple external space domain descriptors, e.g. radii signatures, the recognition strategy is based on correlation or matching of template signatures, rather than on sophisticated parsing techniques.

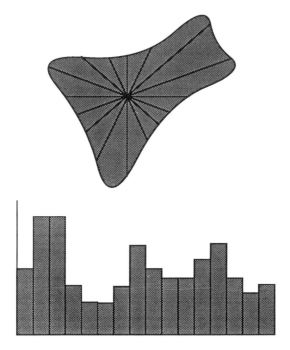

Figure 7.4 Radii signature.

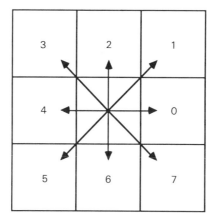

Figure 7.5 Boundary chain code (BCC) directions.

One of the most common external space domain descriptors is the boundary chain code (BCC), introduced in Chapter 5. It should be emphasized, however, that the BCC is more useful for *shape representation* rather than *shape recognition*. The BCC encodes piecewise linear curves as a sequence of straight-line segments called links. A link a_i is a directed straight-line segment of length $T(\sqrt{2})^p$ and of angle

146

$a_i \times 45°$ (referenced to the X-axis of a right-handed Cartesian coordinate system); T is the grid spacing and is normally set equal to unity; a_i may be any integer in the range 0–7 and represent the (coarsely quantized) direction of the link; p is the modulo two value of a_i; i.e. $p = 0$ if a_i is even and $p = 1$ if a_i is odd. Thus, the link length in directions 1, 3, 5, and 7 is equal to $\sqrt{2}$ and is equal to 1 in directions 0, 2, 4, and 6 (see Figure 7.5). However, you should bear in mind the discussion on inter-pixel distances in Chapter 3. Freeman also proposed the inclusion of signal codes in the chain to facilitate, for example, descriptive comments, chain termination, and the identification of the chain origin. Figure 7.6 illustrates a BCC representation of a simple shape.

Although it is widely used as a technique for shape representation, a BCC is *a non-uniformly sampled* function, that is, the distance between the sample points along the boundary may be either 1 or $\sqrt{2}$ depending on whether the neighbouring boundary points are horizontal/vertical neighbours or diagonal neighbours respectively. Thus, a BCC is dependent on the orientation of the object boundary on two distinct bases:

- Each link encodes the *absolute* direction of the boundary at that point.
- The link length (1 or $\sqrt{2}$) varies with the boundary direction.

Any shape descriptor which is derived from this non-uniformly sampled BCC is

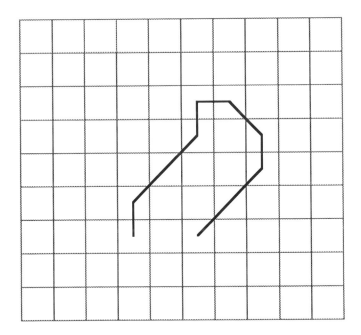

BCC: 2 1 1 2 0 7 6 5 5

Figure 7.6 A BCC representation of a simple shape.

inherently sensitive to changes in orientation. To alleviate this rotational variance it is necessary to remove the dependency on link length, ensuring that the link lengths of the BCC are all equal, specifically by resampling the BCC in uniformly spaced intervals. Note that this resampling technique will generate non-integer coordinate values for the pixels they represent; the actual image pixel values can be obtained for shape reconstruction, which is of interest when displaying the segmented shape, simply by rounding the real-valued coordinates. The fact that the node coordinate values are non-integer is not important if the descriptor is being used for the purposes of shape recognition since one is interested only in correspondence between link values (or the corresponding transformed property) and not the absolute position that they might represent in the image.

Since BCCs are so popular, one simple algorithm for transforming a non-uniformly sampled BCC into a uniformly sampled BCC is presented below. The algorithm, while not as general as others which have been suggested in the computer vision literature, has proven to be adequate for the purposes of constructing rotation-invariant shape descriptors.

7.4.1 An algorithm for resampling boundary chain codes

Let NUS_BCC and US_BCC represent the non-uniformly sampled and uniformly sampled BCCs, respectively. Let a point given by a non-uniformly sampled BCC be represented by (nus_x, nus_y) and let a point given by a uniformly sampled BCC be represented by (us_x, us_y).

NUS_BCC and US_BCC start at the same point on the contour: (nus_x, nus_y) = (us_x, us_y) initially:

```
WHILE there are more NUS_BCC links to be resampled DO

    Generate the next NUS_BCC points: (nus_x, nus_y)

    /* resample */

    REPEAT

        /* generate new US_BCC link and append to US_BCC */

        Generate three candidate uniformly sampled
points:
        (us_x1, us_y1), (us_x2, us_y2), (us_x3, us_y3)
        at a distance of 1 unit from the current uniformly
        sampled point (us_x, us_y)
        in directions corresponding to the NUS_BCC link
        direction, ±1.
```

```
Test all three points and choose the point which
is closest to
    (nus_x, nus_y) (using the Euclidean distance
    metric)

Reassign the current (us_x, us_y) to be this point

Append to the US_BCC a link with a direction
corresponding to this chosen point

UNTIL |us_x - nus_x | < 0.5 AND | us_y - nus_y | < 0.5

/* (us_x, us_y) now lies within the bounds of the      */
/* grid pixel given by (nus_x, nus_y)                   */
```

Figure 7.7 illustrates this resampling process: the original non-uniformly sampled

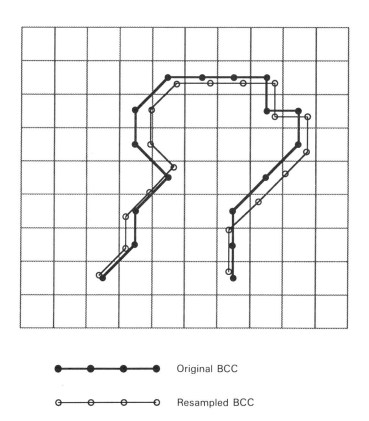

Original BCC

Resampled BCC

Figure 7.7 Resampling a BCC.

boundary is depicted by dots joined by a dotted line and the resampled boundary is depicted by circles joined by a dashed line.

As mentioned above, the BCC is most useful as a method for the representation of shapes and recognition is normally based upon other descriptors derived from the BCC. For example, the moment shape descriptors discussed previously can be generated from the boundary points given by a BCC. Thus, after Wilf (1981), we have:

$$m_{00} = \frac{1}{2} \sum_{i=1}^{n} A_i$$

$$m_{10} = \frac{1}{3} \sum_{i=1}^{n} A_i(y_i - \tfrac{1}{2}\Delta y_i)$$

$$m_{01} = \frac{1}{3} \sum_{i=1}^{n} A_i(x_i - \tfrac{1}{2}\Delta x_i)$$

$$m_{20} = \frac{1}{4} \sum_{i=1}^{n} A_i(x_i^2 - x_i \Delta x_i + \tfrac{1}{3}\Delta x_i^2)$$

$$m_{11} = \frac{1}{4} \sum_{i=1}^{n} A_i(x_i y_i - \tfrac{1}{2}x_i \Delta y_i - \tfrac{1}{2}y_i \Delta x_i + \tfrac{1}{3}\Delta x_i \Delta y_i)$$

$$m_{02} = \frac{1}{4} \sum_{i=1}^{n} A_i(y_i^2 - y_i \Delta y_i + \tfrac{1}{3}\Delta y_i^2)$$

Where x_{i-1} and y_{i-1} are the coordinates of a point on the perimeter of the shape and x_i and y_i are the coordinates of the subsequent point on the perimeter, as given by the BCC; Δx_i is defined to be $(x_i - x_{i-1})$; Δy_i is defined to be $(y_i - y_{i-1})$; and A_i is defined to be $(x_i \Delta y_i - y_i \Delta x_i)$; n is the number of points on the boundary (i.e. the number of BCC links).

7.5 Internal space domain descriptors: spatial organization of the region

Internal space domain techniques comprise descriptors which utilize structural or relational properties derived from the complete shape. The medial axis transform (MAT), which was mentioned in the section on thinning in Chapter 5, is an example of a commonly used space domain descriptor in that it generates a skeletal line-drawing from a two-dimensional shape. A point in the shape is on the medial axis if and only if it is the centre of a circle which is a tangent to the shape boundary at two non-adjacent points. Each point on the medial axis has a value associated with it which indicates the radius of this circle. This represents the minimum distance to the boundary from that point and thus facilitates the reconstruction of the object. There are various methods for generating the medial axis, the most intuitive of which is one that is often referred to as the 'prairie fire technique'; it is analogous to setting fire to the boundary of a dry grassy field and letting the flame burn inwards. The points at which the flame fronts meet are on the medial axis. The MAT is sensitive to local distortions of the contour and small deviations can give rise to extraneous skeletal lines. For example, Figure 7.8 illustrates the MAT of a rectangle with a 'bump'.

Other descriptors can be derived using integral geometry: for example, an object shape can be intersected by a number of chords in different directions and the locations and the length of the intersection can be used in various ways as a shape descriptor. One example of this type of descriptor is the normal contour distance (NCD) shape descriptor (see Vernon, 1987). It is essentially a one-dimensional signature in which each signature value represents an estimate of the distance from a point on an object's boundary, with a local orientation of m, to the opposing boundary point which lies on a path whose direction is normal to m. The NCD signature is evaluated over the length of the available boundary. The NCD signature does not require knowledge of the complete boundary and can be used for recognition of partially occluded objects. Note that, if the contour represents a partial boundary, there may not be another boundary point which lies on a path which is normal to the contour and, hence, some segments of the NCD may be undefined.

To conclude this section on internal space domain descriptors, we will discuss the smoothed local symmetries (SLS) representation, which was introduced by Brady. This is a sophisticated and interesting technique because it represents shape with both region-based descriptors and contour-based descriptors. As such, it is more than an internal space domain descriptor and does not require the entire shape to be visible for extraction of useful shape description primitives. An SLS representation has the following three components:

1. A set of *spines* which are the loci of local symmetries of the boundary of the shape.

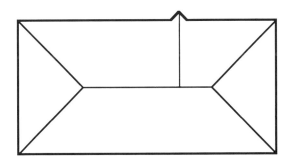

Figure 7.8 Medial axis transform (MAT) of a rectangular shape with a 'bump'.

2. A description of the local shape of the boundary contour in terms of parametric curves (Brady uses circles and spirals) and in terms of primitives of curvature discontinuity. These primitives effectively describe the manner in which the local contour curves are joined together to form the complete boundary shape.

3. A description of the region subtended by two locally symmetric curves. This is effected by a small number of region labels (e.g. cup, sector, wedge, and

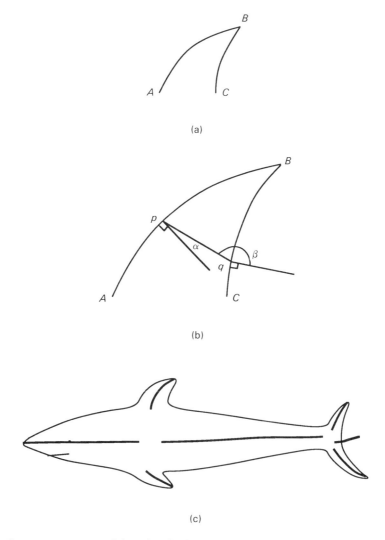

(a)

(b)

(c)

Figure 7.9 (a) Dorsal fin of a shark. (b) Geometry defining a smoothed local symmetry (SLS). (c) Schematic SLS for a complex shape.

so on), each of which has several attributes associated with it. They include the width of the region and the curvature of the associated spine.

For example, consider Figure 7.9(a) which depicts the dorsal fin of a shark. The shape of the fin is defined by two curves *AB* and *BC*:

- The curve *AB* is convex and is described by a circular arc.
- The curve *BC* is concave and is also described by a circular arc.
- The junction between the two curves at *B* is an acute-angled *corner*.

These three items form the contour-based description. The descriptor of the region between the two curves *AB* and *BC* is labelled a *beak* (the labelling that is used is based on the relative concavity/convexity of the two sides of a local symmetry) and the spine curves to the right. This raises the issue of how the spine is identified. Referring to Figure 7.9(b), let α be the angle subtended by the inward normal to the contour at a point p on the curve *AB* and let β be the angle subtended by the outward normal to the contour at a point q on the curve *BC*. A point q on the curve *BC* forms a local symmetry with the point p on the curve *AB* if the sum of their respective angles is equal to $180°$, i.e. if $\alpha + \beta = 180°$. Several such points q can exist for a given point p. The spine of the SLS is effectively formed by the set mid-points of chords pq which satisfy this condition for local symmetry (for an exact formulation, see Brady and Asada, 1984).

At this stage, we might remark on the similarity between the SLS and the MAT. However, the SLS differs in several important ways: the local symmetry which is implicit in the MAT is made explicit in the SLS; global symmetries, such as that which lies between a long fork (see Figure 7.10), are not made explicit by the MAT; and the SLS includes the attributed contour and regions descriptors discussed above – the SLS is more than just a collection of spines. Finally, let us note that the SLS representation is also intended to be used as a descriptor of complex shapes, which can be viewed as a network of locally symmetric parts (see Figure 7.9(c)). The connections in the network are relationships between the sub-parts and carry information (or attributes) which can help disambiguate between similar objects.

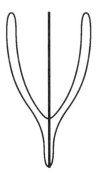

Figure 7.10 Global SLS of a forked object.

Exercises

1. Discuss how an object skeleton would be used as a shape descriptor, paying particular attention to issues of shape recognition.
2. Generate a BCC representing a circle of diameter 10 pixels. Derive a uniformly sampled version and compare the perimeter length of both versions with the theoretical value.
3. Would a radii signature shape descriptor be useful for the recognition of occluded shapes? Why?
4. Bearing in mind that the minimum bounding rectangle of an arbitrarily oriented shape requires the prior estimation of its major axis, how would you go about computing this shape descriptor?

References and further reading

Anderson, R.L. 1985 'Real-time grey-scale video using a moment-generating chip', *IEEE Journal of Robotics and Automation*, Vol. RA-1, No. 2, pp. 79–85.

Ballard, D.H. and Sabbah, D. 1983 'Viewer independent shape recognition', *IEEE Transactions on Pattern Analysis and Machine Intelligence*, Vol. PAMI-5, No. 6, pp. 653–60.

Bamieh, B. and De Figueiredo, R.J.P. 1986 'A general moment-invariants/attributed-graph method for three-dimensional object recognition from a single image', *IEEE Journal of Robotics and Automation*, Vol. RA-2, No. 1, pp. 31–41.

Berman, S., Parikh, P. and Lee, C.S.G. 1985 'Computer recognition of two overlapping parts using a single camera', *IEEE Computer*, pp. 70–80.

Bolles, R.C. 1980 *Locating Partially Visible Objects: The Feature Focus Method*, SRI International, Technical Note No. 223.

Bolles, R.C. and Cain, R.A. 1982 'Recognizing and locating partially visible objects: the local-feature-focus method, *The International Journal of Robotics Research*, Vol. 1, No. 3, 1982, pp. 57–82.

Brady, M. 1983 'Criteria for representations of shape', *Human and Machine Vision*, A. Rosenfeld and J. Beck (eds), Academic Press, New York.

Brady, M. and Asada, H. 1984 'Smoothed local symmetries and their implementation', *The International Journal of Robotics Research*, Vol. 3, No. 3, pp. 36–61.

Freeman, H. 1961 'On the encoding of arbitrary geometric configurations', *IRE Transactions on Electronic Computers*, pp. 260–8.

Freeman, H. 1974 'Computer processing of line-drawing images', *ACM Computing Surveys*, Vol. 6, No. 1, pp. 57–97.

Fu, K-S. (ed.) 1980 *Digital Pattern Recognition*, Springer Verlag, Berlin.

Hu, M.K. 1962 'Visual pattern recognition by moment invariants', *IRE Transactions on Information Theory*, Vol. IT-8, pp. 179–87.

Lin, C.C. and Chellappa, R. 1987 'Classification of partial 2-D shapes using Fourier descriptors', *IEEE Transactions on Pattern Analysis and Machine Intelligence*, Vol. PAMI-9, No. 5, pp. 686–90.

Nackman, L.R. and Pizer, S.M. 1985 'Three-dimensional shape description using the symmetric axis transform 1: Theory', *IEEE Transactions on Pattern Analysis and Machine Intelligence*, Vol. PAMI-7, No. 2, pp. 187–202.

Pavlidis, T. 1978 'A review of algorithms for shape-analysis', *Computer Graphics and Image Processing*, Vol. 7, pp. 243–58.

Pavlidis, T. 1980 'Algorithms for shape analysis of contours and waveforms', *IEEE Transactions on Pattern Analysis and Machine Intelligence*, Vol. PAMI-2, No. 4, pp. 301–12.

Shahraray, B. and Anderson, D.J. 1985 'Uniform resampling of digitized contours', *IEEE Transactions on Pattern Analysis and Machine Intelligence*, Vol. PAMI-7, No. 6, pp. 674–81.

Tang, G.Y. 1982 'A discrete version of Green's theorem', *IEEE Transactions on Pattern Analysis and Machine Intelligence*, Vol. PAMI-4, No. 3, pp. 242–9.

Vernon, D. 1987 'Two dimensional object recognition using partial contours', *Image and Vision Computing*, Vol. 5, No. 1, pp. 21–7.

Wiejak, J.S. 1983 'Moment invariants in theory and practice', *Image and Vision Computing*, Vol. 1, No. 2, pp. 79–83.

Wilf, J.M. 1981 'Chain-code', *Robotics Age*, Vol. 3, No. 2, pp. 12–19.

Wong, R.Y. 1978 'Scene matching with invariant moments', *Computer Graphics and Image Processing*, Vol. 8, pp. 16–24.

Zhan, C.T. and Roskies, R.Z. 1972 'Fourier descriptors for plane closed curves', *IEEE Trans. Computers*, Vol. C-21, pp. 269–81.

8

Robot programming and robot vision

So far, we have discussed in some detail the automatic processing and analysis of images and image data. Any information about position and orientation of objects has been derived in an image frame for reference, that is, with respect to the two-dimensional array of pixels representing the imaged scene. However, objects only exist in the so-called real world (i.e. the world we are imaging) and if we wish to do something useful with the information we have extracted from our digital images, then we have to address the relationship between images and the three-dimensional environment from which they are derived. Even then, this is typically not enough since there is little point in knowing where things are if we don't know how to manipulate and move them. In this chapter, we turn our attention to these issues and we will discuss how we can usefully describe the three-dimensional position and orientation of objects relative to any other object, how to go about configuring a task to effect their manipulation, and how, given their image position and orientation, we can derive their three-dimensional pose.

Recall that imaging is a projective process from a three-dimensional world to a two-dimensional one and, as such, we lose one dimension (typically the object depth or range) when we perform this imaging. As we noted in Chapter 1, much of computer vision is concerned with the recovery of this third dimension but, so far in this book, we have not dealt with it in any detail. Most of the discussion of recovery of depth information is included in the next chapter on image understanding. However, to make this chapter complete and self-contained, we discuss at the end a popular and versatile technique called *structured-light*, which allows us to compute the distance between a camera and objects in the field of view.

Before proceeding, we will briefly review robot programming methodologies to provide a context for the approach that we adopt in this book.

8.1 A brief review of robot programming methodologies

Modern robotic manipulators, which have their origins in telecheric and numerically controlled devices, have been developing for the past twenty-five years. As robots have developed, so too have various methods evolved for programming them and, consequently, modern commercially available robot manipulators make use of many programming techniques which exhibit a wide spectrum of sophistication. There are, broadly speaking, three main categories of robot programming system which are, in order of the level of sophistication: guiding systems; robot-level or explicit-level systems; and task-level systems.

Guiding systems are typified by the manual lead-through approach in which the manipulator is trained by guiding the arm through the appropriate positions using, for example, a teach-pendant, and recording the individual joint positions. Task execution is effected by driving the joints to these recorded positions. This type of manual teaching is the most common of all programming systems, and though several variations on the theme have been developed, such as trajectory control, the explicit interactive nature remains the same.

Robot-level programming systems, for the most part, simply replace the teach-pendant with a robot programming language: manipulator movements are still programmed by explicitly specifying joint positions. However, several languages also facilitate robot control in a three-dimensional Cartesian space, rather than in the joint space. This is effected using the *inverse kinematic solution* of the manipulator arm (the kinematic solution allows you to compute the position of the end-effector or gripper in a three-dimensional Cartesian frame of reference, given the manipulator joint positions; the inverse kinematic solution allows you to compute the joint positions for a given position and orientation of the end-effector). The more advanced of these languages incorporate structured programming control constructs (such as are found in most modern programming languages, e.g. ADA, Modula-2, and Pascal) and they make extensive use of *coordinate transformation* and *coordinate frames*. With this approach, the robot control is defined in terms of transformations on a coordinate frame (a set of *XYZ*-axes) associated with, and embedded in, the robot hand. Off-line programming is more feasible as long as the transformations representing the relationships between the frames describing the objects in the robot environment are accurate. It is this approach which we adopt in this book and these techniques will be discussed in detail in the remainder of the chapter.

Task-level robot programming languages attempt to describe assembly tasks as sequences of goal spatial relationships between objects and, thus, they differ from the other two approaches in that they focus on the objects rather than on the manipulator. The robot is merely a mechanism to achieve these goals. They typically require the use of task planning, path planning, collision avoidance and world-modelling: this level of sophistication is not yet widely available on a commercial basis.

8.2 Description of object pose with homogeneous transformations

Robot manipulation is concerned, in essence, with the spatial relationships between several objects, between objects and manipulators, and with the reorganization of these relationships. We will use *homogeneous transformations* to represent these spatial relationships. However, we first need to review a little vector algebra to ensure that we are equipped with the tools to develop this methodology.

A vector $v = ai + bj + ck$, where i, j and k are unit vectors along the X-, Y-, and Z-axes of a coordinate reference frame (see Figure 8.1), is represented in *homogeneous coordinates* as a column matrix:

$$v = \begin{bmatrix} x \\ y \\ z \\ w \end{bmatrix}$$

where:

$$a = \frac{x}{w}$$

$$b = \frac{y}{w}$$

$$c = \frac{z}{w}$$

Thus, the additional fourth coordinate w is just a scaling factor and means that a single three-dimensional vector can be represented by several homogeneous coordinates. For example, $3i + 4j + 5k$ can be represented by

$$\begin{bmatrix} 3 \\ 4 \\ 5 \\ 1 \end{bmatrix} \text{ or by } \begin{bmatrix} 6 \\ 8 \\ 10 \\ 2 \end{bmatrix}.$$

Note that, since division of zero by zero is indeterminate, the vector

$$\begin{bmatrix} 0 \\ 0 \\ 0 \\ 0 \end{bmatrix}$$

is undefined.

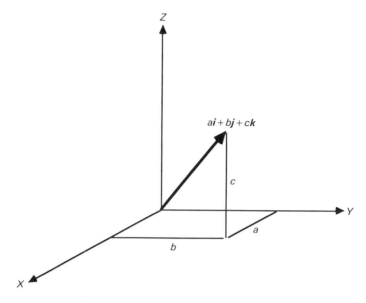

Figure 8.1 Coordinate reference frame.

Vectors can be combined in two simple ways. Given two vectors a and b:

$$a = a_x i + a_y j + a_z k$$
$$b = b_x i + b_y j + b_z k$$

The *vector dot product* is defined:

$$a \cdot b = a_x b_x + a_y b_y + a_z b_z$$

and is a scalar quantity. The *vector cross product* is defined:

$$a \times b = (a_y b_z - a_z b_y)i + (a_z b_x - a_x b_z)j + (a_x b_y - a_y b_x)k$$

It may also be written as:

$$a \times b = \begin{bmatrix} i & j & k \\ a_x & a_y & a_z \\ b_x & b_y & b_z \end{bmatrix}$$

that is, as the expansion of this 3×3 determinant.

A general transformation H, in three-dimensional space, representing translation, rotation, stretching, and perspective distortions, is a 4×4 matrix in homogeneous formulation. Given a point represented by the vector u, its transformation v is represented by the matrix product:

$$v = Hu$$

The transformation H corresponding to a translation by a vector $ai + bj + ck$ is:

$$H = TRANS(a, b, c) = \begin{bmatrix} 1 & 0 & 0 & a \\ 0 & 1 & 0 & b \\ 0 & 0 & 1 & c \\ 0 & 0 & 0 & 1 \end{bmatrix}$$

For example: to transform $u = \begin{bmatrix} x \\ y \\ z \\ w \end{bmatrix}$ by H:

$$v = Hu = \begin{bmatrix} 1 & 0 & 0 & a \\ 0 & 1 & 0 & b \\ 0 & 0 & 1 & c \\ 0 & 0 & 0 & 1 \end{bmatrix} \begin{bmatrix} x \\ y \\ z \\ w \end{bmatrix}$$

$$= \begin{bmatrix} x + aw \\ y + bw \\ z + cw \\ w \end{bmatrix}$$

$$= \begin{bmatrix} x/w + a \\ y/w + b \\ z/w + c \\ 1 \end{bmatrix}$$

Thus, we have the familiar property of translation of a vector by another vector being simply the addition of their respective coefficients.

The transformation corresponding to rotations about the X-, Y-, or Z-axes by an angle θ are:

$$Rot(X, \theta) = \begin{bmatrix} 1 & 0 & 0 & 0 \\ 0 & \cos\theta & -\sin\theta & 0 \\ 0 & \sin\theta & \cos\theta & 0 \\ 0 & 0 & 0 & 1 \end{bmatrix}$$

$$Rot(Y, \theta) = \begin{bmatrix} \cos\theta & 0 & \sin\theta & 0 \\ 0 & 1 & 0 & 0 \\ -\sin\theta & 0 & \cos\theta & 0 \\ 0 & 0 & 0 & 1 \end{bmatrix}$$

$$Rot(Z, \theta) = \begin{bmatrix} \cos\theta & -\sin\theta & 0 & 0 \\ \sin\theta & \cos\theta & 0 & 0 \\ 0 & 0 & 1 & 0 \\ 0 & 0 & 0 & 1 \end{bmatrix}$$

Now, from our point of view, we come to the most important aspect of homogeneous transformations in that we can interpret the homogeneous transformation as a *coordinate reference frame*. In particular, a homogeneous

transformation describes the position and orientation of a coordinate frame with respect to another previously defined coordinate frame. Thus, the homogeneous transformation represents not only transformations of vectors (points) but also positions and orientations.

Specifically, a coordinate frame is defined by four things: the position of its origin and the direction of its X-, Y-, and Z-axes. The first three columns of the homogeneous transformation represent the direction of the X-, Y-, and Z-axes of the coordinate frame with respect to the base coordinate reference frame, while the fourth column represents the position of the origin. This is intuitively appealing: a homogeneous transformation, which can be a combination of many simpler homogeneous transformations, applies equally to other homogeneous trans-formations as it does to vectors (pre-multiplying a 4×1 vector by a 4×4 matrix yields a 4×1 vector; pre-multiplying a 4×4 matrix by a 4×4 matrix yields a 4×4 matrix which is still a homogeneous transformation). Thus, we can take a coordinate reference frame and move it elsewhere by applying an appropriate homogeneous transformation. If the coordinate frame to be 'moved' is originally aligned with the so-called base coordinate reference frame, then we can see that the homogeneous transformation is both a description of how to transform the base coordinate frame to the new coordinate frame and a description of this new coordinate frame with respect to the base coordinate reference frame. For example, consider the following transformation:

$$H = Trans\ (10, 10, 0)\ Rot\ (Y, 90)$$

$$= Trans\ (10, 10, 0) \begin{bmatrix} 0 & 0 & 1 & 0 \\ 0 & 1 & 0 & 0 \\ -1 & 0 & 0 & 0 \\ 0 & 0 & 0 & 1 \end{bmatrix}$$

$$= \begin{bmatrix} 0 & 0 & 1 & 10 \\ 0 & 1 & 0 & 10 \\ -1 & 0 & 0 & 0 \\ 0 & 0 & 0 & 1 \end{bmatrix}$$

The transformation of the three vectors corresponding to the unit vectors along the X-, Y-, and Z-axes are:

$$\begin{bmatrix} 0 & 0 & 1 & 10 \\ 0 & 1 & 0 & 10 \\ -1 & 0 & 0 & 0 \\ 0 & 0 & 0 & 1 \end{bmatrix} \begin{bmatrix} 1 \\ 0 \\ 0 \\ 1 \end{bmatrix} = \begin{bmatrix} 10 \\ 10 \\ -1 \\ 1 \end{bmatrix},$$

$$\begin{bmatrix} 0 & 0 & 1 & 10 \\ 0 & 1 & 0 & 10 \\ -1 & 0 & 0 & 0 \\ 0 & 0 & 0 & 1 \end{bmatrix} \begin{bmatrix} 0 \\ 1 \\ 0 \\ 1 \end{bmatrix} = \begin{bmatrix} 10 \\ 11 \\ 0 \\ 1 \end{bmatrix}, \text{ and}$$

161

$$\begin{bmatrix} 0 & 0 & 1 & 10 \\ 0 & 1 & 0 & 10 \\ -1 & 0 & 0 & 0 \\ 0 & 0 & 0 & 1 \end{bmatrix} \begin{bmatrix} 0 \\ 0 \\ 1 \\ 1 \end{bmatrix} = \begin{bmatrix} 11 \\ 10 \\ 0 \\ 1 \end{bmatrix} \text{ respectively}$$

The direction of these (transformed) unit vectors is formed by subtracting the vector representing the origin of this coordinate frame and extending the vectors to infinity by reducing the scale factor to zero. Thus, the direction of the X-, Y-, and Z-axes of this (new) frame are

$$\begin{bmatrix} 0 \\ 0 \\ -1 \\ 0 \end{bmatrix}, \begin{bmatrix} 0 \\ 1 \\ 0 \\ 0 \end{bmatrix}, \text{ and } \begin{bmatrix} 1 \\ 0 \\ 0 \\ 0 \end{bmatrix}$$

Similarly, the transformation of the null vector, i.e. the vector which performs no translation and thus defines the origin of the base coordinate frame, is given by:

$$\begin{bmatrix} 10 \\ 10 \\ 0 \\ 1 \end{bmatrix} = \begin{bmatrix} 0 & 0 & 1 & 10 \\ 0 & 1 & 0 & 10 \\ -1 & 0 & 0 & 0 \\ 0 & 0 & 0 & 1 \end{bmatrix} \begin{bmatrix} 0 \\ 0 \\ 0 \\ 1 \end{bmatrix}$$

These four results show us that the new origin is at coordinates $(10, 10, 0)$; the new X-axis is directed along the Z-axis of the base coordinate reference frame in the negative direction; the new Y-axis is directed along the Y-axis of the base coordinate reference frame in the positive direction; and the new Z-axis is directed along the X-axis of the base coordinate reference frame in the positive direction. This can be seen in Figure 8.2. You should try to do this transformation graphically but remember when deciding in which sense to make a rotation that: a positive rotation about the X-axis takes the Y-axis *towards* the Z-axis; a positive rotation about the Y-axis takes the Z-axis *towards* the X-axis; a positive rotation about the Z-axis takes the X-axis *towards* the Y-axis.

The rotations and translations we have been describing have all been made relative to the fixed base reference frame. Thus, in the transformation given by:

$$H = \mathit{Trans}(10, 10, 0) \; \mathit{Rot} \; (Y, 90)$$

the frame is first rotated around the reference Y-axis by $90°$, and *then* translated by $10i + 10j + 0k$.

This operation may also be interpreted in reverse order, from left to right, viz: the object (frame) is first translated by $10i + 10j + 0k$; it is then rotated by $90°$ around the *station* frame axis (Y). In this instance, the effect is the same, but in general it will not be. This second interpretation seems to be the most intuitive since we can forget about the base reference frame and just remember 'where we are': our current station coordinate reference frame. We then just need to decide what

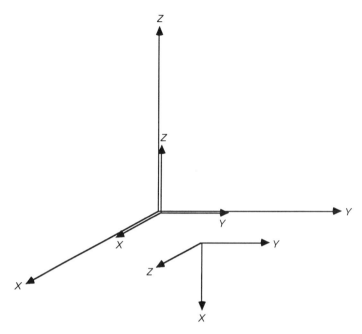

$$H = Trans\,(10, 10, 0)\; Rot\;(Y, 90)$$

Figure 8.2 Interpreting a homogeneous transformation as a coordinate frame.

transformations are necessary to get us to where we want to be based on the orientation of the station axes. In this way, we can get from pose to pose by incrementally identifying the appropriate station transformations, H_1, H_2, H_3, ... H_n, which we apply sequentially, as we go, and the final pose is defined with respect to the base simply as:

$$H = H_1 * H_2 * H_3 * \ldots * H_n.$$

In order to clarify the relative nature of these transformations, each of these frames/transformations is normally written with a leading superscript which identifies the coordinate frame with respect to which the (new) frame/transformation is defined. The leading superscript is omitted if the defining frame is the base frame. Thus the above transform equation is more correctly written:

$$H = H_1 * {}^{H_1}H_2 * {}^{H_2}H_3 * \ldots * {}^{H_{n-1}}H_n.$$

As a general rule, if we post-multiply a transform representing a frame by a second transformation describing a rotation and/or translation we make that rotation/transformation with respect to the frame axis described by the first transformation. On the other hand, if we pre-multiply the frame transformation representing a rotation/transformation then the rotation/transformation is made with respect to the base reference coordinate frame.

At this stage, we have developed a system where we can specify the position and orientation of coordinate reference frames anywhere with respect to each other and with respect to a given base frame. This, in itself, is quite useless since the world you and I know does not have too many coordinate reference frames in it. What we really require is a way of identifying the pose of *objects*. In fact, we are about there. The trick, and it is no more than a trick, is to *attach* a coordinate frame to an object, i.e. symbolically glue an *XYZ*-frame into an object simply by defining it to be there. Now, as we rotate and translate the coordinate frame, so too do we rotate and translate objects. We shall see this at work in the next section on robot programming.

8.3 Robot programming: a wire crimping task specification

Perhaps the best way to introduce robot programming is by example and, so, we will develop our robot programming methodology in the context of a specific application: automated wire crimping.

The wire crimping task requires that a robot manipulator grasp a wire from a tray of wires (see Figure 8.3). The wires are short and curved but they are flexible and the curvature varies from wire to wire. We will assume that, although the wires

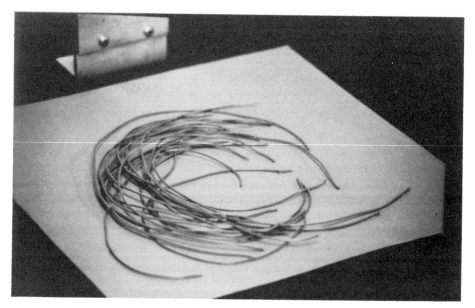

(a)

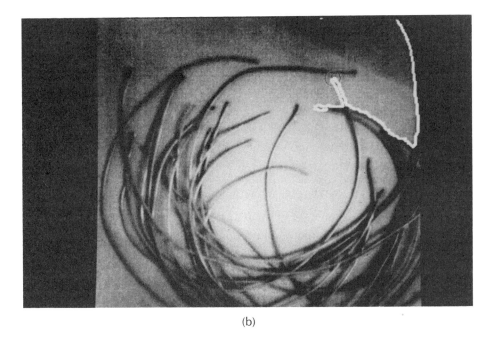

(b)

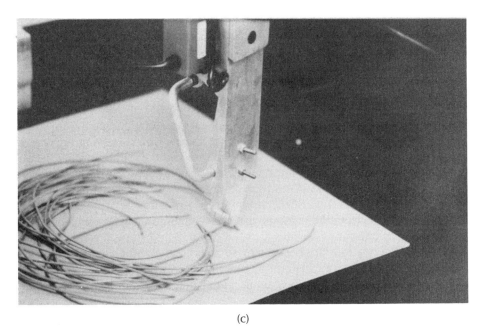

(c)

Figure 8.3 (a) A tray of flexible electrical wires (b) an image of which yields a point on a wire which is suitable for grasping (c) allowing the robot to pick up the wire and manipulate it.

overlap, they all lie flat on the tray. The wire must be grasped near its end by the robot, *at a point which has been identified using a vision system*, and the wire end must be inserted in a crimping machine, and the crimped end then must be inserted in a plastic connector. There are a few other related tasks, such as crimping the other end and inserting it in another connector, but, for the purposes of this example, we will assume that the task is complete once the wire has been crimped the first time. In addition, we must ensure that the manipulator does not obstruct the camera's field of view at the beginning of each crimp cycle and, thus, it must be moved to an appropriate remote position. By defining a series of manipulator end-effector positions *Mn*, say, this task can be described as a sequence of manipulator movements and actions referred to these defined positions. For example, the task might be formulated as follows:

*M*0: Move out of the field of view of the camera.
Determine the position and orientation of the wire-end and the grasp point using the vision system.
*M*1: Move to a position above the centre of the tray of wires.
*M*2: Move to an approach position above the grasp point.
*M*3: Move to the grasp position
      Grasp the wire.
*M*4: Move to the depart position above the grasp point.
*M*5: Move to the approach position in front of the crimp.
*M*6: Move to a position in which the wire-end and the crimp are in contact.
*M*7: Move to a position such that the wire-end is inserted in the crimp.
Actuate the crimping machine.
*M*8: Move to the depart position in front of the crimping machine.
*M*9: Move to a position above the collection bin.
Release the wire.

This process is repeated until there are no more wires to be crimped.

One of the problems with this approach is that we are specifying the task in terms of movements of the robot while it is the wire and the crimp in which we are really interested. The object movements are implicit in the fact that the manipulator has grasped it. However, we will try to make up for this deficiency to some extent when we describe the structure of the task by considering the structure of the task's component objects: the manipulator, the end-effector, the wire grasp position, the wire end, the crimping machine, and the crimp. In particular, we will use the explicit positional relationships between these objects to describe the task structure. Since coordinate frames can be used to describe object position and orientation, and since we may need to describe a coordinate frame in two or more ways (there is more than one way to reach any given position and orientation), we will use transform equations to relate the two descriptions. A simple example, taken from *'Robot manipulators'* by R. Paul (1981), will serve to illustrate the approach.

Consider the situation, depicted in Figure 8.4, of a manipulator grasping a toy block. The coordinate frames which describe this situation are as follows:

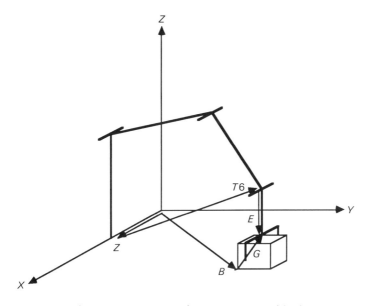

Figure 8.4 A manipulator grasping a block.

Z is the transform which describes the position of manipulator with respect to the base coordinate reference frame.

$^{Z}T6$ describes the end of the manipulator (i.e. the wrist) with respect to the base of manipulator, i.e. with respect to Z.

^{T6}E describes the end-effector with respect to the end of the manipulator, i.e. with respect to $T6$.

B describes a block's position with respect to the base coordinate reference frame.

^{B}G describes the manipulator end-effector with respect to the block, i.e. with respect to B.

In this example, the end-effector is described in two ways, by the transformations leading from the base to the wrist to the end-effector:

$$Z * {}^{Z}T6 * {}^{T6}E$$

and by the transformations leading from the block to the end-effector grip position:

$$B * {}^{B}G$$

Equating these descriptions, we get the following transform equation:

$$Z * {}^{Z}T6 * {}^{T6}E = B * {}^{B}G$$

Solving for $T6$ by multiplying across by the inverse of Z and ^{T6}E:

$$^{Z}T6 = Z^{-1} * B * {}^{B}G * {}^{T6}E^{-1}$$

*T*6 is a function of the joint variables of the manipulator and, if known, then the appropriate joint variables can be computed using the inverse kinematic solution. *T*6, then, is the coordinate which we wish to program in order to effect the manipulation task: an arm position and orientation specified by *T*6 is thus equivalent to our previous informal movement *Mn*:

$$\text{Move } Mn = \text{Move } {}^Z T6$$

and, since we can compute *T*6 in terms of our known frames, we now have an arm movement which is specified in terms of the frames which describe the task structure. Assigning the appropriate value to *T*6 and moving to that position, implicitly using the inverse kinematic solution:

$${}^Z T6 := Z^{-1} * B * {}^B G * {}^{T6} E^{-1}$$

$$\text{Move } {}^Z T6$$

What we have not yet done, and we will omit in this instance, is to fully specify each of these frames by embedding them in the appropriate objects and specifying the transformations which define them. We will do this in full for the wire crimping application.

Before proceeding, it is worth noting that, in this example, as the position of the end-effector with respect to the base reference system is represented by:

$$Z * {}^Z T6 * {}^{T6} E$$

this allows you to generate general-purpose and reusable robot programs. In particular, the calibration of the manipulator to the workstation is represented by *Z*, while if the task is to be performed with a change of tool, only *E* need be altered.

Returning again to the wire crimping application, the transforms (i.e. frames) which are used in the task are as follows.

As before:

Z	is the transform which describes the position of manipulator with respect to the base coordinate reference frame.
${}^Z T6$	describes the end of the manipulator (i.e. the wrist) with respect to the base of manipulator, i.e. with respect to *Z*.
${}^{T6} E$	describes the end-effector with respect to the end of the manipulator, i.e. with respect to *T*6.

We now define:

OOV	the position of the end-effector out of the field of view of the camera and defined with respect to the base coordinate reference system.
CEN	the position of the end-effector centred over table defined with respect to the base coordinate reference system.
WDUMP	the position of the end-effector over the bin of crimped wires, defined with respect to the base coordinate reference system.

W the position of the wire end, defined with respect to the base coordinate reference system.

^{W}WG the position of end-effector holding wire, defined with respect to the wire end.

^{WG}WA the position of end-effector approaching grasp position, defined with respect to the wire-grasp position.

^{WG}WD the position of end-effector departing grasp position (having grasped the wire), defined with respect to the original wire-grasp position.

CM the position of the crimping machine, defined with respect to the base coordinate reference system.

^{CM}C the position of the crimp (ready to be attached), defined with respect to the crimping machine.

^{C}CA the position of the wire end approaching crimp, defined with respect to the crimp.

^{C}CC the position of the wire end in contact with the crimp, defined with respect to the crimp.

^{C}CI the position of the wire end inserted in the crimp, defined with respect to the crimp.

^{C}CD the position of the wire end departing from the crimping machine (the crimp having been attached), defined with respect to the crimp.

The manipulator movements $M0$ through $M9$ can now be expressed as combinations of these transforms:

$$M0: \quad T6 = Z^{-1} * OOV * E^{-1}$$
$$M1: \quad T6 = Z^{-1} * CEN * E^{-1}$$
$$M2: \quad T6 = Z^{-1} * W * WG * WA * E^{-1}$$
$$M3: \quad T6 = Z^{-1} * W * WG * E^{-1}$$
$$M4: \quad T6 = Z^{-1} * W * WG * WD * E^{-1}$$
$$M5: \quad T6 = Z^{-1} * CM * C * CA * WG * E^{-1}$$
$$M6: \quad T6 = Z^{-1} * CM * C * CC * WG * E^{-1}$$
$$M7: \quad T6 = Z^{-1} * CM * C * CI * WG * E^{-1}$$
$$M8: \quad T6 = Z^{-1} * CM * C * CD * WG * E^{-1}$$
$$M9: \quad T6 = Z^{-1} * WDUMP * E^{-1}$$

Note that $WA, WD, CA, CI,$ and CD are all translation transformations concerned with approaching and departing a particular object. In order to allow smooth approach and departure trajectories, these translation distances are iterated from zero to some maximum value or from some maximum value to zero (in integer intervals) depending on whether the effector is approaching or departing. For example: ^{WG}WA is the approach position of the end-effector before grasping the wire and is (to be) defined as a translation, in the negative Z-direction of the WG

frame, of the approach distance *z_approach*, say. Thus:

$$^{WG}WA = Trans(0, 0, -(z\_approach))$$

where:

$$z\_approach = z\_approach\_initial$$
$$z\_approach\_initial - delta$$
$$z\_approach\_initial - 2 * delta$$
$$\vdots$$
$$0$$

It should be noted well that this type of explicit point-to-point approximation of continuous path control would not normally be necessary with a commercial industrial robot programming language since they usually provide facilities for specifying the end-effector trajectory.

To complete the task specification, we now have to define the rotations and translations associated with these transforms/frames. Most can be determined by empirical methods, embedding a frame in an object and measuring the object position and orientation. Others, *W* and *WG* in particular, are defined here and their components determined by visual means at run time.

☐ *Z: The position of the position of manipulator with respect to the base coordinate reference frame*

We will assume that the base coordinate system is aligned with the frame embedded in the manipulator base, as shown in Figure 8.5. Thus:

$$Z = I = \text{Identity transform}$$

Note that the frame defining the manipulator base is dependent on the kinematic model of the robot manipulator.

☐ *T6: the position of the end of the manipulator with respect to its base at Z*

The *T6* frame, shown in Figure 8.6, is a computable function of the joint variables. Again, the frame which defines the end of the manipulator is based on the kinematic model. However, there is a convention that the frame should be embedded in the manipulator with the origin at the wrist, with the *Z*-axis directed outward from the wrist to the gripper, with the *Y*-axis directed in the plane of movement of the gripper when it is opening and closing, and with the *X*-axis making up a right-hand system. This is shown more clearly in Figure 8.7 which depicts a more common two-finger parallel jaw gripper.

It is also worth noting that, although we will specify the orientation of *T6* by solving for it in terms of other frames/transforms in the task specification, there is a commonly used convention for specifying the orientation of objects, in general, and *T6* in particular. This convention identifies three rotations about the station

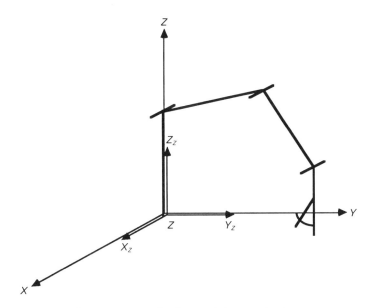

Figure 8.5 *Z* – the base of the manipulator.

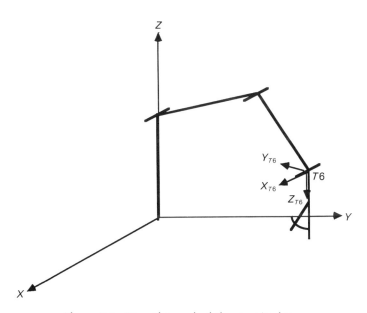

Figure 8.6 *T*6 – the end of the manipulator.

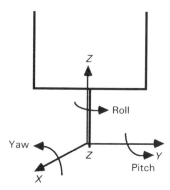

Figure 8.7 Specifying the orientation of $T6$ using roll, pitch, and yaw angles.

coordinate frame embedded in the object which are applied in turn and in a specified order. The rotations are referred to as a *roll* of ϕ degrees about the station Z-axis, a *pitch* of θ degrees about the station Y-axis, and *yaw* of ψ degrees about the station X-axis. The order of rotation is specified as:

$$RPY(\phi, \theta, \psi) = Rot(Z, \phi)Rot(Y, \theta)Rot(X, \psi)$$

Thus, the object is first rotated $\phi°$ about the Z-axis, then $\theta°$ about the current station Y-axis, and finally $\psi°$ about the station X-axis; refer again to Figure 8.7.

☐ *E: the position of the end-effector with respect to the end of the manipulator, i.e. with respect to T6*
The frame E representing a special-purpose end-effector for grasping wires is embedded in the tip of the effector, as shown in Figure 8.8, and hence is defined by a translation 209 mm along the Z-axis of the $T6$ frame and a translation of -15 mm along the Y-axis of the $T6$ frame. Thus:

$$^{T6}E = Trans(0, -15, 209)$$

☐ *OOV: the position of the end-effector out of the field of view of the camera*
This position is defined, with respect to the base coordinate system, such that the end-effector is directed vertically downwards, as shown in Figure 8.9. Thus OOV is defined by a translation (of the origin) to the point given by the coordinates $(150, 300, 150)$ followed by a rotation of $-180°$ about the station X-axis:

$$OOV = Trans(150, 300, 150) \ Rot(X, -180)$$

☐ *CEN: the position of the end-effector centred over the tray, defined with respect to the base coordinate reference frame*
This position is defined such that the end-effector is directed vertically downwards

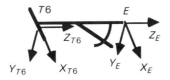

Figure 8.8 E – the end-effector.

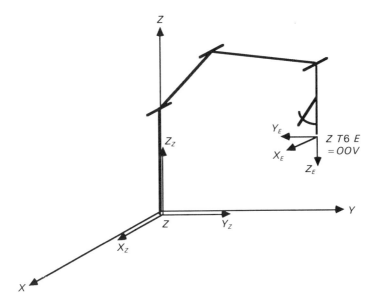

Figure 8.9 *OOV* – the end-effector out of the camera's field of view.

over the centre of the tray, as shown in Figure 8.10. Thus, *CEN* is defined by a translation (of the frame origin) to the point given by the coordinates $(0, 360, 150)$ followed by a rotation of $-180°$ above the station X-axis:

$$CEN = Trans(0, 360, 150) \ Rot(X, -180)$$

☐ *WDUMP: the position of the end-effector over the bin of crimped wires, defined with respect to the base coordinate reference frame*

This position is defined such that the end-effector is directed $-45°$ to the horizontal over the centre of a bin as shown in Figure 8.11. Thus, *WDUMP* is defined by a translation of the frame origin to the point given by the coordinates $(0, 500, 160)$ followed by a rotation of $-135°$ about the station X-axis.

$$WDUMP = TRANS(0, 500, 160) \ Rot(X, -135)$$

☐ *W: the position of the wire end, defined with respect to the base coordinate reference frame*

The origin of the wire frame W is defined to be at the end of the wire, with its

173

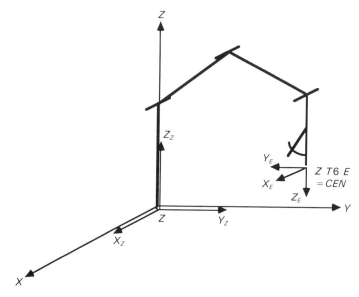

Figure 8.10 *CEN* – the end-effector centred over the tray of wires.

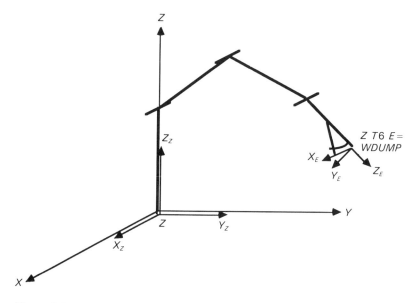

Figure 8.11 *WDUMP* – the end-effector over the bin of crimped wires.

Z-axis aligned with the wire's axis of symmetry. The X-axis is defined to be normal to the tray on which the wires lie, directed vertically upwards. The Y-axis makes up a right-hand system. Since we are assuming that the wires are lying flat on the tray, both the X- and Y-axes lie in the plane of the tray. Furthermore, we will assume that the tray lies in the X–Y plane of the base reference frame. Thus:

$$W = Trans(x, y, 0)Rot(z, \theta)Rot(y, -90)$$

It is the responsibility of the vision system to analyse the image of the wires and to generate the components of this frame automatically, specifically by computing x, y, and θ. W is illustrated in Figure 8.12.

☐ *WG: the position of the end-effector holding the wire, defined with respect to the wire end*

The origin of the wire gripper frame WG is defined to be located a short distance from the origin of W, on the wire's axis of symmetry. The Z-axis is defined to be normal to the plane of the tray, directed downwards. The Y-axis is defined to be normal to the axis of symmetry of the wire, in the plane of the tray. The Y-axis makes up a right-hand system. WG is illustrated in Figure 8.13.

It is important to note that we define the WG frame in this manner since this

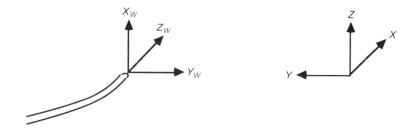

Figure 8.12 *W* – the position of the wire-end.

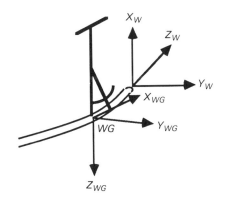

Figure 8.13 *WG* – the wire grasp position.

175

is how the end-effector E will be oriented when grasping the wire, i.e. with the Z-axis pointing vertically downwards and the Y-axis at right-angles to the wire.

As with W, the vision system must return a homogeneous transformation defining this frame; we cannot assume that WG will be a fixed offset from W since we are assuming that the curvature of the wire near the end will vary from wire to wire.

☐ *WA: the position of the end-effector approaching the grasp position, defined with respect to the wire-grasp position*
This is defined to be a position directly above the wire grasp point. As such, it simply involves a translation in the negative direction of the Z-axis of the WG frame. Since it is wished to approach the wire along a known path, many approach positions are used in which the translation distances get successively smaller. This motion, then, approximates continuous path control. Thus:

$$WA = Trans(0, 0, -(z\_approach)),$$

where

$$z\_approach = z\_approach\_initial$$
$$z\_approach\_initial - delta$$
$$z\_approach\_initial - 2 * delta$$
$$\vdots$$
$$0$$

WA is illustrated in Figure 8.14.

☐ *WD: the position of the end-effector departing the grasp position (having grasped the wire), defined with respect to the original wire-grasp position*
In a similar manner to WA, WD is defined as a translation in the negative direction of the Z-axis of the WG frame, except that in this case the translation distance becomes successively greater. Hence:

$$WD = Trans(0, 0, -(z\_depart)),$$

where:

$$z\_depart = 0,$$
$$delta,$$
$$2 * delta,$$
$$\vdots$$
$$z\_depart\_final$$

☐ *CM: the position of the crimping machine, defined with respect to the base coordinate reference system*
The frame CM, representing the crimping machine, is defined to be embedded in

a corner of the machine, as shown in Figure 8.15. Thus:

$$CM = Trans(150, 300, 0)$$

Note that the coordinates of the origin of CM, $(150, 300, 0)$, are determined empirically.

☐ *C: the position of the crimp (ready to be attached), defined with respect to the crimping machine*

The origin of C, representing the crimp, is defined to be at the front of the crimp, of the radial axis; the Z-axis is defined to be coincident with the radial axis (directed in toward the crimp), the X-axis is defined to be directed vertically upward, and the Y-axis makes a right-hand system; see Figure 8.16. Thus:

$$C = Trans(40, 40, 65)Rot(Y, 90)Rot(Y, 180)$$

☐ *CA: the position of the wire end approaching the crimp, defined with respect to the crimp*

CA is a frame embedded in the end of the wire, in exactly the same manner as W, except that it is positioned in front of, i.e. approaching, the crimp. Thus, as shown in Figure 8.17, CA simply involves a translation of some approach distance in the negative direction of the Z-axis of C.

Since, in a similar manner to WA, we want to approach the crimp along a known path, many approach positions are used such that the translation distance gets successively smaller.

Thus:

$$CA = Trans(0, 0, -(z\_approach)),$$

where:

$$z\_approach = z\_approach\_initial$$
$$z\_approach\_initial - delta,$$
$$z\_approach\_initial - 2 * delta$$
$$\vdots$$
$$0$$

☐ *CC: the position of the wire end in contact with the crimp, defined with respect to the crimp*

Since the frames embedded in the end of the wire and the frame embedded in the crimp align when the wire is in contact with the crimp, this transform is simply the identity transform. Had either of these two frames been defined differently, CC would have been used to define the relationship between the end of the wire and the crimp, which would be, in effect, a series of rotations.

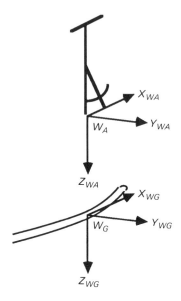

Figure 8.14 *WA* – the position of the end-effector approaching the grasp position.

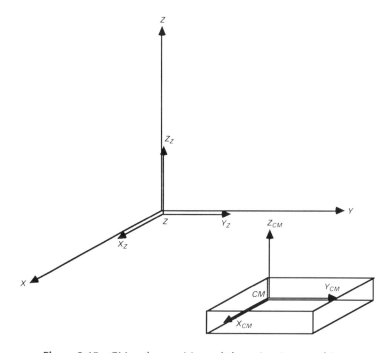

Figure 8.15 *CM* – the position of the crimping machine.

□   *CI: the position of the wire end inserted in the crimp, defined with respect to the crimp*

CI is a frame embedded in the end of the wire, in exactly the same manner as CA, except that it represents the wire inserted in the crimp. Thus, CI simply involves a translation of some insertion distance in the positive direction of the Z-axis of C.

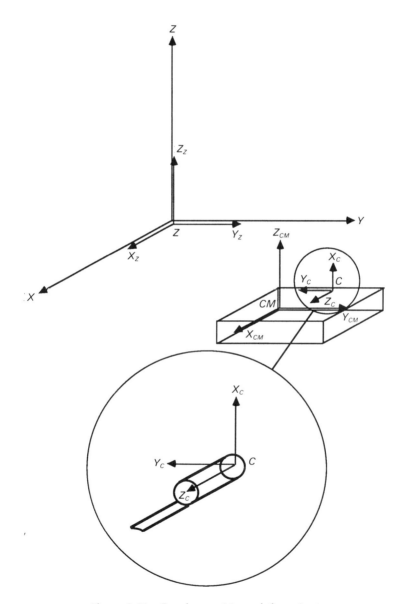

Figure 8.16   C – the position of the crimp.

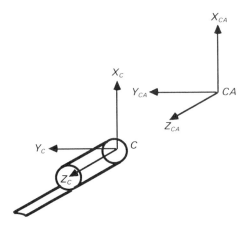

Figure 8.17 *CA* – the position of the wire end approaching the crimp.

In a similar manner to *CA*, many insertion positions are used such that the translation distances get successively greater. Thus:

$$CI = Trans(0, 0, z\_insert),$$

where:

$$z\_insert = 0,$$
$$delta,$$
$$2 * delta,$$
$$:$$
$$z\_insert\_final$$

☐ *CD: the position of the wire end departed from the crimping machine (the crimp having been attached), defined with respect to the crimp*

In a similar manner to *CA*, *CD* is defined as a translation in the negative direction of the Z-axis of the *C* frame, except that in this case the translation distance becomes successively greater. Hence:

$$CD = Trans(0, 0, -(z\_depart)),$$

where:

$$z\_depart = 0,$$
$$delta,$$
$$2 * delta,$$
$$:$$
$$z\_depart\_final$$

The task specification is now complete and it simply remains to program the robot by implementing these transform equations. We will accomplish this in terms of a simple robot programming language described in the next section.

8.4 A simple robot-programming language

We introduce here a very simple robot-programming language to illustrate how this manipulator task might be coded. The robot language, RCL, is not intended to be a fully fledged programming language. It is, rather, intended to facilitate the direct implementation of the manipulator task specifications, described in the preceding section, in a structured programming environment. As such, it is intended to facilitate the representation of coordinate frames and computations on frames, to provide an elegant and simple interface to robot vision facilities, and to provide structured programming control constructs. RCL is an interpretative language, implemented using a simple recursive descent algorithm. The philosophy behind the specification of the language syntax is that an RCL program should be almost identical in appearance to the task specification. Thus, both arithmetic and frame/transform expressions are allowed; a built-in frame data-type is provided and several predefined functions are provided for the specification of translations and rotations. The robot vision interface is facilitated by providing two built-in functions which return, among other things, frames defining the position and orientation of the required objects. A complete RCL program comprises two parts: a frame variable definition part and a series of statements. These statements may be either arithmetic expression statements, frame expression statements, built-in functional primitives, or structures programming control construct statements. Since the language components divide naturally into these five distinct sections, each of these topics will be described and discussed in turn.

☐ *Data-types and variable declarations*

There are only two data-types in RCL: an integer type and a predefined frames type. Variables of integer type are declared implicitly when the variable identifier is used in the program; there is no need (indeed, no facility exists) to declare integer variables explicitly in the program. However, variables of the frame type must be explicitly declared at the beginning of the program. Frame variables are functionally important and this is recognized by the requirement to define them explicitly. Frame variables are declared in the frame declaration part, introduced by the keyword FRAME, and by listing all the required frame variables. Since frame variables have such an important and central function in the program, they are distinguished by a leading character ^ i.e. all frame variables begin with the character ^.

☐ *Functional primitives*

Several built-in functional primitives have been incorporated in RCL. These functions are broadly concerned with the three categories of system initialization, robot motion, and visual sensing. The system initialization primitives include the functions **LOAD_ROB** which loads the robot parameters from file allowing RCL to control two different robots, and **LOAD_CAM** which loads the twelve coefficients of the camera model (to be discussed in Section 8.6) from file. The robot motion primitives include the functions GRASP, RELEASE, HOME, DELAY, and MOVE. The GRASP and RELEASE functions simply cause the end-effector gripper to close and open fully; the HOME function causes the robot manipulator to return to a predefined home position; and the DELAY function causes the robot program to be suspended for a specified period of time. The MOVE function accepts the one parameter, a frame expression, and causes the robot manipulator to move to a particular position and orientation as specified by the *T*6 frame definition given by the frame expression parameter. Thus, in typical situations, the *T*6 frame is assigned the value of transform/frame equation (as discussed in the preceding section on task specification) and the appropriate manipulator movement is effected by passing this *T*6 variable to the MOVE function.

The visual sensing primitive of interest here is the function WIRE which provides the interface to the robot vision sub-system, specifically to determine the position and orientation of a suitable wire for grasping, based on the heuristic grey-scale image analysis techniques detailed in Section 8.5. It returns two frame variables corresponding to the frames *W* and *WG* of the wire-crimping task discussed above.

□   *Arithmetic expression statements*

This type of statement simply provides the facility to evaluate integer expressions, involving any or all of the standard multiplication, division, addition, and division operators ($*, /, +$, and $-$, respectively) and to assign the value of this expression to an integer variable. This expression may be parenthesized and the normal precedence relations apply. The expression operands may be either integer variables or integer constant values.

□   *Frame expression statements*

The frame expression statement type is a central feature of RCL. It allows frame variables and frame functions to be combined by homogeneous transformation matrix multiplication, represented in RCL by the infix operator *, and the resultant value to be assigned to a frame variable. Additionally, frame expressions can be used directly as parameters in the MOVE function. The syntax of the frame statement, expressed in Backus–Naur form, is as follows:

```
<frame_statement>  ::= <frame_variable>:= <frame_expression>
<frame_expression> ::= <frame_entity>      {* <frame_entity>}
<frame_entity>     ::= <frame_variable>  | <frame_function>
<frame_function>   ::= <inv_function>    |
                       <rotx_function>   |
                       <roty_function>   |
                       <rotz_function>   |
                       <rpy_function>    |
                       <trans_function>  |
```

Thus, the frame expression allows the combination of a frame variable and/or any of the six in-built frame functions. These functions, INV, ROTX, ROTY, ROTZ, RPY and TRANS, implement transforms corresponding to a homogeneous transformation inversion, rotation about the x-, y-, and z-axes, manipulator orientation specification using the standard roll, pitch and yaw convention, and translation, respectively.

The INV function takes one parameter, a frame expression, and returns frame value equivalent to the inverse of the frame parameter value.

The ROTX, ROTY, and ROTZ functions take one parameter, an integer expression representing the values of the rotation in degrees, and return frame value equivalent to the homogeneous transformation corresponding to this rotation.

The RPY function takes three parameters, all integer expressions, representing the values of the roll, pitch and yaw rotations. Again, it returns frame value equivalent to the homogeneous transformation corresponding to the combination of these rotations.

The TRANS function takes three parameters, again all integer expressions, representing the x-, y-, and z-coordinates to the translation vector. It returns a frame value equivalent to the homogeneous transformation corresponding to this translation.

To illustrate the use of the frame expression, consider the first move in the wire-crimping task. This is represented by a move corresponding to the frame *T6*, given by the expression:

$$T6 = Z^{-1} * OOV * E^{-1}$$

where:

$$Z = \text{identity transform}$$
$$OOV = Trans(150, 300, 150)Rot(x, -180)$$
$$E = Trans(0, -15, 209)$$

Assuming the frames ^T6, ^Z, ^OOV, and ^E have been declared, this is written in RCL as:

```
^Z   := TRANS(0,0,0);
^OOV := TRANS(150,300,150)*ROTX(-180);
^E   := TRANS(0,-15,209);
^T6  := INV(^Z) * OOV * INV(^E);
```

and a move to this position is effected by the statement:

```
MOVE(^T6);
```

☐   *Structured programming control constructs*

The structured programming control constructs include a REPEAT-UNTIL statement, an IF-THEN-ELSE-ENDIF statement, a FOR statement, and a

WHILE statement. These statements adhere to the normal functionality of such structured control constructs.

Since the syntax and semantics of the RCL language are based on the task specification methodology described in detail in the preceding section, the implementation of the wire-crimping task becomes a very simple translation process. This was illustrated in the preceding section by the implementation of the first move of the task. The remaining moves are equally amenable to translation and understanding and the final wire-crimping program follows:

☐   *An RCL implementation of the wire-crimping task*

```
/ ****************************************************** /
/ *                                                      *
/ *   RCL Wire Crimping Program For 6R/600 Manipulator  */
/ *                                                      *
/ ****************************************************** /

/* Frame Declarations */

FRAME ^wire,
      ^wiregrasp,
      ^wireapproach,
      ^wiredepart,
      ^crimp,
      ^crimpapproach,
      ^crimpdepart,
      ^crimpcontact,
      ^crimpinsert,
      ^crimpmachine,
      ^wiredump,
      ^centre,
      ^outofview,
      ^Z,
      ^T6,
      ^effector;

/* the position of the manipulator is coincident */

/* with the base coordinate reference frame */

^Z := TRANS(0,0,0);

/* the end-effector is at the tip of the */
/* wire gripper; a position defined with */
/* respect to the end of the manipulator */

ey := -15;
ez := 195;
^effector := TRANS(0,ey,ez);
```

184

```
/* the position of the end-effector */
/* out of the field-of-view of the camera */

oovx := 150;
oovy := 300;
oovz := 150;
^outofview := TRANS(oovx,oovy,oovz) * RPY(0,0,-180);

/* the position of the end-effector over */
/* the bin of crimped wires             */

wdumpx := 0;
wdumpy := 550;
wdumpz := 160;
^wiredump := TRANS(wdumpx,wdumpy,wdumpz) *
             RPY(0,0,-135);

/* the position of the end-effector */
/* centred over the tray of wires */

centrex := 0;
centrey := 360;
centrez := 150;
^centre := TRANS(centrex,centrey,centrez) *
           RPY(0,0,-180);

/* the position of the crimping machine */

cmx := 150;
cmy := 300;
cmz := 0;
^crimpmachine := TRANS(cmx,cmy,cmz);

/* the position of the crimp, ready to be */
/* attached; as position defined with */
/* respect to the crimping machine */

cx := 55;
cy := 55;
cz := 85;
^crimp := TRANS(cx,cy,cz) * ROTY(90) * ROTZ(180);

/* the position of the wire-end in contact with */
/* the crimp */

^crimpcontact := TRANS(0,0,0);

/* the position of the wire-end inserted in the crimp */
```

```
insertionlength := 5;
^crimpinsert := TRANS(0,0,insertionlength);

/* load the robot model of the Smart Arms */
/* 6R/600 manipulator from file */

LOAD_ROB;

/* load the components of the camera model from file */

LOAD_CAM;

/* incremental distances for point-to-point */
/* approximation to continuous path movement */

delta := 3;

/* time delay between gross manipulator */
/* point-to-point movements */

lag := 20;

REPEAT

  /* move out of the field-of-view of the camera */

  ^T6 := INV(^Z) * ^outofview * INV(^effector);
  MOVE(^T6);
  DELAY(lag);

  /* determine the position and orientation of the */
  /* wire-end and wire grasping point using vision */

  WIRE(^wire,^wiregrasp);

  /* if not error in the robot vision routine */
  /* proceed with the task */

  IF errcode = 0
    THEN

      /* move to a position above the centre of the tray*/

      ^T6 := INV(^Z) * ^centre * INV(^effector);
      MOVE(^T6);
      DELAY(lag);
      RELEASE;
```

```
/* when grasping, the end-effector is defined */
/* to be between the jaws of the gripper */

ey := 5;
^effector := TRANS(0,ey,ez);

/* move to an approach point above the grasp point */

approachdistance := 30;
^wireapproach := TRANS(0,0,-approachdistance);
^T6 := INV(^Z) * ^wire * ^wiregrasp * ^wireapproach
 * INV (^effector);
MOVE(^T6);
DELAY(lag);

/* move to the grasp point through */
/* successive approach points */

approachdistance := approachdistance - delta;

REPEAT
 ^wireapproach := TRANS(0,0,-approachdistance);
 ^T6 := INV(^Z) * ^wire * ^wiregrasp*
  ^wireapproach * INV(^effector);
 MOVE(^T6);
 approachdistance := approachdistance - delta;

UNTIL approachdistance <= 0;

/* move to the final grasp point and grasp the wire */

^T6 := INV(^Z) * ^wire * ^wiregrasp * INV(^effector);
MOVE(^T6);
GRASP;

/* move to the depart position through */
/* successive depart points */

departdistance := delta;

REPEAT
 ^wiredepart := TRANS(0,0,-departdistance);
 ^T6 := INV(^Z) * ^wire * ^wiregrasp * ^wiredepart
  * INV(^effector);
 MOVE(^T6);
 departdistance := departdistance + delta;
UNTIL departdistance > 30;
```

```
approachdistance := 40;

/* the end-effector is defined to be at the */
/* inside of the upper jaw of the gripper */
/* now that the wire has been grasped */

ey := -15;
^effector := TRANS(0,ey,ez);

^crimpapproach := TRANS(0,0,-approachdistance);
/* move to an approach position */
/* in front of the crimp */

^T6 := INV(^Z) * ^crimpmachine * ^crimp *
 ^crimpapproach * ^wiregrasp * INV(^effector);
MOVE(^T6);
DELAY(lag);

/* bring the wire into contact with the crimp */
/* by moving through successive approach points */

approachdistance := approachdistance - delta;

REPEAT
 ^crimpapproach := TRANS(0,0,-approachdistance);
 ^T6 := INV(^Z) * ^crimpmachine * ^crimp *
  ^crimpapproach * ^wiregrasp * INV(^effector);
 MOVE(^T6);
approachdistance := approachdistance - delta;
UNTIL approachdistance <= 0;

/* final contact position */

^T6 := INV(^Z) * ^crimpmachine * ^crimp *
 ^crimpcontact * ^wiregrasp * INV(^effector);
MOVE (^T6);

/* insert wire in crimp */

^T6 := INV(^Z) * ^crimpmachine * ^crimp *
 ^crimpinsert * ^wiregrasp * INV(^effector);
MOVE(^T6);

/* actuate the crimping machine */
/** this is a virtual action **/

DELAY(lag);
```

```
/* withdraw with the crimped wire */
/* through successive depart positions */

departdistance := delta;

REPEAT
 ^crimpdepart := TRANS(0,0,-departdistance);
 ^T6 := INV(^Z) * ^crimpmachine * ^crimp *
  ^crimpdepart * ^wiregrasp * INV(^effector);
 MOVE(^T6);
 departdistance := departdistance + delta;
UNTIL departdistance > 35;

/* move to a position above the collection bin */

^T6 := INV(^Z) * ^wiredump * INV(^effector);
MOVE(^T6);
DELAY(lag);

RELEASE;

/* return to the position above the */
/* centre of the tray */

^T6 := INV(^Z) * ^centre * INV(^effector);
MOVE(^T6);
DELAY)lag);

ENDIF;

/* this is repeated until there are no more wires */
/* to be crimped; WIRE returns error code 20 */

UNTIL errcode = 20;
```

8.5 Two vision algorithms for identifying ends of wires

8.5.1 A binary vision algorithm

The main problem in this application is to identify the position and orientation of both a wire end and of a suitable grasp point to allow the robot manipulator to pick up the wire and insert it in a crimp. If we assume that the wires are well-scattered and lie no more than one or two deep, then all the requisite information may be gleaned from the silhouette of the wire and, hence, binary vision techniques can be used. In order to facilitate simple image analysis, we threshold the image and thin the resultant segmented binary image.

The original image is acquired at the conventional 512×512 pixel resolution with eight-bit grey-scale resolution (see Figure 8.18). To ensure fast processing and analysis, we first reduce the resolution to 128×128 pixels (see Figure 8.19) resulting in a reduction of the complexity of subsequent operations by a factor of sixteen. This reduction is important as the computational complexity of thinning operations is significant. There are essentially two ways in which this reduced resolution image may be generated: by sub-sampling the original image every fourth column and every fourth line or by evaluating the average of pixel values in a 4×4 window. As

Figure 8.18 512×512 image.

Figure 8.19 128×128 image.

we saw in Chapter 4, it is desirable to reduce the image noise and, since this can be accomplished by local averaging, the reduced resolution image in this implementation is generated by evaluating the local average of a 4×4 (non-overlapping) region in the 512×512 image. This also minimizes the degradation in image quality (referred to as *aliasing*) which would result from sub-sampling.

The image is then segmented by thresholding in the manner discussed in Chapter 4; the threshold value is automatically selected using the approach associated with the Marr–Hildreth edge detector (see Section 4.1.9). Figure 8.20 shows the binary image generated by thresholding the original grey-scale image at the automatically determined threshold.

Once the binary image has been generated, the next step is to model the wires in some simple manner. The skeleton is a suitable representation of electrical wires, objects which display obvious axial symmetry. In this instance, we use the thinning technique described in Section 4.2.3; Figure 8.21 illustrates the application of this thinning algorithm to the binary image shown in Figure 8.20.

Having processed the image, we now proceed to its analysis. There are essentially two features that need to be extracted from the image:

(a) the position of a point at which the robot end-effector should grasp the wire and the orientation of this point on that wire;

(b) the position and orientation of the wire end in relation to the point at which the wire is to be grasped.

The orientations are required because unless the wire is gripped at right-angles to the tangent at the grasp point, the wire will rotate in compliance with the finger grasping force. The orientation of the endpoint is important when inserting the wire in the crimping-press as the wire is introduced along a path coincident with the tangent to the wire at the endpoint. Based on the skeleton model of the wires, a wire

Figure 8.20 Binary image.

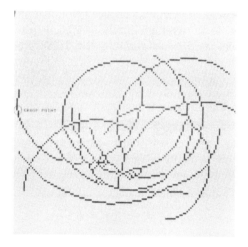

Figure 8.21 Thinned image.

segment may be defined as a subsection of a wire bounded at each end by either a wire-crossing or by an arc-end (wire segment end). Thus, a wire segment with two valid endpoints, at least one of which is an arc-end, and with a length greater than some predefined system tolerance, contains a feasible grasp point. This is a point some suitable fixed distance (15 mm) from the wire end.

Once the positions of both the grasp-point and the endpoint are known, the orientations or tangential angles of these two points are estimated. The tangent to the wire at the grasp-point is assumed to be parallel to the line joining two skeletal points equally displaced by two pixels on either side of the grasp-point. The tangent to the wire end is assumed to be parallel to a line joining the endpoint and a skeletal point three pixels from the end. Both of these tangential angles are estimated using the world coordinates corresponding to these pixel positions; these world coordinates are obtained using the camera model and inverse perspective transformation to be described in Section 8.6.

A typical selected grasp-point is shown in the thinned image (Figure 8.21) of the original image of a tray of wires (Figure 8.20).

8.5.2 A grey-scale vision algorithm

If the organization of the wires becomes more complex than assumed in the preceding section, with many layers of wires occluding both themselves and the background, the required information can no longer be extracted with binary imaging techniques. The grey-scale vision system described in this section addresses these issues and facilitates analysis of poor contrast images. It is organized as two levels, comprising a peripheral level and a supervisory level. All shape identification and analysis is based on boundary descriptors built dynamically by the peripheral level. The supervisory level is responsible for overall scheduling of activity, shape description, and shape matching. The use of an area-of-interest operator facilitates efficient image analysis by confining attention to specific high-interest sub-areas in the image. Thus, the algorithm described here uses three key ideas: dynamic boundary following (see Chapter 5); planning based on reduced resolution images, and a two-level organization based on peripheral and supervisory hierarchical architecture. These three ideas facilitate efficient analysis and compensate for the additional computational complexity of grey-scale techniques. The system is based on 256×256 pixel resolution images; the reduced resolution image is generated by local averaging in every 2×2 non-overlapping region in the acquired 512×512 image. The choice of resolution was based on a consideration of the smallest objects that need to be resolved and the minimum resolution required to represent these objects.

□   *The peripheral level*

The peripheral level corresponds to conventional low-level visual processing, specifically edge detection and the generation of edge and grey-scale information at several resolutions, and segmentation using boundary detection. The Prewitt gradient-based edge operator described in Chapter 5 is used as it provides reasonable edges with minimal computational overhead, especially in comparison to other edge operators. The edge detector operates on both 256×256 and 64×64 resolution images. High-resolution edge detection is used for image segmentation and low-resolution edge detection is used by an area-of-interest operator.

The ability of any edge detector to segment an image depends on the size of the objects in the image with respect to the spatial resolution of the imaging system. The system must be capable of explicitly representing the features (edges) that define the objects, in this case electrical wires. When dealing with long cylinder-like objects, the constraining object dimension is the cylinder diameter. At least three pixels are required to represent the wire (across the diameter) unambiguously: one for each edge and for the wire body. Using wires of diameter 1.0 mm imposes a minimum spatial resolution of 2 pixels/mm or a resolution of 256×256 for a field of view of 128×128 mm. Using a spatial resolution of 1 pixel/mm will tend to smear the object (given that we are reducing the resolution by local averaging and not by sub-sampling). Edge detection tests at this resolution showed that such smearing does not adversely affect the boundary/feature extraction performance if the wire is isolated (i.e. the background is clearly visible) but in regions of high occlusion where there are many wires in close proximity to the edge or boundary, quality does degrade significantly. Tests using a spatial resolution of 0.5 pixels/mm indicated that a detector's ability to segment the image reliably is severely impaired in most situations.

There are several approaches which may be taken to boundary building; this system uses a dynamic contour following algorithm and is the same one described in detail in Chapter 5. As the algorithm traces around the boundary, it builds a boundary chain code (BCC) representation of the contour; see Chapter 7. The complete BCC represents the segmented object boundary and is then passed to the supervisory level for analysis. Figure 8.22 illustrates the boundary following process at various points along the wire contours. The disadvantage of the contour following technique is that, because the algorithm operates exclusively on a local basis using no *a priori* information, the resulting segmentation may not always be reliable and the resulting contour may not correspond to the actual object boundary. In particular, the presence of shading and shadows tends to confuse the algorithm.

The boundary following algorithm, which effects the object's segmentation, is guided by processes at the supervisory level on two distinct bases. Firstly, the supervisory level defines a sub-section of the entire image to which the boundary following process is restricted: this sub-area is effectively a region within the image in which the vision system has high interest. Secondly, the supervisory level supplies the coordinates of a point at which the boundary following procedure should begin. This is typically on the boundary of the object to be segmented.

□ *The supervisory level*

The supervisory phase is concerned with overall scheduling of activity within the vision system and with the transformation and analysis of the boundaries passed to it by the peripheral level.

In guiding the peripheral level, its operation is confined to specific areas of high interest and it is supplied, by the supervisory level, with start coordinates for the boundary following algorithm. An interest operator was used which identifies

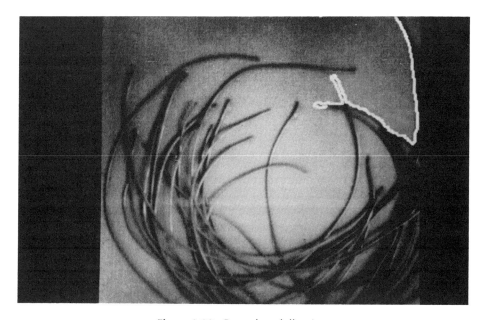

Figure 8.22 Boundary following.

a sequence of sub-areas within the image, ordered in descending levels of interest. This operator is based on the analysis of the edge activity in a reduced resolution image and allows the system to avoid cluttered areas with many (occluding) wires and concentrate on points of low scene population which are more likely to contain isolated and accessible wires. The area of interest is one-sixteenth of the size of the original image and is based on a 4×4 division of a 64×64 pixel resolution image.

The approach taken to the wire-crimping application is to extract a contour, representing the boundary of a group of wires, in a specific area of interest in the image and to analyse this boundary to determine whether or not it contains a boundary segment describing a wire end. What is required of the supervisory processes is to ascertain which part of the contour, if any, corresponds to the wire-end template and subsequently to determine the position and orientation of both the end of the wire and a suitable grasp-point. As we noted in Chapter 7, the use of BCC-based shape descriptors to identify shapes is not reliable and, instead, the wire end is identified by heuristic analysis, formulated as follows.

A boundary segment characterizing a wire end is defined to be a short segment (20 units in length) in which the boundary direction at one end differs by $180°$ from the direction at the other end, and in which the distance between the endpoints is less than or equal to 5 units. In addition, the wire end should be isolated, i.e. there should be no neighbouring wires which might foul the robot end-effector when grasping the wire. This condition is identified by checking that the edge magnitude in the low-resolution image in a direction normal to the boundary direction is less than the usual threshold used by the edge detection process. Figure 8.23 illustrates a wire end extracted from a boundary using this heuristic technique.

8.5.3 The vision/manipulator interface

Once the wire end shape has been identified, it is necessary to determine the components of the homogeneous transformations representing the two frames, W and WG, which denote the position and orientation of the wire end and the position and orientation of the grasp position with respect to the wire end. In the task specification discussed above, we defined the origin of the wire frame W to be at the end of the wire, with its Z-axis aligned with the wire's axis of symmetry, directed away from the end. The X-axis of W was defined to be normal to the tray on which the wires lie (and, hence, is normal to image plane) directed vertically upwards. The Y-axis makes up a right-hand system. The origin of the wire gripper frame WG was defined to be located on the Z-axis of the W frame, in the negative Z-direction, and located a short distance from the origin of W. The Z-axis of WG is defined to be normal to the plane of the tray, directed downwards. The Y-axis is defined to be normal to the axis symmetry of the wire, in the plane of the tray. The X-axis makes up a right-hand system. Refer again to Figures 8.11 and 8.12.

We can see that, to determine the components of the frame W, we only need to identify the position of the end of the wire and orientation of the axis of symmetry of the wire at its end, which gives us the direction of the Z-axis. The

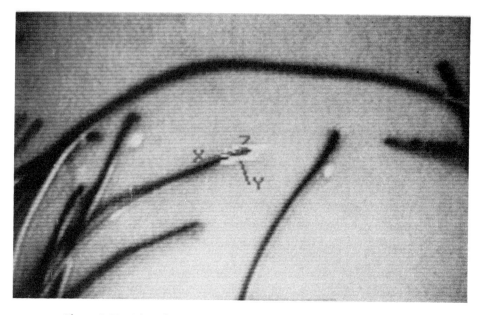

Figure 8.23 Identification of a wire-end (with *W* frame attached).

Y-axis is at right-angles to it and the *X*-axis has already been defined. Similarly, we only need to identify the orientation of the axis of symmetry of the wire at the grasp-point to determine *WG*; this gives us the direction of the *X*-axis; the *Y*-axis is at right-angles to it and the *Z*-axis has already been defined.

The main problem at this stage is that any orientation and position will be computed in the image frame of reference, i.e. using pixel coordinates. This is not satisfactory since the robot task specification is formulated in the real-world frame of reference. Obviously, the relationship between these two reference frames must be established. Once it is, we can transform the relevant image positions (the end of the wire and other points on its axis) to the real-world frame of reference and then compute the required orientations. This relationship is the subject to which we now turn our attention.

8.6 The camera model and the inverse perspective transformation

Generally speaking, when we use machine vision to identify the position and orientation of objects to be manipulated by a robot, we must do so with reference to real-world coordinates, i.e. in the real-world frame of reference. However, all the techniques we have dealt with in preceding chapters have been confined to the image frame of reference; we now need to establish the relationship between this image coordinate reference frame and the real-world coordinate reference frame.

For any given optical configuration, there are two aspects to the relationship: the *camera model*, which maps a three-dimensional world point to its corresponding two-dimensional image point, and the *inverse perspective transformation*, which is used to identify the three-dimensional world point(s) corresponding to a particular two-dimensional image point. Since the imaging process is a projection (from a three-dimensional world to a two-dimensional image), the inverse process, i.e. the inverse perspective transformation, cannot uniquely determine a single world point for a given image point; the inverse perspective tranformation thus maps a two-dimensional image point into a line (an infinite set of points) in the three-dimensional world. However, it does so in a useful and well-constrained manner.

For the following, we will assume that the camera model (and, hence, the inverse perspective transformation) is linear; this treatment closely follows that of Ballard and Brown (1982). Details of non-linear models can be found in the references to camera models in the bibliography at the end of the chapter.

8.6.1 The camera model

Let the image points in question be given by the coordinates

$$\begin{bmatrix} U \\ V \end{bmatrix}$$

which, in homogeneous coordinates, is written

$$\begin{bmatrix} u \\ v \\ t \end{bmatrix}.$$

Thus:

$$U = \frac{u}{t}$$

and:

$$V = \frac{v}{t}$$

Let the desired camera model, a transformation which maps the three-dimensional world point to the corresponding two-dimensional image point, be C. Thus:

$$C \begin{bmatrix} x \\ y \\ z \\ 1 \end{bmatrix} = \begin{bmatrix} u \\ v \\ t \end{bmatrix}$$

Hence C must be a 3×4 (homogeneous) transformation:

$$C = \begin{bmatrix} C_{11} & C_{12} & C_{13} & C_{14} \\ C_{21} & C_{22} & C_{23} & C_{24} \\ C_{31} & C_{32} & C_{33} & C_{34} \end{bmatrix}$$

and:

$$\begin{bmatrix} C_{11} & C_{12} & C_{13} & C_{14} \\ C_{21} & C_{22} & C_{23} & C_{24} \\ C_{31} & C_{32} & C_{33} & C_{34} \end{bmatrix} \begin{bmatrix} x \\ y \\ z \\ 1 \end{bmatrix} = \begin{bmatrix} u \\ v \\ t \end{bmatrix}$$

Expanding this matrix equation, we get:

$$C_{11}x + C_{12}y + C_{13}z + C_{14} = u \tag{1}$$

$$C_{21}x + C_{22}y + C_{23}z + C_{24} = v \tag{2}$$

$$C_{31}x + C_{32}y + C_{33}z + C_{34} = t \tag{3}$$

but:

$$u = Ut$$
$$v = Vt$$

so:

$$u - Ut = 0 \tag{4}$$

$$v - Vt = 0 \tag{5}$$

Substituting (1) and (3) for u and t, respectively, in (4) and substituting (2) and (3) for v and t, respectively, in (5):

$$C_{11}x + C_{12}y + C_{13}z + C_{14} - UC_{31}x - UC_{32}y - UC_{33}z - UC_{34} = 0 \tag{6}$$

$$C_{21}x + C_{22}y + C_{23}z + C_{24} - VC_{31}x - VC_{32}y - VC_{33}z - VC_{34} = 0 \tag{7}$$

Remember that these two equations arose from the association of a particular world point

$$\begin{bmatrix} x \\ y \\ z \\ 1 \end{bmatrix}$$

with a particular and corresponding image point

$$\begin{bmatrix} u \\ v \\ t \end{bmatrix}.$$

If we establish this association (i.e. if we measure the values of x, y, z, U, and V), we will have two equations in which the only unknowns are the twelve camera model coefficients (which we require). Since a single observation gives rise to two equations, six observations will produce twelve simultaneous equations which we can solve for the required camera coefficients C_{ij}. Before we proceed, however, we need to note that the overall scaling of C is irrelevant due to the homogeneous formulation and, thus, the value of C_{34} may be set arbitrarily to 1 and we can rewrite (6) and (7), completing the equations so that terms for each coefficient of C are included, as follows:

$$C_{11}x + C_{12}y + C_{13}z + C_{14} + C_{21}0 + C_{22}0$$
$$+ C_{23}0 + C_{24}0 - UC_{31}x - UC_{32}y - UC_{33}z = U$$

$$C_{11}0 + C_{12}0 + C_{13}0 + C_{14}0 + C_{21}x + C_{22}y$$
$$+ C_{23}z + C_{24} - VC_{31}x - VC_{32}y - VC_{33}z = V$$

This reduces the number of unknowns to eleven. For six observations, we now have twelve equations and eleven unknowns: i.e. the system of equations is over-determined. Reformulating the twelve equations in matrix form, we can obtain a least-square-error solution to the system using the pseudo-inverse method which we described in Chapter 4.

Let

$$X = \begin{bmatrix}
x^1 & y^1 & z^1 & 1 & 0 & 0 & 0 & 0 & -U^1x^1 & -U^1y^1 & -U^1z^1 \\
0 & 0 & 0 & 0 & x^1 & y^1 & z^1 & 1 & -V^1x^1 & -V^1y^1 & -V^1z^1 \\
x^2 & y^2 & z^2 & 1 & 0 & 0 & 0 & 0 & -U^2x^2 & -U^2y^2 & -U^2z^2 \\
0 & 0 & 0 & 0 & x^2 & y^2 & z^2 & 1 & -V^2x^2 & -V^2y^2 & -V^2z^2 \\
x^3 & y^3 & z^3 & 1 & 0 & 0 & 0 & 0 & -U^3x^3 & -U^3y^3 & -U^3z^3 \\
0 & 0 & 0 & 0 & x^3 & y^3 & z^3 & 1 & -V^3x^3 & -V^3y^3 & -V^3z^3 \\
x^4 & y^4 & z^4 & 1 & 0 & 0 & 0 & 0 & -U^4x^4 & -U^4y^4 & -U^4z^4 \\
0 & 0 & 0 & 0 & x^4 & y^4 & z^4 & 1 & -V^4x^4 & -V^4y^4 & -V^4z^4 \\
x^5 & y^5 & z^5 & 1 & 0 & 0 & 0 & 0 & -U^5x^5 & -U^5y^5 & -U^5z^5 \\
0 & 0 & 0 & 0 & x^5 & y^5 & z^5 & 1 & -V^5x^5 & -V^5y^5 & -V^5z^5 \\
x^6 & y^6 & z^6 & 1 & 0 & 0 & 0 & 0 & -U^6x^6 & -U^6y^6 & -U^6z^6 \\
0 & 0 & 0 & 0 & x^6 & y^6 & z^6 & 1 & -V^6x^6 & -V^6y^6 & -V^6z^6
\end{bmatrix}$$

$$c = \begin{bmatrix}
C_{11} \\ C_{12} \\ C_{13} \\ C_{14} \\ C_{21} \\ C_{22} \\ C_{23} \\ C_{24} \\ C_{31} \\ C_{32} \\ C_{33}
\end{bmatrix}$$

$$
y = \begin{bmatrix} U^1 \\ V^1 \\ U^2 \\ V^2 \\ U^3 \\ V^3 \\ U^4 \\ V^4 \\ U^5 \\ V^5 \\ U^6 \\ V^6 \end{bmatrix}
$$

where the trailing superscript denotes the observation number.
Then:

$$
\begin{aligned}
c &= (X^TX)^{-1}X^Ty \\
&= X^\dagger y
\end{aligned}
$$

We assumed above that we make six observations to establish the relationship between six sets of image coordinates and six sets of real-world coordinates.[*] This is, in fact, the central issue in the derivation of the camera model, that is, the identification of a set of corresponding *control points*. There are several approaches. For example, we could present the imaging system with a calibration grid, empirically measure the positions of the grid intersections, and identify the corresponding points in the image, either inactively or automatically. The empirical measurement of these real-world coordinates will be prone to error and this error will be manifested in the resultant camera model. It is better practice to get the robot itself to calibrate the system by fitting it with an end-effector with an accurately located calibration mark (e.g. a cross-hairs or a surveyor's mark) and by programming it to place the mark at a variety of positions in the field of view of the camera system. The main benefit of this approach is that the two components of the manipulation environment, the robot and the vision system, both of which are reasoning about coordinates in the three-dimensional world, are effectively coupled and, if the vision system 'sees' something at a particular location, that is where the robot manipulator will go.

8.6.2 *The inverse perspective transformation*

Once the camera model *C* has been determined, we are now in a position to determine an expression for the coordinates of a point in the real world in terms of the coordinates of its imaged position.

---

[*] In general, it is better to overdetermine the system of equations significantly by generating a larger set of observations than the minimal six.

Camera model and inverse perspective transformation

Recalling equations (1)–(5):

$$C_{11}x + C_{12}y + C_{13}z + C_{14} = u = Ut$$
$$C_{21}x + C_{22}y + C_{23}z + C_{24} = v = Vt$$
$$C_{31}x + C_{32}y + C_{33}z + C_{34} = t$$

Substituting the expression for t into the first two equations gives:

$$U(C_{31}x + C_{32}y + C_{33}z + C_{34}C_{11}x) = C_{11}x + C_{12}y + C_{13}z + C_{14}$$
$$V(C_{31}x + C_{32}y + C_{33}z + C_{34}C_{11}x) = C_{21}x + C_{22}y + C_{23}z + C_{24}$$

Hence:

$$(C_{11} - UC_{31})x + (C_{12} - UC_{32})y + (C_{13} - UC_{33})z + (C_{14} - UC_{34}) = 0$$
$$(C_{21} - VC_{31})x + (C_{22} - VC_{32})y + (C_{23} - VC_{33})z + (C_{24} - VC_{34}) = 0$$

Letting:

$$a_1 = C_{11} - UC_{31}$$
$$b_1 = C_{12} - UC_{32}$$
$$c_1 = C_{13} - UC_{33}$$
$$d_1 = C_{14} - UC_{34}$$

and:

$$a_2 = C_{21} - VC_{31}$$
$$b_2 = C_{22} - VC_{32}$$
$$c_2 = C_{23} - VC_{33}$$
$$d_2 = C_{24} \quad VC_{34}$$

we have:

$$a_1x + b_1y + c_1z + d_1 = 0$$
$$a_2x + b_2y + c_2z + d_2 = 0$$

These two equations are, in effect, equations of two planes; the intersection of these planes determines a line comprising the set of real-world points which project onto the image point

$$\begin{bmatrix} U \\ V \end{bmatrix}.$$

Solving these plane equations simultaneously (in terms of z):

$$x = \frac{z(b_1c_2 - b_2c_1) + (b_1d_2 - b_2d_1)}{(a_1b_2 - a_2b_1)}$$

$$y = \frac{z(a_2c_1 - a_1c_2) + (a_2d_1 - a_1d_2)}{(a_1b_2 - a_2b_1)}$$

Thus, for any given z_0, U, and V, we may determine the corresponding x_0 and y_0, i.e the real-world coordinates.

8.6.3 Recovery of the third dimension

The camera model and the inverse perspective transformation which we have just discussed allow us to compute the x- and y- real-world coordinates corresponding to a given position in the image. However, we must assume that the z-coordinate, i.e. the distance from the camera, is known. For the wire-crimping application in which the wires lie on a table at a given and constant height (i.e. at a given z_0), this is quite adequate. In general, however, we will *not* know the coordinate of the object in the third dimension and we must recover it somehow. As we have already noted, a significant part of computer vision is concerned with exactly this problem and three techniques for determining depth information will be discussed: one in the next section of this chapter and two in Chapter 9. The purpose of this section is to show how we can compute z_0 if we have a second image of the scene, taken from another viewpoint, and if we know the image coordinates of the point of interest (e.g. the wire end) in this image also.

In this instance, we have two camera models and, hence, two inverse perspective transformations. Instead of solving two plane equations simultaneously, we solve four plane equations. In particular, we have:

$$a_1 x + b_1 y + c_1 z + d_1 = 0$$
$$a_2 x + b_2 y + c_2 z + d_2 = 0$$
$$p_1 x + q_1 y + r_1 z + s_1 = 0$$
$$p_2 x + q_2 y + r_2 z + s_2 = 0$$

where

$$a_1 = C1_{11} - U1C1_{31} \qquad a_2 = C1_{21} - V1C1_{31}$$
$$b_1 = C1_{12} - U1C1_{32} \qquad b_2 = C1_{22} - V1C1_{32}$$
$$c_1 = C1_{13} - U1C1_{33} \qquad c_2 = C1_{23} - V1C1_{33}$$
$$d_1 = C1_{14} - U1C1_{34} \qquad d_2 = C1_{24} - V1C1_{34}$$
$$p_1 = C2_{11} - U2C2_{31} \qquad p_2 = C2_{21} - V2C2_{31}$$
$$q_1 = C2_{12} - U2C2_{32} \qquad q_2 = C2_{22} - V2C2_{32}$$
$$r_1 = C2_{13} - U2C2_{33} \qquad r_2 = C2_{23} - V2C2_{33}$$
$$s_1 = C2_{14} - U2C2_{34} \qquad s_2 = C2_{24} - V2C2_{34}$$

and $C1_{ij}$ and $C2_{ij}$ are the coefficients of the camera model for the first and second images respectively. Similarly, $U1$, $V1$ and $U2$, $V2$ are the coordinates of the point of interest in the first and second images respectively. Since we now have four equations and three unknowns, the system is overdetermined and we compute a least-square-error solution using the pseudo-inverse technique discussed in Chapter 4.

It should be noted that the key here is not so much the mathematics which allow us to compute x_0, y_0, and z_0 but, rather, the image analysis by which we identify the corresponding point of interest in the two images. It is this correspondence problem which lies at the heart of most of the difficulties in recovery of depth information. To complete the chapter, the next section describes a simple, popular, and useful technique for analysing images and computing depth information.

8.7 Three-dimensional vision using structured light

Active ranging using structured light is one of the most popular ranging techniques in industrial vision. The essential idea is to illuminate the object in such a way so that

(a) we know the position and direction of the source of illumination;
(b) the point being illuminated is easily identifiable (e.g. we illuminate a very small part of the surface of the object with a dot of light);
(c) we know the position of the sensor (camera) and can compute the direction to the illuminated part of the object surface.

Thus, we can draw two lines, one along the ray of illumination from the light source to the object surface and the other from the position of the sensed illumination on the image through the focal point to the object surface. The object surface is at the intersection of these two lines (see Figure 8.24) and to compute the three-dimensional position of this point on the surface of the object, we just have to compute the point of intersection of these two lines.

The basis of the approach is that it solves, in a simple but contrived way, the correspondence problem to which we alluded in the preceding section. The solution is not without problems, however. Since the approach will yield the range to only one small point on the object's surface, we either have to scan the surface with the dot of light, computing the range at each point, or illuminate more than one point

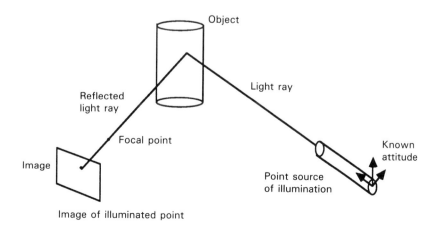

Figure 8.24 Active triangulation.

at the same time. The former approach is not normally employed, except in specialized laser-scanning applications, since one would have a significant overhead in image acquisition; the latter approach popularly utilizes stripes of light (and is hence referred to as *light striping*) or grids of light to illuminate the object. In these cases, the derivation of range involves the computation of the point of intersection of the plane of light and the line from an image point on the sensed line through the focal point (see Figures 8.25 and 8.26).

If we calibrate the vision system and determine the camera model, then, for any point in the image, we can derive the equation of a single line in the real world. To identify the coordinates of the single point which reflected light causing the imaged point, we need an additional constraint. One such constraint might be the knowledge that the real-world point lies on some plane (which is not coincident with the line of sight). For example, in Section 8.6 where we derived the inverse perspective transformation, we assumed that the point lay on the plane given by $z = z_0$. In the case of light striping, use the same idea and illuminate the object with a single plane of light and, if we know the equation of this plane, then the identification of the three-dimensional world point coordinates simply requires the computation of the intersection of the line of sight (given by the inverse perspective transformation) and this plane. In order to determine the equation of the light plane, one can locate several points on it, identify their three-dimensional coordinates and fit a plane through these points. One simple way of identifying points in the plane of light is to place blocks of different known heights on the work surface in the path of the light beam. Knowing the real z-coordinate, the real-world x- and y-coordinates of points on the resulting stripe are then computed by imaging the stripe and applying the inverse perspective transformation of the camera to the measured points.

Having identified a number (M, say) of points on the plane at several different heights, one can use these x, y, and z values to generate a set of simultaneous plane

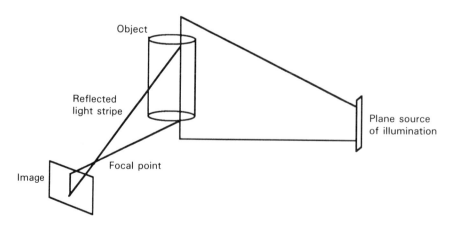

Figure 8.25 Light striping.

Three-dimensional object

Structured light
pattern

Object reflecting
light pattern

Imaged light pattern
(viewed from an
oblique angle)

Figure 8.26 'Structured light'.

equations:

$$a_1 x_i + a_2 y_i + a_3 z_i + a_4 = 0, \quad i = 1 \ldots M$$

and solve them using the pseudo-inverse method. Unfortunately, this equation has a degenerate solution in which all the coefficients are zero. To avoid this possibility, we can reformulate (1) (from Bolles *et al.*, 1981) by dividing across by a_3 and letting:

$$\frac{a_1}{a_3} = b_1$$

$$\frac{a_2}{a_3} = b_2$$

$$\frac{a_4}{a_3} = b_3$$

Thus:

$$b_1 x_i + b_2 y_i + z_i + b_3 = 0$$

and hence:

$$b_1 x_i + b_2 y_i + b_3 = z_i$$

A least-square-error solution to this set of equations, written in matrix form as:

$$
\begin{bmatrix}
x_1 & y_1 & 1 \\
x_2 & y_2 & 1 \\
x_3 & y_3 & 1 \\
\vdots & & \\
x_M & y_M & 1
\end{bmatrix}
*
\begin{bmatrix}
b_1 \\
b_2 \\
b_3
\end{bmatrix}
=
\begin{bmatrix}
-z_1 \\
-z_2 \\
-z_3 \\
\vdots \\
-z_M
\end{bmatrix}
\quad M > 3
$$

can now be generated using the pseudo-inverse method.

The only restriction in this case is that the plane of light cannot be normal to the Z-axis since an equation of this form cannot be used to represent such a plane (i.e. Z cannot be constant).

The equation of the plane of light is thus:

$$b_1 x_i + b_2 y_i + z_i + b_3 = 0$$

and the three-dimensional position of a point in an imaged light stripe can be found by solving the set of simultaneous equations given by the two plane equations

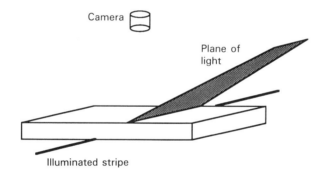

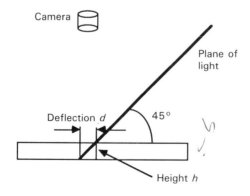

Figure 8.27 Height measurement using light stripes.

provided by the inverse perspective transformation:

$$x(c_{11} - uc_{31}) + y(c_{12} - uc_{32}) + z(c_{13} - uc_{33}) = uc_{34} - c_{14}$$
$$x(c_{21} - vc_{31}) + y(c_{22} - vc_{32}) + z(c_{23} - vc_{33}) = vc_{34} - c_{24}$$

and the light plane:

$$b_1 x + b_2 y + z = -b_3$$

The plane of light can be generated either using a laser scanner or it can be generated by projecting a collimated light source through a slit. The advantage of using a laser is that it can illuminate the object in the presence of ambient lighting, e.g. by using an infra-red laser and an infra-red sensitive sensor (CCD sensor), while the slit projection approach will typically require a somewhat darkened environment or an extremely bright light source. Furthermore, this approach suffers from a problem common to all so-called triangulation systems of this type: that only surface points which are visible from both illumination source and sensor can be used to yield range measurements. Hence, hidden parts in concavities will cause some problems.

As a final note, it is worth remarking that this structured light approach is quite general in the sense that it allows you to generate all three real-world coordinates for points on an imaged light stripe. If you are only interested in deriving the height of the object rather than its range, then you can adopt a simpler approach. Consider a plane of light which is incident to the work surface at an angle of $45°$ (see Figure 8.27). An object on the work surface in the path of the beam will cause the illuminated stripe to be deflected by an amount which is proportional to the height of the block. In fact, for the example shown, the deflection will be equivalent to the height of the block (in an image frame of reference). Thus, to measure the height you merely need to calibrate the system by computing the relationship between a deflection d and a height h in the real world (using a block of known height) and subsequently measure deflections.

Exercises

1. Describe the use of transform equations in robot task specification, illustrating your answer with at least one example.

2. What is meant by the camera model and the inverse perspective transformation? How do these transformations relate to the transform equations used in the robot task specification?

3. Cylindrical steel ingots, held in a clamp after they have been cut from a bar, require chamfering (i.e. trimming the edge of the cut) to minimize the possibility of jamming when they are introduced into a cast. This can be accomplished by a robot with a high-speed rotating

grinding wheel mounted on the end effector. Identify a sequence of end-effector movements which will effect this chamfering task and generate a complete task specification by:
  (i) identifying the appropriate coordinate frames for each distinct object/end-effector position;
  (ii) specifying the task transform equations; and
  (iii) solving the task transform equations to achieve an explicit sequence of movements for the end effector.

Each coordinate frame specified in (i) above should be explicitly defined and you should use figures where appropriate.

How would you exploit CAD (computer aided design) information regarding the clamp position and the ingot diameter?

4. In some industrial quality control tasks, the objects to be checked and assured are three-dimensional and all the visible surfaces must be viewed and inspected. In what circumstances would it be useful to deploy an articulated robot-mounted camera system rather than several distinct cameras?

Using homogeneous transformations and task transform equations to specify object position and orientation, describe with the aid of diagrams how one would configure a robot program to inspect all five visible faces of a cubic object using a camera mounted on the end effector of the robot.

References and further reading

Adams, R. 1983 'Welding apparatus with vision correction', *Robotics age*, Nov/Dec, pp. 43–6.

Adorni, G. and Di Manzo, M. 1980 *A Natural Language as a Means of Communications between Men and Robots*, Internal Report, Institute of Electrotechnics, University of Genoa, 1980.

Agin, G. 1979 *Real-time Control of a Robot with a Mobile Camera*, SRI International, Technical Report No. 179.

Agin, G.J. 1985 *Calibration and Use of a Light Stripe Range Sensor Mounted on the Hand of a Robot*, CMU-RI-TR-20, The Robotics Institute, Carnegie-Mellon University.

Ayache, N., Faverjon, B., Boissonnat, J.D. and Bollack, B. 1984 'Manipulation Automatique de Pieces Industrielles en Vrac Planaire', *Proceedings of the First Image Symposium, CESTA, Biarritz*, pp. 869–75.

Bogaert, M. and Ledoux, O. 1983 '3-D perception in industrial environment', *Proceedings of SPIE*, Vol. 449, pp. 373–80.

Bolles, R.C. 1981 *Three-Dimensional Locating of Industrial Parts*, SRI International, Technical Note No. 234.

Bolles, R.C., Kremers, J.H. and Cain, R.A. 1981 *A Simple Sensor to Gather 3-D Data*, SRI International, Technical Note No. 249.

Bonner, S. and Shin, K.G. 1982 'A comparative study of robot languages', *Computer*, Vol. 15, No. 12, pp. 82–96.

Brooks, R.A. 1983 'Planning collision-free motions for pick-and-place operations', *The International Journal of Robotics Research*, Vol. 2, No. 4, pp. 19–44.

Chiang, M.C., Tio, J.B.K. and Hall, E.L. 1983 'Robot vision using a projection method, *Proceedings of SPIE*, Vol. 449, pp. 74–81.

Drezner, Z. and Nof, S.Y. 1984 'On optimizing bin picking and insertion plans for assembly robots', *IIE Transactions*, Vol. 16, No. 3, pp. 262–70.

El-Hakim, S.F. 1985 'A photogrammetric vision system for robots', *Photogrammetric Engineering and Remote Sensing*, Vol. 51, No. 5, pp. 545–52.

Goldman, R. 1982 *Design of an Interactive Manipulator Programming Environment*, Department of Computer Science, Stanford University, Stanford, STAN-CS-82-955.

Grossman, D.D. 1977 *Programming of a Computer Controlled Industrial Manipulator by Guiding through the Motions*, IBM Research Report RC6393, IBM T.J. Watson Research Centre, Yorktown Heights, N.Y.

Guo, H-L., Yachida, M. and Tsuji, S. 1986 'Three dimensional measurement of many line-like objects', *Advanced Robotics*, Vol. 1, No. 2, pp. 117–30.

Hall, E.L., Tio, J.B.K., McPherson, C.A. and Sadjadi, F. 1982 'Measuring curved surfaces for robot vision', *Computer*, Vol. 15, No. 12, pp. 42–54.

Jarvis, R.A. 1983 'A perspective on range finding techniques for computer vision', *IEEE Transactions on Pattern Analysis and Machine Intelligence*, Vol. PAMI-5, No. 2, pp. 122–39.

Lavin, M.A. and Lieberman, L.I. 1982 'AML/V: An industrial machine vision programming system', *The International Journal of Robotics Research*, Vol. 1, No. 3, pp. 42–56.

Lozano-Perez, T. 1982 *Robot Programming*, MIT AI Memo No. 698.

Luh, J.Y.S. and Klaasen, J.A. 1983 'A real-time 3-D multi-camera vision system', *Proceedings of SPIE*, Vol. 449, pp. 400–8.

Luh, J.Y.S. and Klaasen, J.A. 1985 'A three-dimensional vision by off-shelf system with multi-cameras', *IEEE Transactions on Pattern Analysis and Machine Intelligence*, Vol. PAMI-7, No. 1, pp. 35–45.

Mujtaba, M. 1982 'Motion sequencing of manipulators', Ph.D. Thesis, Stanford University, Report No. STAN-CS-82-917.

Mujtaba, M. and Goldman, R. 1979 *The AL User's Manual*, STAN-CS-79-718, Stanford University.

Nagel, R.N. 1984 'Robots: Not yet smart enough', *IEEE Spectrum*, Vol. 20, No. 5, pp. 78–83.

Paul, R. 1979 'Robots, models, and automation', *Computer*, July, pp. 19–27.

Paul, R. 1981 *Robot Manipulators: Mathematics, Programming, and Control*, MIT Press, Cambridge, Massachusetts, 1981.

Summers, P.D. and Grossman, D.D. 1984 'XPROBE: An experimental system for programming robots by example', *The International Journal of Robotics Research*, Vol. 3, No. 1, pp. 25–39.

Taylor, R.H. 1983 *An Integrated Robot System Architecture*, IBM Research Report.

Taylor, R.H., Summers, P.D. and Meyer, J.M. 1982 'AML: A manufacturing language', *The International Journal of Robotics Research*, Vol. 1, No. 3, pp. 19–41.

Tsai, R.Y. 1987 'A versatile camera calibration technique for high-accuracy 3D machine vision metrology using off-the-shelf TV cameras and lenses', *IEEE Journal of Robotics and Automation*, Vol. RA-3, No. 4, pp. 323–44.

Vernon, D. 1985 'A hierarchically-organized robot vision system', *Proceedings of AI EUROPA*, Wiesbaden, West Germany.

Volz, R.A., Mudge, T.N. and Gal, D.A. 1983 *Using Ada as a Programming Language for Robot-Based Manufacturing Cells*, RSD-TR-15-83. Centre of Robotics and Integrated Manufacturing, Robot Systems Division, College of Engineering, University of Michigan.

Yachida, M., Tsuji, S. and Huang, X. 1982 'Wiresight – a computer vision system for 3-D measurement and recognition of flexible wire using cross stripe light', *Proceedings of the 6th International Conference on Pattern Recognition*, Vol. 1, pp. 220–2.

9

Introduction to image understanding

9.1 Representations and information processing: from images to object models

This book began by borrowing a phrase from David Marr and defining computer vision as the endeavour to 'say what is where in the world by looking' by the automatic processing and analysis of images by computer. We immediately distinguished between industrial machine vision and image understanding, identifying the former as the heavily engineered pragmatic application of a small sub-set of the broad spectrum of imaging techniques in quite restricted, and often two-dimensional, domains. Image understanding, on the other hand, addresses general three-dimensional environments where one lifts the restrictions on the possible organization of the visual domain. Thus, image understanding must take into consideration the considerable loss of information which arises when a three-dimensional world is imaged and represented by two-dimensional digital images. In particular, it must address the recovery of range or depth information. We noted that a considerable amount of effort is expended in accomplishing this. Again, approaches which are associated with image understanding endeavour to avoid intrusive sensing techniques, i.e. imaging systems which depend on the transmission of appropriate signals (infra-red, laser, or ultrasonic beams; or grids of structured light) to facilitate the process. Instead, a more passive approach is adopted, using whatever ambient information exists, in an *anthropomorphic* manner.

There is, however, more to image understanding than just the recovery of depth information. If we are going to be able to identify the structure of the environment, we need to do more than develop a three-dimensional range map since this is still an image and the information which we need is still *implicit*. We require an *explicit* representation of the structure of the world we are imaging. Hence, we still need the process of segmentation and object recognition that we dealt with in the preceding chapters. Our difficulty is that now the data we are dealing with is much more complex than before and the simplistic image segmentation, template matching or feature extraction and classification paradigms are wholly inadequate. To be able to proceed from raw two-dimensional images of the world to explicit three-dimensional structural representations, we must adopt a much more sophisticated stance and we must acknowledge that no single process or representation is going to be generally adequate. Thus, there is one central theme which runs through the current, and now conventional, approach to image understanding: that we require intermediate representations to bridge the gap between raw images and the abstracted structural model.

These representations should make different kinds of knowledge explicit and should expose various kinds of constraint upon subsequent interpretations of the scene. It is the progressive integration of these representations and their mutual constraint to facilitate an unambiguous interpretation of the scene that most characterizes the branch of vision known as image understanding. It is perhaps useful to note that most of the progress that has been made in the past few years has not, in fact, been in this area of representation integration, or *data fusion* as it is commonly known, but rather in the development of formal and well-founded computational models for the generation of these representations in the first place. As we shall see, this is no accident. Nevertheless, there remains a great deal of work to be done in the area of data fusion.

In summary then, we can characterize image understanding as a sequence of processes concerned with successively extracting visual information from one representation (beginning with digital images), organizing it, and making it explicit in the representation to be used by other processes. From this perspective, vision is computationally modular and sequential. What we must now proceed to look at are the possible organizations of visual processes, the representations, and the visual processes themselves. We will begin with the organization of visual processes, emphasizing one particular approach and giving an overview of the area; we will then proceed to the other two component topics.

9.2 Organization of visual processes

At present, it is not clear how information in one representation should influence the acquisition and generation of information in another representation. Some possibilities include the following three:

1. A bottom-up flow of data in which information is made explicit without recourse to *a priori* knowledge. Thus, we form our structural representation purely on the basis of the data implicit in the original images.
2. Heterarchical constraint propagation. This is similar to the bottom-up approach but we now have the additional constraint that cues, i.e. a given information representation, at any one level of the hierarchical organization of representations can mutually interact to delimit and reduce the possible forms of interpretation at that level and, hence, the generation of the

information representations at the next level of the hierarchy. Perhaps one of the simplest examples is the integration of depth values generated by two independent processes such as binocular stereo and parallax caused by a moving camera. This approach typifies much current thinking in image understanding.

3. A top-down, *model driven*, information flow whereby early vision is guided by firm expectations of what is to be seen. It should be noted that this model-based vision is quite different from the knowledge-based approach which was fashionable in artificial intelligence a decade ago, in which the effort was to design control processes that could utilize the appropriate knowledge at the appropriate time, with inadequate attention being paid to the representations used, the processes using them, and, indeed, the reasons for utilizing those representations.

We will restrict our attention in the remainder of this chapter to the first approach to image understanding. It should be noted that this emphasis is more by way of convenience than by way of making a statement about the relative importance of the three approaches. Model-based vision, for example, is currently a very popular paradigm and there is a wealth of interesting work being done in the area. The present enthusiasm for data fusion, too, in the computer vision community reflects the importance of the approach of heterarchical constraint propagation. Both these topics would require a volume each to do them justice. We choose the bottom-up approach here because it is often an essential component of the other two paradigms and it will serve to highlight the fundamental visual representations and processes without clouding the issue with additional considerations, however important they might be.

David Marr, at MIT, exerted a major influence on the development of this new computational approach to vision. Marr modelled the vision process as an information processing task in which the visual information undergoes different hierarchical transformations at and between levels, generating representations which successively make more three-dimensional features explicit. He indicated that there are three distinct levels at which the problem must be understood: a computational level, a representational and algorithmic level, and an implementation level. The computational level is concerned with the 'what' and 'why' of the problem: what is to be computed, why it is to be computed, and what is the best strategy for computing it? The representational and algorithmic levels address the 'how' of the problem: how is this theory to be implemented? This necessitates a representation for the input and the output. The third level, hardware implementation, addresses the problem of how to realize these representations and algorithms physically. Thus, this approach removes one from the image environment and addresses the more fundamental problems of the task, formulating a theory of computation and then putting this theory into effect by applying the available visual abilities.

The importance of a computational theory is stressed very strongly by Marr and he illustrates his case by pointing out that attempting to understand perception solely from the neurological standpoint is as fruitless as trying to understand bird flight from the study of feathers. One must first understand aerodynamics; only then does the structure of the feathers make sense. Marr's contribution was not simply confined to championing this new, and now popular, approach; he also detailed techniques for implementing these philosophies. His idea was, in essence, to generate successive representations of information, each representation being richer in the type of information it makes explicit. We shall now have a brief look at each of these representations.

9.3 *Visual representations*

9.3.1 *The raw primal sketch*

Beginning with a grey-level image, Marr proposed the generation of a *Raw Primal Sketch*, which consists of primitives of *edges, terminations, blobs*, and *bars* at different scales. We will explain each of these four terms shortly. Each primitive has certain associated properties: orientation, width, length, position, and strength. The computation of the raw primal sketch requires both the measurement of intensity gradients of different scale and the accurate measurement of location of these changes. This causes a problem, however, since no single measuring device can be optimal simultaneously at all scales. For example, a watchmaker will use a micrometer for very fine measuring work and calipers for coarse work, both of which are useless to a surveyor measuring up a building site. Thus, we need an edge detector which can operate at different scales and is well-localized in the frequency domain, that is, the spatial frequencies (the rate of variation of image intensity with distance) to which it is sensitive are confined to given ranges. Since edges are also localized in space (i.e. in the image), this means that the measuring device must also be spatially localized.

Obviously, the requirements of spatial localization and confinement in spatial frequency are at variance: devices for measuring variation over large distances must themselves be large. Marr and Hildreth proposed a compromise. They suggested that one should use smoothing filters to select information in the grey-level intensity image at different scales, but choose a type of smoothing that optimizes these two opposing demands (of spatial frequency and positional localization). The Gaussian distribution is the only appropriate smoothing distribution with these properties. Marr suggested that the raw primal sketch should be generated using the Marr–Hildreth theory of edge detection (which we discussed in Chapter 5), i.e. by convolving the image with Laplacian-of-Gaussian functions, each Gaussian having a different standard deviation (hence the facility for analysis at different scales). Points at which the resultant image go from positive to negative, i.e. zero-crossings, are isolated; see Figures 9.1–9.4. These points correspond to instances of sharp intensity change in the original image. Note that these images have been automatically post-processed to remove spurious noisy zero-crossings. This is

Figure 9.1 A grey-scale image.

accomplished by analysing various features of the contour points and comparing their values to statistics of these features collected from the entire image (see Vernon, 1988).

By analysing the coincidence of zero-crossings in particular positions at different scales, one can infer evidence of physical reality, i.e. of a real physical edge, and it is these spatially coincident and hence (hopefully) real physically meaningful zero-crossings that are then represented by the primitives of the raw primal sketch. We can now define each of the four primitives.

Edge primitives are, effectively, local line segment approximations of the zero-crossing contours (see Figure 9.5); curves comprise a sequence of edges, delimited at either end by the *termination* primitives (see Figure 9.6). Instances of local parallelism of these edges are represented by *bars* (see Figure 9.7), while blobs represent the zero-crossing contours which are not present, i.e. which have no spatial coincidence, in *all* of the zero-crossing images derived at the different scales, i.e. using different standard deviations for the Gaussian smoothing (see Figure 9.8).

9.3.2 The full primal sketch

As the information made explicit in the raw primal sketch is still local and spatially restricted, i.e. it does not convey any global information about shape in an explicit manner, we now wish to group these primitives so that the groups correspond to physically meaningful objects. In this sense, the grouping process is exactly what

(a)

(b)

Figure 9.2 Zero-crossings derived by convolving the image with a Laplacian of Gaussian filter in which the standard deviation of the Gaussian is 3.0 pixels: (a) all zero-crossings; (b) after removal of noisy zero-crossings.

216

(a)

(b)

Figure 9.3 Zero-crossings derived by convolving the image with a Laplacian of Gaussian filter in which the standard deviation of the Gaussian is 6.0 pixels: (a) all zero-crossings; (b) after removal of noisy zero-crossings.

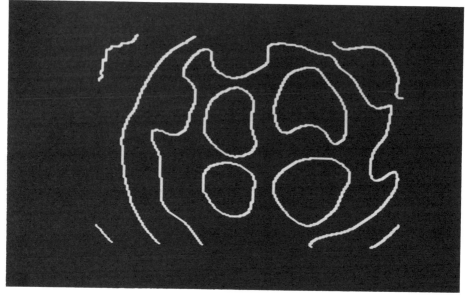

(a)

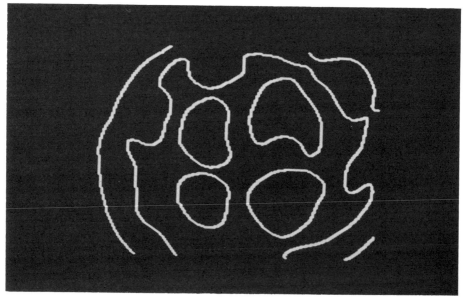

(b)

Figure 9.4 Zero-crossings derived by convolving the image with a Laplacian of Gaussian filter in which the standard deviation of the Gaussian is 9.0 pixels: (a) all zero-crossings; (b) after removal of noisy zero-crossings.

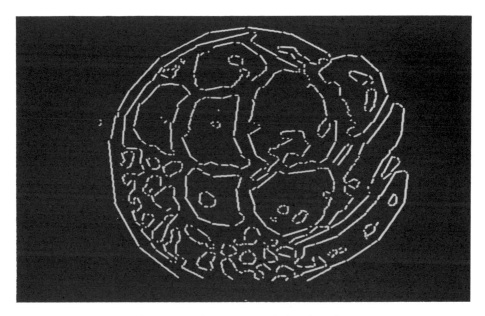

Figure 9.5 The raw primal sketch: edges.

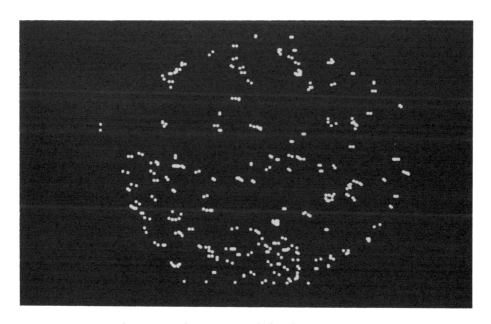

Figure 9.6 The raw primal sketch: terminations.

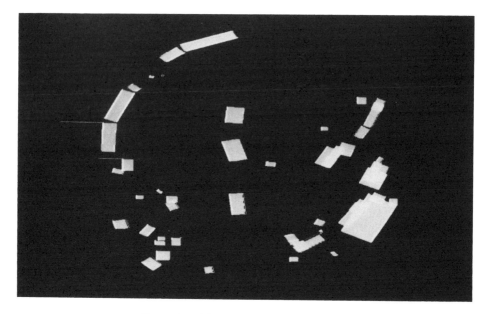

Figure 9.7 The raw primal sketch: bars.

Figure 9.8 The raw primal sketch: blobs.

we mean by segmentation, which we described in Chapter 5. Since we are now dealing with more complex data, the segmentation processes must be more sophisticated. Many of them are based on Gestalt 'figural grouping principles', named after the Gestalt school of psychology formed in the early part of this century. For example, primitives can be grouped according to three criteria: *continuity, proximity*, and *similarity*. In the first case, for instance, lines bounded by terminations which are co-linear would be grouped. Primitives which are spatially proximate are also candidates for the formation of groups, while so too are primitives which belong to the same class, i.e which are similar. These criteria are not independent and the final groupings will be based on the relative weights attached to each criterion.

The contrived example shown in Figure 9.9, comprising three types of fictitious token, illustrates these three criteria. The horizontal row would be grouped on the basis of spatial proximity and continuity; the vertical columns would be grouped on the basis of similarity and, to an extent, continuity, whereas the single diagonal group is formed on the basis of continuity of absence of tokens. This may seem a little strange: grouping entities which do not exist. However, it becomes a little more sensible when we note that, apart from the criteria of grouping, there are also definite grouping principles. The first, *the principle of explicit naming*, states that grouped entities are to be treated as single entities and given an explicit name. This means that they become tokens or primitives in their own right and can be subsequently grouped. Thus, grouping to form the primal sketch is essentially a recursive process; the same grouping principles and criteria applying to all levels of the group hierarchy. Now the situation in Figure 9.9 becomes a little clearer. The groups we identified are not necessarily achieved in one pass of the grouping algorithm; typically, it would take two: one to form the groups identified in Figure 9.10 and a second pass to group the new horizontal groups into the horizontal groups originally shown in Figure 9.9. Now, however, we have new tokens comprising the termination points of these intermediate horizontal tokens; it is the grouping of these terminations, on the basis of continuity, that forms the diagonal group.

There is a second grouping principle, the *principle of least commitment*, which is pragmatic in nature. It addresses the problem that, since grouping can be applied recursively to tokens, groups can be formed which do not segment the physical objects successfully, and it may be necessary to backtrack and undo a grouping process. The principle of least commitment states that these 'mistakes' are expensive and, therefore, grouping should be applied conservatively.

In summary the outcome of such grouping, the full primal sketch, makes region boundaries, object contours and primitive shapes explicit. It is a segmented representation and it exploits processes which are knowledge-free.

9.3.3 *The two-and-a-half-dimensional sketch*

The next level of representation is the two-and-a-half dimensional sketch. This is

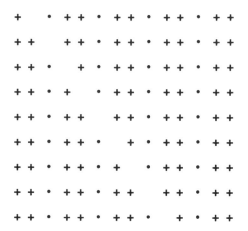

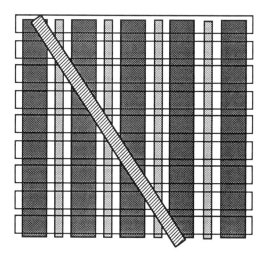

Figure 9.9 Grouping processes.

derived both from the full primal sketch and from the grey-level image by using many visual cues, including stereopsis, apparent motion, shading, shape, and texture. We will have a brief look at the first three of these visual processes in Sections 9.4.1, 9.4.2 and 9.4.3. The two-and-a-half-dimensional sketch is a rich viewer-centred representation of the scene containing not only primitives of spatial organization and surface discontinuity, but also of the local surface orientation at each point and an estimate of the distance from the viewer. The surface orientation is usually represented by a unit vector which is normal to the surface; this is commonly referred to as the 'surface normal vector' (see Figure 9.11).

Recall from Chapter 8 that there are three degrees of freedom in the general

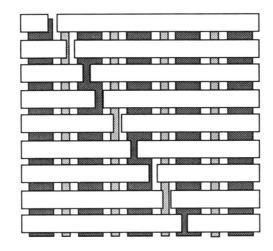

Figure 9.10 Recursive grouping.

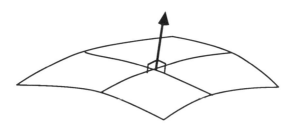

Figure 9.11 The surface normal vector.

specification of orientation of a vector. For example, we used the roll, pitch, and yaw angles to specify the orientation of the robot end effector. In this case, however, we only require two angles since the vector is symmetric and the roll angle is redundant. Thus, the two-and-a-half-dimensional sketch can be thought of as a two-dimensional array of 3-valued entities, representing the distance from the camera to the surface and the two angles specifying the surface normal vectors.

Figure 9.12 shows a schematic of the two-and-a-half-dimensional sketch for a spherical object; the surface normal vectors are projected on to the image plane so that vectors at the boundary of the sphere are the longest and those at the centre, facing the viewer, are the shortest and, in effect, have no length. The intensity with which the vectors are drawn is proportional to their distance from the camera so that the boundary vectors are the brightest and the central vectors are the darkest. It is important to realize that this array-based, or *iconic*, representation is not the complete two-and-a-half-dimensional sketch; since it is also based on the full primal sketch, it integrates the information about grouping and segmentation. Thus, it is a *viewer-centred* three-dimensional model, in that all distances are defined with

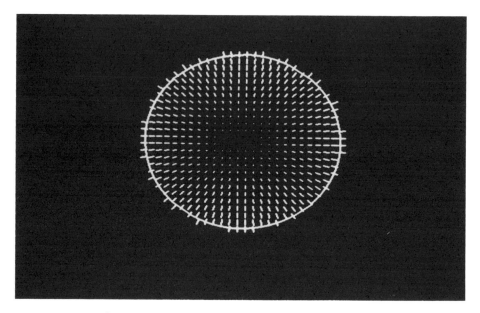

Figure 9.12 The two-and-a-half-dimensional sketch.

respect to the camera coordinate system, with integrated surface-based object representations.

Some of the visual processes which are involved in deriving local surface orientation and depth are discussed in Section 9.4.

9.3.4 Three-dimensional model

The final stage of this information processing organization of visual processes lies in the analysis of the two-and-a-half-dimensional sketch and the production of an explicit three-dimensional representation. There are two issues which must be addressed:

1. The conversion from a viewer-centred representation to an object-centred representation. This is, in effect, the transformation between a camera coordinate system and the real-world coordinate system and is exactly the process we discussed in Chapter 8 in the section on the camera model.
2. The type of three-dimensional representation we choose to model our objects. There are three types of three-dimensional representation based on volumetric, skeletal, and surface primitives.

9.3.4.1 Volumetric representations

Volumetric representations work on the basis of spatial occupancy, delineating the segments of a three-dimensional workspace which are, or are not, occupied by an object. The simplest representation utilizes the concept of a *voxel image* (voxel derives from the phrase volumetric element) which is a three-dimensional extension of a conventional two-dimensional binary image. Thus, it is typically a uniformly sampled three-dimensional array of cells, each one belonging either to an object or to the free space surrounding the object. Because it is a three-dimensional data-structure, voxel image requires a significant amount of memory and, hence, tends to be quite a coarse representation. For example, a 1 m^3 work space comprising 1 cm^3 voxels will require approximately 1 Mbyte of memory (assuming that a voxel is represented by one byte; although eight voxels could be packed into a single byte, you do not then have simple direct access to each voxel).

The oct-tree is another volumetric representation. However, in this instance, the volumetric primitives are not uniform in size and you can represent the spatial occupancy of a work space to arbitrary resolution in a fairly efficient manner. The oct-tree is a three-dimensional extension of the quad-tree which we discussed in Chapter 5. In the same way as a quad-tree described the occupancy of a two-dimensional image by identifying large homogeneous areas in the image and representing them as single nodes in a tree, the position in the tree governing the size of the region, so too is the three-dimensional spatial occupancy represented by such a tree. Initially, the work space is represented by a single cubic volume. If the work space is completely occupied by an object (a very unlikely situation), then the work space is represented by a single root node in the oct-tree. In the more likely situation that the volume is not completely occupied, the cube is divided into eight sub-cubes of equal volume. Again, if any of these sub-cubes are completely occupied then that volume is represented by a node at the second level in the tree; alternatively, the sub-cube is further sub-divided into another eight cubes and the same test for complete spatial occupancy is applied. This process is reiterated until we reach the required resolution for spatial occupancy, i.e. the smallest required cubic volume: this is equivalent to the voxel in the preceding representation.

Note that, because the sub-division of volumes, and hence the generation of new nodes in the oct-tree, only takes place at the boundary between the object and the free-space surrounding it, this representation is extremely efficient (in terms of storage requirements) for regular solids since the interior of the object is represented by a few nodes close to the root of the tree. Furthermore, the coarseness of the object representation is easily controlled by limiting the depth to which the tree can grow, i.e. by placing a limit on the size of the smallest volumes.

9.3.4.2 Skeletal representations

The generalized cylinder, also referred to as the 'generalized cone', is among the most common skeletal three-dimensional object representations. A generalized cylinder is defined as the surface created by moving a cross-section along an axis. The cross-section may vary in size, getting larger or smaller, but the shape remains the same and the axis may trace out any arbitrary three-dimensional curvilinear path. Thus, a single generalized cylinder can represent, e.g., a cone (circular cross-section; linear decrease in diameter; linear axis), a sphere (circular cross-section; sinusoidal variation in diameter; linear axis), or a washer (rectangular cross-section; constant area; circular axis). However, a general three-dimensional model comprises several generalized cones and is organized in a modular manner with each component subsequently comprising its own generalized cylinder-based model. Thus, the three-dimensional model is a hierarchy of generalized cylinders; see Figure 9.13.

9.3.4.3 Surface representations

Finally, we come to the third type of three-dimensional model which is based on surface representations. We immediately have a choice to make and to decide which type of surface primitives (or surface patches) we will allow: planar patches or curved patches. Although there is no universal agreement about which is the better, the planar patch approach is quite popular and yields polyhedral approximations

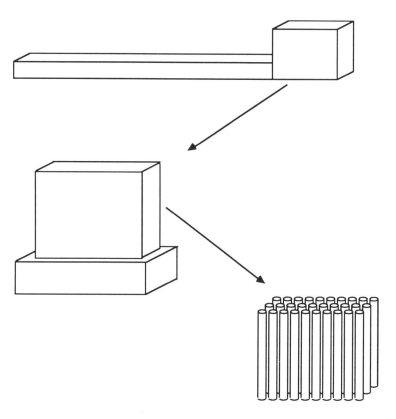

Figure 9.13 Generalized cylinder representation of a tooth-brush.

of the object being modelled. This is quite an appropriate representation for man-made objects which tend predominantly to comprise planar surfaces. It is not, however, a panacea for three-dimensional representational problems and it would appear that many of the subtleties of three-dimensional shape description cannot be addressed with simplistic first-order planar representations. Nevertheless, it does have its uses and, even for naturally curved objects, it can provide quite a good approximation to the true shape, if an appropriate patch size is used. For example, Figure 9.14 shows a sphere comprised of triangular planar patches.

To conclude this brief overview of three-dimensional object representations, it should be noted that we have not addressed the usefulness of these models for object recognition. The subject of three-dimensional shape representation and matching is a difficult one and there are at present no entirely satisfactory answers to the problems it poses. At the same time, we can make a few short comments about the representations which we have discussed. Note first, however, that these comments are made in the context of ideal object representations: as we will see in the next few sections, the three-dimensional models that we build directly from two-dimensional images tend to be incomplete, noisy and often are only approximations to the expected form.

The voxel image represents the three-dimensional shape in an implicit manner (in the same way as a two-dimensional binary image represents two-dimensional shapes) and recognition can be effected by three-dimensional template matching. However, all the problems associated with this technique (see Chapter 6) still apply and, indeed, they are exacerbated by the increase in the dimensionality of the model.

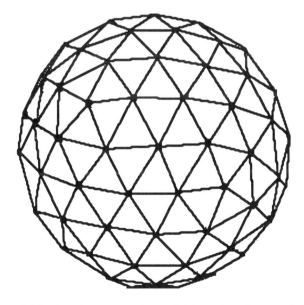

Figure 9.14 A sphere comprised of triangular planar patches.

Object recognition using oct-trees essentially requires a graph (or tree) matching algorithm. However, since the oct-tree will vary with the orientation of the object, especially at the lower levels, the matching algorithm must be able to detect structural similarities in sub-sets of the tree.

Similarly, a tree matching technique can be used to facilitate matching models based on generalized cylinders, since the representation is a hierarchical structure of nodes comprising three parametric entities: the axis, the cross-section, and the variation of cross-section.

Finally, it is difficult to accomplish object recognition using planar surface models for anything except the simplest of regular objects since the size and position of each patch, and the total number of patches, will vary considerably with the orientation of the original object and the completeness of the data. Instead, object recognition can be effected by backtracking somewhat and regenerating an iconic (array-based) version of the two-and-a-half-dimensional sketch. The recognition process is accomplished by matching this two-dimensional representation with a template. It assumes, however, that the template and object poses have first been registered; otherwise, several (indeed a very large number) of object templates will have to be used in the template matching process, each one generated by projecting the three-dimensional model on to the two-and-a-half-dimensional sketch at different orientations. It is this task of three-dimensional pose estimation to which we now turn.

9.3.5 *The extended Gaussian image*

The two-and-a-half-dimensional sketch provides us with the local orientation at each point on the surface of the object. These surface normals can be represented on a unit sphere called a Gauss map. If we attach a unit mass to each endpoint, we now observe a distribution of mass over the Gaussian sphere and this distribution is called the 'extended Gaussian image' (EGI) of the object. The EGI is effectively a two-dimensional histogram of surface normal orientations, distributed on a sphere, and the attitude, or pose, of an object is greatly constrained by the global distribution of EGI mass over the visible Gaussian hemisphere. Constraints on the viewer direction can be derived from the position of the EGI mass centre, and from the directions of the EGI axis of inertia. To determine object pose, we simply match partial EGIs, derived from the observed scene, with template EGIs derived from our stored prototypical model.

For example, Figure 9.15 shows a contrived, e.g. artificial, object in several poses, together with the associated EGIs. In this case, the mass at a point on the EGI (which is proportional to the surface area of the object with that attitude) is coded by grey-level. Note that the distribution of mass is not uniform; this is caused by quantization errors in the orientation of the facets of both the Gaussian sphere and the object surfaces.

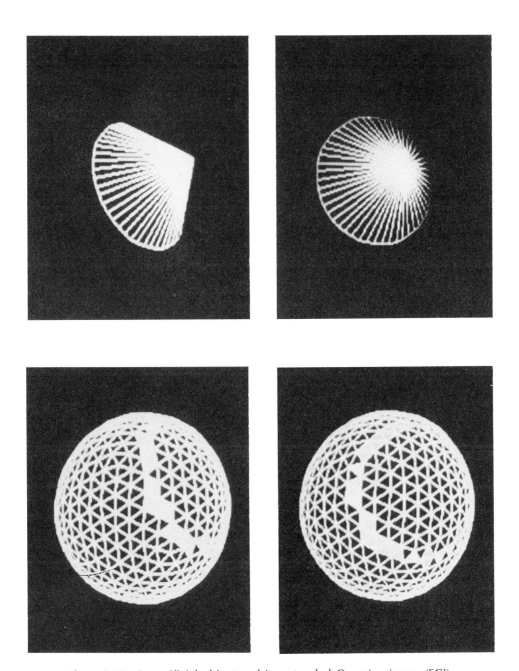

Figure 9.15 An artificial object and its extended Gaussian image (EGI).

9.4   *Visual processes*

We began this chapter by suggesting that there is a great deal more to image understanding than the recovery of depth information from two-dimensional images, and we then proceeded to look at the representations and organization of visual processes which comprise an image understanding system. Nevertheless, as we have stated several times, the recovery of depth information is important and so we return now to the visual processes which are involved constructing the two-and-a-half-dimensional sketch: the computation of depth information and of local surface orientation.

9.4.1 *Stereopsis*

Our interest here is in the use of two views of a scene to recover information about the distance of objects in the scene from the observer (the cameras). In a sense, we have already discussed stereopsis, or stereo for short, in the last chapter when we dealt with the camera model, the inverse perspective transformation, and the recovery of depth information. We discussed in detail how the inverse perspective transformation allows us to construct a line describing all the points in the three-dimensional world which could have been projected onto a given image point. If we have two images acquired at different positions in the world, i.e. a stereo pair, then for the two image coordinates *which correspond to a single point in three-dimensional space*, we can construct two lines, the intersection of which identifies the three-dimensional position of the point in question. Thus, there are two aspects to stereo imaging:

(a)   the identification of corresponding points in the two stereo images;
(b)   the computation of the three-dimensional coordinates of the world point which gives rise to these two corresponding image points.

Since we have already covered the second aspect in detail (and you are encouraged to review these techniques in Chapter 8), the main problem in stereo is to find the corresponding points in the left and right images and this is what we will discuss here. Before we proceed, however, it is perhaps worth while noting that quite often stereo techniques are presented without discussing the inverse perspective transformation formally; instead, stereo is discussed in the context of the computation of the stereo disparity (i.e. the relative shift in position of an imaged point in the two stereo images) and the subsequent computation of depth on the basis of knowledge of the geometry of the two camera systems, i.e. the focal length of the lens, the distance between the lens centres, the size of the sensor, and the relative attitude of the focal axes of the two cameras. We have not done this here because it neglects the calibration of the camera systems: it is difficult to measure the distance between lens centres empirically, the relative attitude of focal axes, and the focal length quoted on camera lenses is only nominal; quite often, two 'identical' lenses will have slightly different focal lengths.

We return now to the stereo correspondence problem. In characterizing a stereo system, we must address the following:

(a) the kind of visual entities on which the stereo system works;
(b) the mechanism by which the system matches visual entities in one image with corresponding entities on the other.

Typically, the possible visual entities from which we can choose include, at an iconic level, zero-crossing points, patches (small areas) in the intensity image, and patches in filtered images; or, at a more symbolic level, line segment tokens, such as are made explicit in the raw primal sketch.

The matching mechanism which establishes the correspondence will depend on the type of visual entities which we have chosen: iconic entities will normally exploit some template matching paradigm, such as normalized cross-correlation (see Chapter 6), while token entities can be used with more heuristic search strategies. As an example, the stereo disparity image shown in Figure 9.16,* in which disparity is inversely proportional to grey-level, is derived by convolving the stereo pair (see Figure 9.17) with a Laplacian of Gaussian filter, computing the zero-crossings, and correlating patches in the convolved image, centred on the zero-crossing points at discrete intervals along the zero-crossing contour.

9.4.2 Camera motion

The analysis of object motion in sequences of digital images, or of apparent motion in the case of a moving observer, to provide us with information about the structure of the imaged scene, is an extremely topical and important aspect of current image understanding research. However, the general object motion problem is difficult, since the motion we perceive can be due to either the rotation of the object, a translation of the object, or both. We will not attempt to address this problem here and the interested reader will find references to some seminal work in the area in the bibliography at the end of the book. We confine our attention to the somewhat easier problem of camera motion and, in particular, to the study of apparent motion of objects in a scene arising from the changing vantage point of a moving camera. This restriction is not necessarily a limitation on the usefulness of the technique; on the contrary, the concept of a camera mounted on the end-effector of a robot, providing hand–eye coordination, or on a moving autonomously guided vehicle (AGV), providing navigation information, is both appealing and plausible.

---

* This disparity representation, which is based on the zero-crossings of Laplacian of Gaussian filtered images, is merely a short-hand way of summarizing the relative position of corresponding points in the two images. Given a zero-crossing point, we can compute its corresponding position in the second stereo image from its disparity, represented here as intensity. This assumes that we know the direction in which the corresponding point lies; for a stereo pair of cameras which have parallel focal axes, the direction is horizontal.

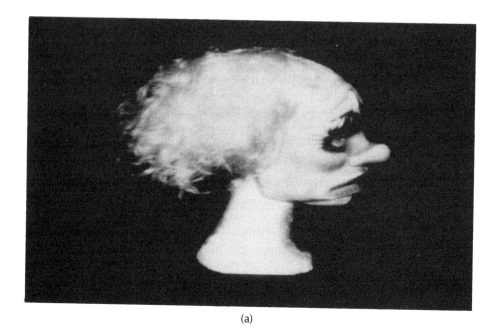

(a)

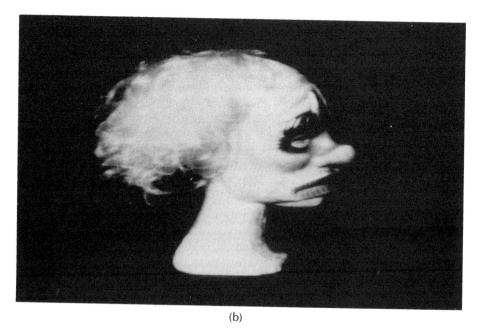

(b)

Figure 9.16 (a) Left stereo image. (b) Right stereo image.

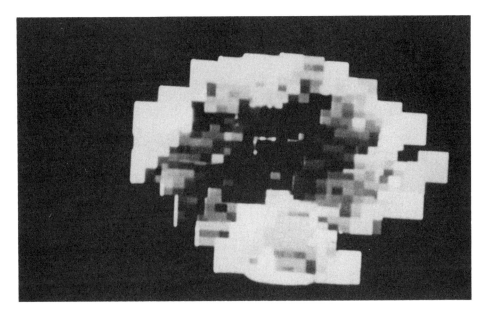

Figure 9.17 Disparity of a stereo pair of images.

From an intuitive point of view, camera motion is identical to the stereo process in that we are identifying points in the image (e.g. characteristic features on an object) and then tracking them as they appear to move due to the changing position (and, perhaps, attitude) of the camera system. At the end of the sequence of images, we then have two sets of corresponding points, connected by *optic flow vectors*, in the first and last images of the sequence. Typically, we will also have a sequence of vectors which tack the trajectory of the point throughout the sequence of images. The depth, or distance, of the point in the world can then be computed in the manner discussed in Chapter 8 and in the preceding section.

However, there are a number of differences. First, the tracking is achieved quite often, not by a correlation technique or by a token matching technique, but by differentiating the image sequence with respect to time to see how it changes from one image to the next. There is often a subsequent matching process to ensure the accuracy of the computed image change, and sometimes it is not the grey-scale image which is differentiated but, rather, a filtered version of it. Nevertheless, the information about change is derived from a derivative (or, more accurately, a first difference) of the image sequence. Second, the 'correspondence' between points is established incrementally, from image to image, over an extended sequence of images. Thus, we can often generate accurate and faithful maps of point correspondence which are made explicit by a two-dimensional array of flow vectors which describe the trajectory of a point over the image sequence.

In this book, we will confine our attention to two simple types of camera motion in order to illustrate the approach. The first describes a trajectory along the

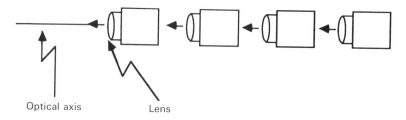

Optical axis   Lens

Figure 9.18 Translational motion along the optic axis.

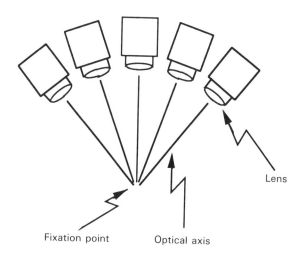

Lens

Fixation point   Optical axis

Figure 9.19 Rotational motion about a fixation point.

optical axis of the camera (see Figure 9.18), while in the second the camera is rotated about a fixation point (see Figure 9.19). The optic flow field resulting from this first type of egocentric motion is very easy to compute as all flow vectors are directed radially outward from the focus of expansion (FOE),* i.e. the centre of the image. For camera motion in rotation about a fixation point, the rotational component of optical flow can be determined directly from the known camera trajectory and the direction of the translational component is also constrained by the camera motion. Knowing the direction of the flow vector, the magnitude of the visual motion is directly derived from a time-derivative of a sequence of images acquired at successive points along the camera trajectory.

---

* The focus of expansion is the point which defines the direction from which all the optic flow vectors appear to emanate, i.e. all flow vectors are co-linear with a line joining the FOE and the origin of the flow vector.

There is one main difficulty when attempting to compute the true optical flow, i.e. the visual motion, of a point in the image. It is generally referred to as the *aperture problem*. Consider a contour in an image and let us say that we only have a small local window of visibility around the point of interest on the contour (see Figure 9.20). If the position of the contour changes due to the camera motion, then we cannot say with any certainty in which direction it moved, based purely on the local information available in this small local window. The only thing we can compute with certainty is the *orthogonal component of the velocity vector*, i.e. the component which is normal to the local contour orientation. This vector component is referred to as $v^\perp$, and the second component is referred to as the tangential component, v^T. Thus, the true velocity vector v is given by:

$$v = v^\perp + v^\mathsf{T}$$

If the luminance intensity does not change with time (i.e. there are no moving light sources in the environment) the component of the orthogonal velocity vector for each image point is given by:

$$v^\perp = \frac{-\partial I/\partial t}{|\nabla I|}$$

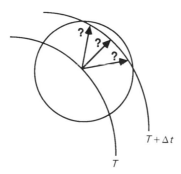

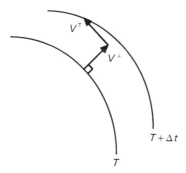

Figure 9.20 The aperture problem.

235

where ∂ indicates the partial derivative operator and $|\nabla I|$ is the local intensity gradient.

In the technique described here, we compute the time derivative of a $\nabla^2 G$ filtered image instead of the raw intensity image and compute the optical flow at zero-crossing contours. This means that the amount of data to be processed is limited and, furthermore, the effects of noise are less pronounced.

The computation of $v^{\perp}$ (the orthogonal component of velocity) is based on a computation of the time derivative using image subtraction, in the same way as we saw that gradient-based edge detectors can be affected by local pixel differences, according to the relationship described above.

The computation of the true velocity depends on the prior knowledge of the parameters of the camera motion: the position of the camera at time T and $T + \Delta t$ from the fixation point; θ the rotational angle of the camera around the Y-axis, and W_x and W_z the components of the translational velocity of the camera along the X-axis and the Z-axis respectively. The velocities W_x and W_z are defined with respect to the coordinate system of the camera at time T (see Figure 9.21). Using basic trigonometric relations, we find:

$$W_x = \frac{D_2 \sin \theta}{\Delta t}$$

$$W_y = 0$$

$$W_z = \frac{D_1 - D_2 \cos \theta}{\Delta t}$$

where D_1 and D_2 are the distances of the camera from the fixation point at time T and $T + \Delta t$ respectively.

These computed egomotion parameters are used to determine the true image velocity vector v. Note that v comprises two components, v_t and v_r, one due to camera translation $W = (W_x, W_y, W_z)$ and the other to camera rotation $\omega = (\omega_x, \omega_y, \omega_z)$:

$$v_t = \left(\frac{xW_z - FW_x}{Z}, \quad \frac{yW_z - FW_y}{Z} \right)$$

$$v_r = \left(\frac{xy\omega_x - (x^2 + F^2)\omega_y + y\omega_z}{F}, \quad \frac{(y^2 + F^2)\omega_x - xy\omega_y - x\omega_z}{F} \right)$$

$$v = v_t + v_r$$

where:

F is the focal length of the lens,

x and y are the coordinates of the point in the image plane at time T, and

Z is the distance from the camera to the world point corresponding to image point (x, y).

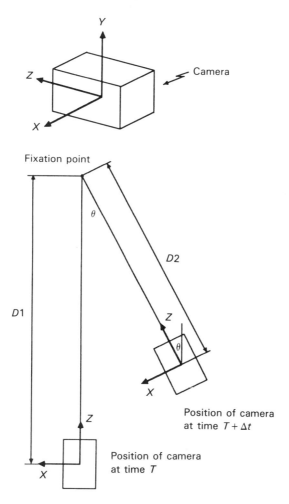

Figure 9.21 Camera coordinate system and the parameters associated with camera motion.

For the constrained camera motion shown in Figure 9.19, the camera translational velocity is given by the equations for W_x, W_y and W_z above, while the rotational velocity ω is $(0, \theta/\Delta t, 0)$.

$$v_t = \left(\frac{x(D_1 - D_2 \cos \theta) - FD_2 \sin \theta}{Z \, \Delta t}, \quad \frac{y(D_1 - D_2 \cos \theta)}{Z \, \Delta t} \right)$$

$$v_r = \left(\frac{-(x^2 + F^2)\theta}{F \, \Delta t}, \quad \frac{-xy\theta}{F \, \Delta t} \right)$$

In these two equations for v_t and v_r, the only unknown is Z (which is what we wish to determine). Thus, to determine v_t and v_r, and hence Z, we exploit the value of $v^\perp$, the orthogonal component of velocity, computed at an earlier stage. This can be accomplished directly by solving the attendant system of equations or by a geometrical construction.

In the solution by geometrical construction, v is determined from the intersection of three straight lines derived from v_r (for which all terms are known), $v^\perp$ (which was computed previously), and the position of the FOE.

First, v_r defines the first line of the construction (refer to Figure 9.22).

Second, the position of the FOE defines the direction of v_t, since v_t is parallel to the line joining the FOE and the point (x, y) in question. Thus, the second line is parallel to v_t and passes through the point given by v_r(see Figure 9.22). The coordinates of the FOE are given by:

$$(x_{FOE}, y_{FOE}) = \left(\frac{FW_x}{W_z}, \frac{FW_y}{W_z}\right)$$

where W_x, W_y, and W_z are the known velocities of the camera in the x-, y-, and z-directions respectively.

Finally, we note again that v is also given by the sum of the orthogonal component and the tangential component of velocity:

$$v = v^\perp + v^T$$

Since these two vectors are orthogonal to one another, and since $v^\perp$ is known, this relationship defines a third line through the point given by $v^\perp$ and normal to the direction of $v^\perp$. Hence, v is given by the intersection of the second and the third lines: see Figure 9.22.

In the simpler case of translatory motion along the optic axis, θ is equal to

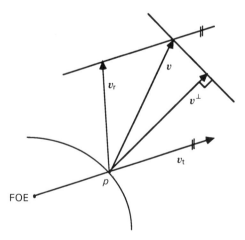

Figure 9.22 Computation of true velocity v from $v^\perp$, $v_t v_r$ at a point P on a zero-crossing contour.

zero and the translational component of velocity reduces to:

$$v_t = \left(\frac{x(D_1 - D_2)}{Z}, \quad \frac{y(D_1 - D_2)}{Z} \right)$$

while the rotational component v_r is now zero.

Computing v in this manner and, in particular, computing $v^{\perp}$ using image differences, errors can still be recorded in the final flow. A significant improvement can be achieved by performing a contour-to-contour matching between successive frames, along the direction of the flow vectors, tuning the length of the flow vectors to the correct size. The tracking procedure searches in the direction of the flow vector until the next contour is found, then it searches in the direction of the new flow vector, and so forth until the whole image sequence is processed. Although a small difference between successive frames is required to guarantee the accuracy in the computation of the orthogonal component $v^{\perp}$, a long baseline is required for the depth measurement. For this reason, many images are normally considered and the flow field obtained for a sequence of images is used for range computation: the flow vector from the first image to the last image being employed in the computation of depth.

The algorithm for computing the optical flow can be summarized as follows:

```
Convolve the images with a Laplacian of Gaussian
operator

Extract the zero-crossings

Compute the difference between the ∇²G of successive
frames of the sequence

Compute the velocity component in the direction
perpendicular to the orientation of the contour

Compute the velocity along the contour using the known
motion parameters

Search for the zero-crossings of the second frame
projected from the first frame in the direction of the
velocity vector.
```

The depth, for each contour point, is computed as before by applying the inverse perspective transformation, derived from camera models corresponding to the initial and final camera positions, to the two points given by the origin of the optical flow vector and the end of the optical flow vector.

To illustrate this approach to inferring the depth of objects, motion sequences of two different scenes were generated, each comprising nine images. These scenes were of a white 45° cone with black stripes at regular intervals and a 'toy-town'

Figure 9.23 A black and white cone.

environment (see Figures 9.23, 9.24, 9.26 and 9.27). For the purposes of illustration, Figures 9.23 through 9.28 depict the results of the rotational motion only. Each of the constituent images in these image sequences were then convolved with a Laplacian of Gaussian mask (standard deviation of the Gaussian function = 4.0) and the zero-crossings contours were extracted. Since the Laplacian of Gaussian operator isolates intensity discontinuities over a wide range of edge contrasts, many of the resultant zero-crossings do not correspond to perceptually significant physical edges. As before, an adaptive thresholding technique was employed to identify these contours and to exclude them from further processing.

The zero-crossings contour images and their associated convolution images were then used to generate six time derivatives; since the time derivative utilizes a five-point operator combining the temporal difference with temporal averaging, the time derivative can only be estimated for images 3, 4, 5, 6, and 7; the associated orthogonal component of velocity was then computed, followed by the true optical flow vectors. An extended flow field was then estimated by tracking the flow vectors from image 3 through images 4, 5 to image 6 on a contour-to-contour basis, i.e. tracking a total of three images (see Figures 9.25 and 9.28). Depth images (representing the distance from the camera to each point on the zero-crossing contour) were generated for each scene (Figures 9.25 and 9.28) from the tracked velocity vectors. Finally, a range image representing the range of all visible points on the surface was generated by interpolation (again, Figures 9.25 and 9.28).

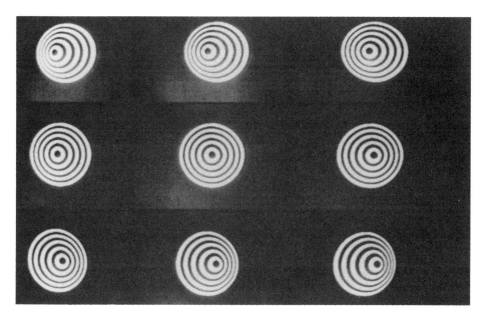

Figure 9.24 The nine views of the black and white cone.

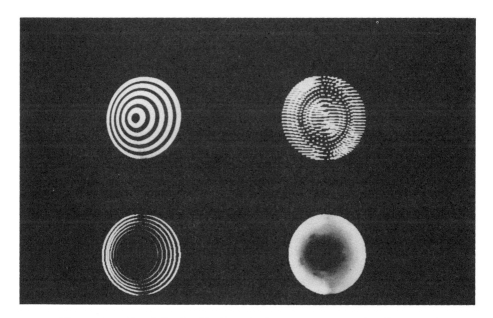

Figure 9.25 Top left: the black and white cone. Top right: the optical flow vectors. Bottom left: zero-crossings with intensity proportional to distance from camera. Bottom right: range image with intensity proportional to distance from camera.

Figure 9.26 A toy-town scene.

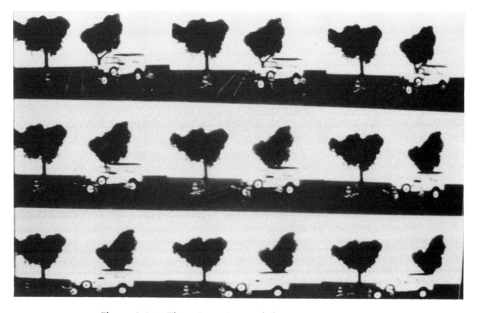

Figure 9.27 The nine views of the toy-town scene.

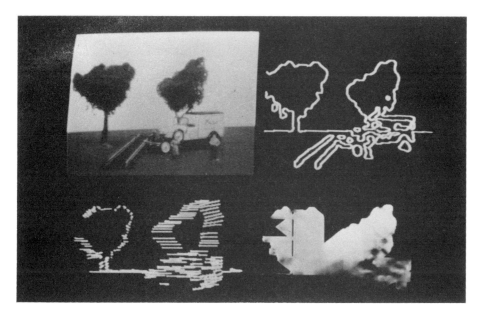

Figure 9.28 Top left: the toy-town scene. Top right: the optical flow vectors. Bottom left: zero-crossings with intensity proportional to distance from camera. Bottom right: range image with intensity proportional to distance from camera.

9.4.3 Shading

The construction of the two-and-a-half-dimensional sketch requires one further element: the computation of the local orientation of a point, i.e. the surface normal vector. The analysis of the shading of a surface, based on assumed models of the reflectivity of the surface material, is sometimes used to compute this information.

The amount of light reflected from an object depends on the following (referring to Figure 9.29):

(a)   the surface material;
(b)   the emergent angle, e between the surface normal and the viewer angle;
(c)   the incident angle, i, between the surface normal and light source direction.

There are several models of surface reflectance, the simplest of which is the Lambertian model. A Lambertian surface is a surface that looks equally bright from all viewpoints, i.e. the brightness of a particular point does not change as the viewpoint changes. It is a perfect diffuser: the observed brightness depends only on the direction to the light source, i.e. the incident angle i.

Let E be the observed brightness, then for a Lambertian surface:

$$E = \rho \cos i$$

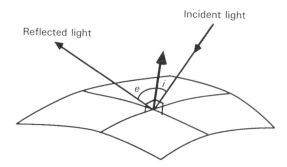

Figure 9.29 Incident and emergent angles.

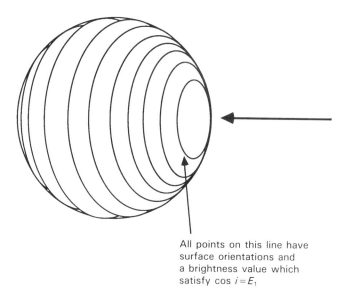

All points on this line have
surface orientations and
a brightness value which
satisfy $\cos i = E_1$

Figure 9.30 Lambertian sphere and iso-brightness lines.

where ρ is a constant called the 'surface albedo' and is peculiar to the surface material under analysis.

The reflectance properties of Lambertian surfaces are encapsulated by images of Lambertian spheres of radius 1 upon which we draw (for convenience) lines joining points of equal brightness, i.e. iso-brightness lines. There will, in general, be many points on the surface of the sphere which satisfy $E = \rho \cos i$ for a given brightness E_1; see Figure 9.30. More often, a projection of these iso-brightness values onto a plane is used. This is called a *reflectance map*. The most commonly used projection is one onto a plane which is parallel to the viewer's image plane and is a tangent to the sphere; see Figure 9.31. This is effected by drawing a line from the point on the sphere opposite the viewer, through the point to be projected.

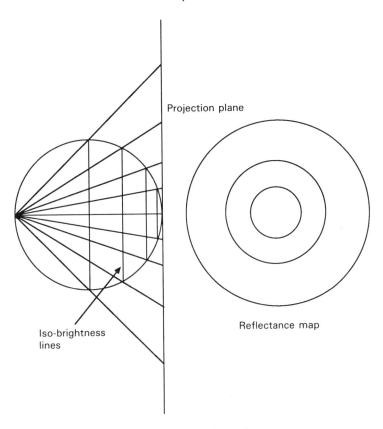

Figure 9.31 Generation of the reflectance map.

A brightness value determines only a curve on the reflectance map rather than a single point, since there will be several points on the sphere having equal brightness, i.e. the points on an iso-brightness line. Thus, an extra constraint is required to determine uniquely the orientation of the imaged point from the brightness: this is supplied by assumptions of surface smoothness (or continuity) that *the surface should not vary much from the surface direction at neighbouring parts*. Obviously, we need some coordinates on the reflectance map to anchor the process and from which we can infer the orientation of neighbouring points.

On occluding boundaries of objects without sharp edges, the surface direction is perpendicular to the viewer's line of sight. All such directions project onto a circle of radius 2 on the reflectance map and, thus, we know immediately the surface orientation of every occluding contour point and, more importantly, the correspondence between a given occluding boundary point and the point to which it maps on the reflectance function. This is achieved by observing that the required point of the reflectance map must correspond to the surface normal direction at the occluding boundary. Since the surface orientation changes smoothly, all points on

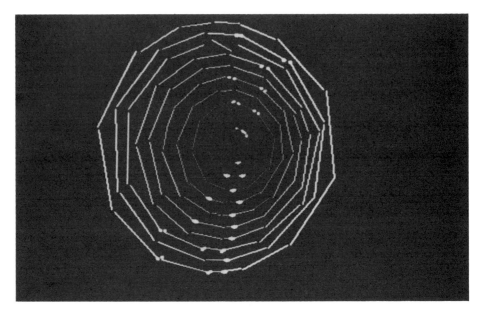

Figure 9.32 Three-dimensional raw primal sketch of a striped cone.

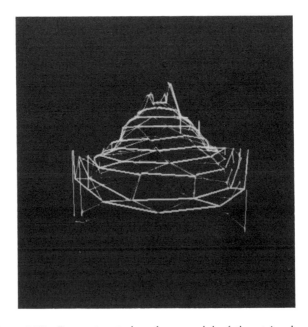

Figure 9.33 Reconstructed surface model of the striped cone.

Figure 9.34 Extended Gaussian image depicting the distribution of
surface normals on the polyhedral model of the cone.

the surface close to the occluding boundary must have an orientation which is not
significantly different from that of the occluding boundary. The surface orientation
of each point adjacent to the occluding boundary can now be computed by
measuring the intensity value and reading off the corresponding orientation from
the reflectance map *in a local area surrounding the point on the map which
corresponds to the current occluding boundary anchor point*. This scheme of local
constraint is reiterated using these newly computed orientations as constraints, until
the orientation of all points on the surface have been computed.

This technique has been studied in depth in the computer vision literature and
it should be emphasized that this description is intuitive and tutorial in nature; you
are referred to the appropriate texts cited in the bibliography at the end of the
chapter. As we have noted, however, there are a number of assumptions which
must be made in order for the technique to work successfully, e.g. the surface
orientation must vary smoothly and, in particular, it must do so at the occluding
boundary (the boundary of the object at which the surface disappears from sight).
Look around the room you are in at present. How many objects do you see which
fulfil this requirement? Probably very few. Allied to this are the requirements that
the reflective surface has a known albedo and that we can model its reflective
properties, or, alternatively, that we can calibrate for a given reflective material,
and, finally, that one knows the incident angle of light. This limits the usefulness
of the techniques for *general* image understanding.

There are other ways of estimating the local surface orientation. As an example of one *coarse* approach, consider the situation where we have a three-dimensional raw primal sketch, i.e. a raw primal sketch in which we know the depth to each point on the edge segments, and if these raw primal sketch segments are *sufficiently close*, we can compute the surface normal by interpolating between the edges, generating a succession of planar patches, and effectively constructing a polyhedral model of the object (see Section 9.3.4.3). The surface normal is easily computed by forming the vector cross-product of two vectors in the plane of the patch (typically two non-parallel patch sides). For example, the three-dimensional raw primal sketch of the calibration cone which is shown in Figure 9.32 yields the polyhedral model shown in Figure 9.33, the extended Gaussian image of which is shown in Figure 9.34.

9.5 Concluding remarks

Having read this book, and this chapter in particular, you could be excused for thinking that computer vision is an end in itself, that is, that the task is complete once we arrive at our unambiguous explicit three-dimensional representation of the world. This is quite wrong. Vision is no such thing; it is merely part of a larger system which might best be characterized by a dual two-faced process of *making sense of/interacting with* the environment. Without action, perception is futile; without perception, action is futile. Both are complementary, but highly related, activities. Any intelligent action in which the system engages in the environment, i.e. anything it does, it does with an understanding of its action, and quite often it gains this by on-going visual perception.

In essence, image understanding is as concerned with cause and effect, with purpose, with action and reaction as it is with structural organization. That we have not advanced greatly in this aspect of image understanding and computer vision yet is not an indictment of the research community; in fact, given the disastrous consequences of the excessive zeal and ambition in the late 1970s, it is perhaps no bad thing that attention is currently focused on the formal and well-founded bases of visual processes: without these, the edifice we construct in image understanding would be shaky, to say the least. However, the issues we have just raised, in effect the temporal semantics of vision in contribution to and in participation with physical interactive systems, will not go away and must be addressed and understood someday. Soon.

Exercises

1. What do you understand by the term 'subjective contour'? In the context of the full primal sketch, explain how such phenomena arise

and suggest a technique to detect the occurrence of these contours. Are there any limitations to your suggestion? If so, identify them and offer plausible solutions.

2. Given that one can establish the correspondence of identical points in two or more images of the same scene, where each image is generated at a slightly different viewpoint, explain how one can recover the absolute real-world coordinates of objects, or points on objects, with suitably calibrated cameras. How can one effectively exploit the use of more than two such stereo images? How would you suggest organizing the cameras for this type of multiple camera stereo in order to minimize ambiguities?

3. Describe, in detail, one approach to the construction of the two-and-a-half-dimensional sketch and identify any assumptions exploited by the component processes.

4. Is the two-and-a-half-dimensional sketch a useful representation in its own right or is it merely an intermediate representation used in the construction of higher-level object descriptions?

5. 'The sole objective of image understanding systems is to derive unambiguous, four-dimensional (spatio-temporal) representations of the visual environment and this can be accomplished by the judicious use of early and late visual processing.' Evaluate this statement critically.

6. 'Image understanding systems are *not* intelligent; they are *not* capable of perception, and, in effect, they do *not* understand their environment.' Discuss the validity of this statement.

7. Do exercise 1 in Chapter 1.

References and further reading

Ahuja, N., Bridwell, N., Nash, C. and Huang, T.S. 1982 *Three-Dimensional Robot Vision*, Conference record of the 1982 workshop on industrial application of machine vision, Research Triangle Park, NC, USA, pp. 206–13.

Arun, K.S., Huang, T.S. and Blostein, S.D. 1987 'Least-squares fitting of two 3-D point sets', *IEEE Transaction on Pattern Analysis and Machine Intelligence*, Vol. PAMI-9, No. 5, pp. 698–700.

Bamieh, B. and De Figueiredo, R.J.P. 1986 'A general moment-invariants/attributed-graph method for three-dimensional object recognition from a single image', *IEEE Journal of Robotics and Automation*, Vol. RA-2, No. 1, pp. 31–41.

Barnard, S.T. and Fischler, M.A. 1982 *Computational Stereo*, SRI International, Technical Note No. 261.

Ben Rhouma, K., Peralta, L. and Osorio, A. 1983 'A "K2D" perception approach for assembly robots', *Signal Processing II: Theory and Application*, Schurrler, H.W. (ed.), Elsevier Science Publishers B.V. (North-Holland), pp. 629–32.

Besl, P.J. and Jain, R. 1985 'Three-dimensional object recognition', *ACM Computing Surveys*, Vol. 17, No. 1, pp. 75–145.

Bhanu, B. 1984 'Representation and shape matching of 3-D objects', *IEEE Transactions on Pattern Analysis and Machine Intelligence*, Vol. PAMI-6, No. 3, pp. 340–51.

Brady, M. 1982 'Computational approaches to image understanding', *ACM Computing Surveys*, Vol. 14, No. 1, pp. 3–71.

Brooks, R.A. 1981 'Symbolic reasoning among 3-D models and 2-D images', *Artificial Intelligence*, Vol. 17, pp. 285–348.

Brooks, R.A. 1983 'Model-based three-dimensional interpretations of two-dimensional images', *IEEE Transactions on Pattern Analysis and Machine Intelligence*, Vol. PAMI-5, No. 2, pp. 140–50.

Dawson, K. and Vernon, D. 1990 'Implicit model matching as an approach to three-dimensional object recognition', *Proceedings of the ESPRIT Basic Research Action Workshop on 'Advanced Matching in Vision and Artificial Intelligence'*, Munich, June 1990.

Fang, J.Q. and Huang, T.S. 1984 'Some experiments on estimating the 3-D motion parameters of a rigid body from two consecutive image frames', *IEEE Transactions on Pattern Analysis and Machine Intelligence*, Vol. PAMI-6, No. 5, pp. 545–54.

Fang, J.Q. and Huang, T.S. 1984 'Solving three-dimensional small rotational motion equations: uniqueness, algorithms and numerical results', *Computer Vision, Graphics and Image Processing*, No. 26, pp. 183–206.

Fischler, M.A. and Bolles, R.C. 1986 'Perceptual organisation and curve partitioning', *IEEE Transactions on Pattern Analysis and Machine Intelligence*, Vol. PAMI-8, No. 1, pp. 100–5.

Frigato, C., Grosso, E., Sandini, G., Tistarelli, M. and Vernon, D. 1988 'Integration of motion and stereo', *Proceedings of the 5th Annual ESPRIT Conference, Brussels*, edited by the Commission of the European Communities, Directorate-General Telecommunications, Information Industries and Innovation, North-Holland, Amsterdam, pp. 616–27.

Guzman, A. 1968 'Computer Recognition of Three-Dimensional Objects in a Visual Scene', Ph.D. Thesis, MIT, Massachusetts.

Haralick, R.M., Watson, L.T. and Laffey, T.J. 1983 'The topographic primal sketch', *The International Journal of Robotics Research*, Vol. 2, No. 1, pp. 50–72.

Hall, E.L. and McPherson, C.A. 1983 'Three dimensional perception for robot vision', *Proceedings of SPIE*, Vol. 442, pp. 117–42.

Healy, P. and Vernon, D. 1988 'Very coarse granularity parallelism: implementing 3-D vision with transputers', *Proceedings Image Processing '88*, Blenheim Online Ltd, London, pp. 229–45.

Henderson, T.C. 1983 'Efficient 3-D object representations for industrial vision systems', *IEEE Transactions on Pattern Analysis and Machine Intelligence*, Vol. PAMI-5, No. 6, pp. 609–18.

Hildreth, E.C. 1983 *The Measurement of Visual Motion*, MIT Press, Cambridge, USA.

Horaud, P., and Bolles, R.C. 1984 '3DPO's strategy for matching 3-D objects in range data', *International Conference on Robotics, Atlanta, GA, USA*, pp. 78–85.

Horn, B.K.P. and Schunck, B.G. 1981 'Determining optical flow', *Artificial Intelligence*, **17**, Nos 1–3 pp. 185–204.

Horn, B.K.P. and Ikeuchi, K. 1983 *Picking Parts out of a Bin*, AI Memo No. 746, MIT AI Lab.

Huang, T.S. and Fang, J.Q. 1983 'Estimating 3-D motion parameters: some experimental results', *Proceedings of SPIE*, Vol. 449, Part 2, pp. 435–7.

Ikeuchi, K. 1983 *Determining Attitude of Object From Neddle Map Using Extended Gaussian Image*, MIT AI Memo No. 714.

Ikeuchi, K., Nishihara, H.K., Horn, B.K., Sobalvarro, P. and Nagata, S. 1986 'Determining grasp configurations using photometric stereo and the PRISM binocular stereo system', *The International Journal of Robotics Research*, Vol. 5, No. 1, pp. 46–65.

Jain, R.C. 1984 'Segmentation of frame sequences obtained by a moving observer', *IEEE Transactions on Pattern Analysis and Machine Intelligence*, Vol. PAMI-6, No. 5, pp. 624–9.

Kanade, T. 1981 'Recovery of the three-dimensional shape of an object from a single view', *Artificial Intelligence*, Vol. 17, pp. 409–60.

Kanade, T. 1983 'Geometrical aspects of interpreting images as a 3-D scene', *Proceedings of the IEEE*, Vol. 71, No. 7, pp. 789–802.

Kashyap, R.L. and Oomen, B.J. 1983 'Scale preserving smoothing of polygons', *IEEE Transactions on Pattern Analysis and Machine Intelligence*, Vol. PAMI-5, No. 6, pp. 667–71.

Kim, Y.C. and Aggarwal, J.K. 1987 'Positioning three-dimensional objects using stereo images', *IEEE Journal of Robotics and Automation*, Vol. RA-3, No. 4, pp. 361–73.

Kuan, D.T. 1983 'Three-dimensional vision system for object recognition', *Proceedings of SPIE*, Vol. 449, pp. 366–72.

Lawton, D.T. 1983 'Processing translational motion sequences', *CVGIP*, **22**, pp. 116–44.

Lowe, D.G. and Binford, T.O. 1985 'The recovery of three-dimensional structure from image curves', *IEEE Transactions on Pattern Analysis and Machine Intelligence*, Vol. PAMI-7, No. 3, pp. 320–6.

Marr, D. 1976 'Early processing of visual information', *Philosophical Transactions of the Royal Society of London*, **B275**, pp. 483–524.

Marr, D. and Poggio, T. 1979 'A computational theory of human stereo vision', *Proceedings of the Royal Society of London*, **B204**, pp. 301–28.

Marr, D. 1982 *Vision*, W.H. Freeman and Co., San Francisco.

Martin, W.N. and Aggarwal, J.K. 1983 'Volumetric descriptions of objects from multiple views', *IEEE Transactions on Pattern Analysis and Machine Intelligence*, Vol. PAMI-5, No. 2, pp. 150–8.

McFarland, W.D. and McLaren, R.W. 1983 'Problem in three dimensional imaging', *Proceedings of SPIE*, Vol. 449, pp. 148–57.

McPherson, C.A., Tio, J.B.K., Sadjadi, F.A. and Hall, E.L. 1982 'Curved surface representation for image recognition', *Proceedings of the IEEE Computer Society Conference on Pattern Recognition and Image Processing, Las Vegas, NV, USA*, pp. 363–9.

McPherson, C.A. 1983 'Three-dimensional robot vision', *Proceedings of SPIE*, Vol. 449, part 4, pp. 116–26.

Nishihara, H.K. 1983 'PRISM: a practical realtime imaging stereo matcher', *Proceedings of SPIE*, Vol. 449, pp. 134–42.

Pentland, A. 1982 The Visual Inference of Shape: Computation from Local Features, Ph.D. Thesis, Massachusetts Institute of Technology.

Poggio, T. 1981 *Marr's Approach to Vision*, MIT AI Lab., AI Memo No. 645.

251

Pradzy, K. 1980 'Egomotion and relative depth map from optical flow', *Biol. Cybernetics*, **36**, pp. 87–102.

Ray, R., Birk, J. and Kelley, R.B. 1983 'Error analysis of surface normals determined by radiometry', *IEEE Transactions on Pattern Analysis and Machine Intelligence*, Vol. PAMI-5, No. 6, pp. 631–71.

Roberts, L.G. 1965 'Machine perception of three-dimensional solids' in *Optical and Electro-Optical Information Processing*, J.T. Tippett *et al.* (eds), MIT Press, Cambridge, Massachusetts, pp. 159–97.

Safranek, R.J. and Kak, A.C. 1983 'Stereoscopic depth perception for robot vision: algorithms and architectures', *Proceedings of IEEE International Conference on Computer Design: VLSI in Computers (ICCD '83), Port Chester, NY, USA*, pp. 76–9.

Sandini, G. and Tistarelli, M. 1985 'Analysis of image sequences', *Proceedings of the IFAC Symposium on Robot Control*.

Sandini, G. and Tistarelli, M. 1986 *Recovery of Depth Information: Camera Motion Integration Stereo*, Internal Report, DIST, University of Genoa, Italy.

Sandini, G. and Tistarelli, M. 1986 'Analysis of camera motion through image sequences', in *Advances in Image Processing and Pattern Recognition*, V. Cappellini and R. Marconi (eds), Elsevier Science Publishers B.V. (North-Holland), pp. 100–6.

Sandini, G. and Vernon, D. 1987 'Tools for integration of perceptual data', in *ESPRIT '86: Results and Achievements*, Directorate General XIII (eds), Elsevier Science Publishers B.V. (North-Holland), pp. 855–65.

Sandini, G., Tistarelli, M. and Vernon, D. 1988 'A pyramid based environment for the development of computer vision applications', *IEEE International Workshop on Intelligent Robots and Systems, Tokyo*.

Sandini, G. and Tistarelli, M. 1990 'Active tracking strategy for monocular depth inference from multiple frames', *IEEE Transactions on Pattern Analysis and Machine Intelligence*, Vol. 12, No. 1, pp. 13–27.

Schenker, P.S. 1981 'Towards the robot eye: isomorphic representation for machine vision', *SPIE*, Vol. 283, '3-D machine reception', pp. 30–47.

Shafer, S.A. 1984 *Optical Phenomena In Computer Vision*, Technical Report TR 135, Computer Science Department, University of Rochester, Rochester, NY, USA.

Vernon, D. and Tistarelli, M. 1987 'Range estimation of parts in bins using camera motion', *Proceedings of SPIE's 31st Annual International Symposium on Optical and Optoelectronic Applied Science and Engineering, San Diego, California, USA*, 9 pages.

Vernon, D. 1988 *Isolation of Perceptually-Relevant Zero-Crossing Contours in the Laplacian of Gaussian-filtered Images*, Department of Computer Science, Trinity College, Technical Report No. CSC-88-03 (17 pages).

Vernon, D. and Sandini, G. 1988 'VIS: A virtual image system for image understanding', *Software Practice and Experience*, Vol. 18, No. 5, pp. 395–414.

Vernon, D. and Tistarelli, M. 1991 'Using camera motion to estimate range for robotic parts manipulation', accepted for publication in the *IEEE Transactions on Robotics and Automation*.

Wertheimer, M. 1958 'Principles of perceptual organisation', in D.C. Beardslee and M. Wertheimer (eds), *Readings in Perception*, Princeton, Van Nostrand.

Wu, C.K., Wang, D.Q. and Bajcsy, R.K. 1984 'Acquiring 3-D spatial data of a real object', *Computer Vision, Graphics, and Image Processing*, Vol. 28, pp. 126–33.

Appendix: Separability of the Laplacian of Gaussian operator

The *Laplacian of Gaussian* operator is defined:

$$\nabla^2\{I(x, y) * G(x, y)\} = \nabla^2 G(x, y) * I(x, y)$$

where $I(x, y)$ is an image function and $G(x, y)$ is the two-dimensional Gaussian function defined as follows:

$$G(x, y) = \frac{1}{2\pi\sigma^2} \exp[-(x^2 + y^2)/2\sigma^2]$$

The Laplacian is the sum of the second-order unmixed partial derivatives:

$$\nabla^2 = \frac{\partial^2}{\partial x^2} + \frac{\partial^2}{\partial y^2}$$

This two-dimensional convolution is separable into four one-dimensional convolutions:

$$\nabla^2\{I(x, y) * G(x, y)\} = G(x) * \left\{ I(x, y) * \frac{\partial^2}{\partial y^2} G(y) \right\}$$

$$+ G(y) * \left\{ I(x, y) * \frac{\partial^2}{\partial x^2} G(x) \right\}$$

This can be shown as follows:

$$\nabla^2\{I(x, y) * G(x, y)\} = \left(\frac{\partial^2}{\partial x^2} + \frac{\partial^2}{\partial y^2} \right) \left(I(x, y) * \frac{1}{2\pi\sigma^2} \exp[-(x^2 + y^2)/2\sigma^2] \right)$$

$$= \frac{\partial^2}{\partial x^2} \left(I(x, y) * \frac{1}{2\pi\sigma^2} \exp[-(x^2 + y^2)/2\sigma^2] \right)$$

$$+ \frac{\partial^2}{\partial y^2} \left(I(x, y) * \frac{1}{2\pi\sigma^2} \exp[-(x^2 + y^2)/2\sigma^2] \right)$$

$$= \frac{\partial^2}{\partial x^2} \left(I(x, y) * \frac{1}{2\pi\sigma^2} \exp(-x^2/2\sigma^2) \exp(-y^2/2\sigma^2) \right)$$

$$+ \frac{\partial^2}{\partial y^2} \left(I(x, y) * \frac{1}{2\pi\sigma^2} \exp(-x^2/2\sigma^2) \exp(-y^2/2\sigma^2) \right)$$

$$= \left(\frac{1}{\sqrt{2\pi}\,\sigma} \exp(-y^2/2\sigma^2) \left(\frac{\partial^2}{\partial x^2} \frac{1}{\sqrt{2\pi}\,\sigma} \exp(-x^2/2\sigma^2) \right) \right) * I(x, y)$$

$$+ \left(\frac{1}{\sqrt{2\pi}\,\sigma} \exp(-x^2/2\sigma^2) \left(\frac{\partial^2}{\partial y^2} \frac{1}{\sqrt{2\pi}\,\sigma} \exp(-y^2/2\sigma^2) \right) \right) * I(x, y)$$

$$= \left\{ G(x) \frac{\partial^2}{\partial y^2} G(y) \right\} * I(x, y) + \left\{ G(y) \frac{\partial^2}{\partial x^2} G(x) \right\} * I(x, y)$$

Let $(\partial^2/\partial x^2)G(x)$ be $A(x)$ and let $(\partial^2/\partial y^2)G(y)$ be $A(y)$, then we can rewrite the above as:

$$= \{G(x)\, A(y)\} * I(x, y) + \{G(y)\, A(x)\} * I(x, y)$$

Noting the definition of the convolution integral:

$$f(x, y) * h(x, y) = \int_{-\infty}^{\infty} \int_{-\infty}^{\infty} f(x - m, y - n)\, h(m, n)\, dm\, dn$$

we can expand the above:

$$= \int_{-\infty}^{\infty} \int_{-\infty}^{\infty} G(x - m)\, A(y - n)\, I(m, n)\, dm\, dn$$

$$+ \int_{-\infty}^{\infty} \int_{-\infty}^{\infty} G(y - n)\, A(x - m)\, I(m, n)\, dm\, dn$$

$$= \int_{-\infty}^{\infty} G(x - m) \int_{-\infty}^{\infty} A(y - n)\, I(m, n)\, dn\, dm$$

$$+ \int_{-\infty}^{\infty} G(y - n) \int_{-\infty}^{\infty} A(x - m)\, I(m, n)\, dm\, dn$$

$$= G(x) * \left\{ I(x, y) * \frac{\partial^2}{\partial y^2} G(y) \right\} + G(y) * \left\{ I(x, y) * \frac{\partial^2}{\partial x^2} G(x) \right\}$$

Index